THE CENTRAL THEME OF
BLACK HISTORY

THE CENTRAL THEME OF BLACK HISTORY

by

Earl E. Thorpe

PRINTED BY SEEMAN PRINTERY
DURHAM, NORTH CAROLINA

E
175
.T48

TO

The memory of Ethel Thorpe Rogers, Gracie Dean Fletcher,
Pattie Short Rigsbee, and Nellie Ruth Cooke Jones.

ACKNOWLEDGMENTS

For permission to quote from works published by them appreciation is hereby extended to the following: the Association for the Study of Negro Life and History and the Associated Publishers; American Historical Association; *Phylon*; *Negro History Bulletin*; *Quarterly Review of Higher Education among Negroes*; *American Historical Review*; *Mississippi Valley Historical Review* (now *Journal of American History*; *American Journal of Sociology*; *Journal of Southern History*; *Yale Review*; *New Republic*; *The Nation*, Prentice-Hall, Columbia University Press, Dell Publishing Co., Bantam Books, A. A. Knopf, Rinehart and Company, Little, Brown and Company, Ray Long and R. R. Smith, Dodd, Mead, Harpers, Macmillan, Grosset and Dunlap, Houghton-Mifflin, Doubleday, Ronald Press, The Dial Press, McGraw-Hill Co., Louisiana State University Press, University of Chicago Press, University of North Carolina Press, Harvard University Press, Indiana University Press, George Braziller Co., Johns Hopkins University Press, Northern Michigan University Press, Cordon Press, H. Regnery Co., Scribners, American Book Company, G. P. Putnam's Sons, Random House, D. Appleton-Century, and Harcourt, Brace and World.

CONTENTS

PREFACE

Black historiography and the theory and philosophy of Afro-American history are fields in which very little writing by scholars has been done. It is this reason which is offered as justification for bringing together the essays in this volume. Four of the essays, revised somewhat, are taken from three of the author's previous books. These books, and the chapters from them, are: "The Why and What of Negro Historiography" and "The Father of Negro History," from *Negro Historians in the United States (1958)*; "The Philosophy of Black History," from *The Mind of the Negro: An Intellectual History of Afro-Americans (1961)*; and "The Negro and the Central Theme of Southern History," from *Eros and Freedom in Southern Life and Thought (1967)*.

There is need for much more to be written on black historiography and the theory and philosophy of Afro-American history. Carter G. Woodson ought to be the subject of at least one good full-length biography.

Since the appearance of Ulrich B. Phillips' famous essay on the subject, the quest for the central theme of Southern history has been vigorously debated. It is hoped that the subject of essays herein, entitled "The Central Theme of Black History" and "The Negro and the Central Theme of Southern History" also will be vigorously debated. The essay on the work of Carter G. Woodson is included also because Dr. Woodson's contribution needs to be better known, especially to the younger generation of black and white historians. The two essays which seek to interpret aspects of Afro-American history from perspectives gained through reading some of Marshall McLuhan's writings are presented because black history,—like all other fields of historical specialization—, is ever in need of fresh points of view.

The great contribution of W. E. B. Du Bois to Black history earns for him a special place in a book on the theory and philosophy of this field, and makes him an appropriate subject for concluding such a volume.

In this book, at times I have attempted to go beyond commentary on the central theme of Black history, and to ponder themes central to Being and to remaining human while we seek to diminish and end racial conflict.

—Earl E. Thorpe
August, 1969

THE CENTRAL THEME OF
BLACK HISTORY

CHAPTER I

THE CENTRAL THEME OF BLACK HISTORY

Black history may be defined as American history with the accent and emphasis on the point of view, attitude, and spirit of Afro-Americans, as well as on the events where Black Americans have been either the actors or the objects of action. Because Blacks have been forcibly kept in a subordinate degraded status, so that they have held a much smaller portion of America's wealth and power than their numbers would command, the point of view, attitude, and spirit of Black Americans are often different from those held by white Americans. In similar vein the history of the South or West is American history with a primary focus on the South or West, while North Carolina history is American history with a primary focus on North Carolina. The national,—and even the international context—, must not be lost.

Black history is that American history which, until the 1960s, largely was either viewed by White America with contempt and disdain or ignored altogether. This history was viewed and treated with contempt and disdain because Blacks themselves largely were so viewed and treated. It was ignored for this reason, plus the factor of psychological repression. Men tend either to deny or force out of consciousness the evil that they do. Much of Black history, then, is the story of the cruelties and inhumanities which a powerful White majority has inflicted on a defenseless Black minority.

As fields of historical specialization, before 1945 Afro-American history and the history of Africa shared the common fate of not having won wide respectability and acceptance. In Service Center for Teachers of History Pamphlet No. 56, entitled, AFRICAN HISTORY, Philip Curtin makes the statement: "Before the Second World War, most of the important contributions to African history were made by non-historians." Today, the fact that one can earn the Ph.D. with a specialty in African or Negro history is perhaps the strongest proof that these fields have won wide acceptance. This has been a source of both pleasure and concern for the pioneers in these fields. At annual meetings of the Association for the Study of Negro Life and History since 1945, lengthy discussions have centered about the question of whether the new acceptance of Negro history makes the work of the Association obsolete.

The black scholars who pioneered in establishing Afro-American history as a respectable field of historical endeavor had motivations which stemmed in large part, but by no means completely, from the condition and status of their race in this nation. Negro history is still studied, taught, and written, by both white and black Americans, in part for these reasons. But more than ever, today Black history is studied, taught, and written for the same reasons that all other fields of historical specialization are studied, taught, and written.

The forces of industrialization and urbanization which were changing the South during the 1920's and 30's caused Southerners to become more concerned than ever with the question of their identity. The blurring of regional lines led to a search for the central theme of Southern history. The famous essay on this subject by Ulrich Bonnell Phillips has been supplemented with essays by C. Vann Woodward, David Potter, George B. Tindall, and others.

A similar situation exists where areas of historical specialization are concerned, for here, too, when one area comes close to others the problem of identity becomes more acute. Before 1945 there was less need for a discourse on the central theme of Black history. Today, this need exists.

The central theme of Black History is the quest of Afro-Americans for freedom, equality, and manhood.

It is not necessary to cite many instances where black spokesmen before 1865 used the words "freedom" or "liberty." "Free Negroes" and "freedom" were terms of pride. The first Negro newspaper was called *Freedom's Journal.* Recently the "Freedom Riders" had their busses burned as they made sacrifices in the cause of advancing civil rights. "Freedom" has been one of the black American's most often-used words.

Nor is it necessary to recite many instances before and since 1865 when black spokesmen used the word "equality." In Georgia, near the opening of this century, Negroes called one of their organizations "The Equal Rights League." Among other things and along with other groups, the National Association for the Advancement of Colored People has fought for equality before the law, while the National Urban League has sought equal employment opportunities. "Equality" has been among the words most often-used by black Americans. The same is true of the words "manhood" and "dignity."

The Negro male is unique in the extent to which he has been subjected to female authoritativeness in the home. Throughout the Caribbean area and in North America, the slave family was often a matriarchy. The husband was less respected by his wife and children because slavery prevented him from playing the role of a real authoritarian father-figure. Since 1865, due to low wages often paid Negro males, their wives have been forced to work more. Also, more Black households have had female heads than has been the case among white Americans.

In addition to the Negro male being subjected longer to female authoritativeness in the home, he has been subjected to unique forces of emasculation outside the home. Throughout the United States of America, ideology and practice in the Black-White relationship often have tried to deny the Black male the right and opportunity to be a man, to be aggressive, competitive, and to hold high positions.

Manhood means to have freedom, pride, and courage for maximum growth, self-expression, and personal and social health. Slavery was manhood's greatest antithesis.

A Kentucky court ruled in one case that "a slave by our code, is not a person, but a thing." But the law of slavery was ambiguous, and in practice there were both ambiguity and consistency. The main recognition of slaves as persons was in the area of crime,—to protect the white man's life and property. In other words, it was largely for the white man's convenience that the black man was ever regarded or treated as a person.

A judge in a Georgia court stated in 1854:

> . . . it is not true that slaves are only chattels, . . . and therefore, it is not true that it is not possible for them to be prisoners . . . The Penal Code has them in contemplation . . . in the first division . . . as persons capable of committing crimes; and as a consequence . . . as capable of becoming prisoners.

A few years later, another Southern judge declared:

> Because they are rational *human beings*, they are capable of committing crimes; and, in reference to acts which are crimes, are regarded as *persons*. Because they are *slaves*, they are . . . incapable of performing civil acts; and in reference to all such, they are *things*; not persons.

By law, a male slave was a more degraded being than a female slave, for the latter could be legally recognized as a mother. Since marriage between slaves had no legal standing, no offspring of slaves was ever recognized as having a legal father.

The speeches and other statements of black Americans reveal the extent to which they have felt that slavery and compulsory racial segregation and discrimination constituted denials of their manhood.

Concern about manhood is seen in Frederick Douglass's description of slaves as "beings deprived of every right, stripped of every privilege, ranked with four-footed beasts and creeping things, with no power over their own bodies and souls, . . . compelled to live in grossest ignorance, herded together . . . without marriage, without God, and without hope." The same is true of the statement by Douglass that nothing could keep the Negro satisfied in slavery. "Give him a *bad* master," Douglass declared, "and he aspires to a *good* master; give him a good master, and he wishes to become his *own* master."

In his famous 1829 appeal to the slaves, David Walker said several times to white America: "Treat us like men." At one point Walker added to this: "Treat us like men and we will like you more than we do now hate you." In an 1843 address to the slaves, made at the National Convention of Colored Citizens convening in New York, Henry Highland Garnet said many times: "You had far better all die—*die immediately*, than live slaves." To this he added, "Let your motto be resistance! *Resistance!* RESISTANCE!" Many times he recounted the evils borne by the slave. "In the name of God," Garnet cried, "We ask, are you men?"

The Fugitive Slave Law of 1850 so angered Charles Lenox Remond that he hoped for the breakup of the Union. Yet, in an 1854 speech before the New England Anti-Slavery Convention, Remond could say to white Americans: "Friends! God has made us men. If you will recognize us as such, we will conduct ourselves in a manner worthy of your regard and protection." Adult Black males long have resented being referred to as "boy," and of course, "a nigger" is not a man.

Although the Thirteenth Amendment to the federal constitution lifted black Americans above the level of chattel property, they were far from their goal of equality of status and opportunity.

In an article entitled, "The Relation of the Whites to the Negroes," published in the July, 1901 issue of *The Annals of the American Academy of Political and Social Science,* the president of North Carolina's white land-grant college expressed the long-prevailing views of many white Americans. Throughout a lengthy article this southern leader repeated such statements as the following: "The Negro is a child race . . . the Negro here is bound to be under the tutelage and control of the whites." He continued:

> It would be a cruelty greater than slavery to leave this helpless race, this child race, to work out its own salvation . . . the Negro . . . must aim at white civilization, and must reach it through the support, guidance, and control of the white people among whom he lives.

At another point, this college president repeated once more: "The Negro race is a child race and must remain in tutelage for years to come." It is noteworthy here that, in such minds as this one, the Negro had progressed from being classified as chattel property—along with horses, cows, and barns—, to the classification of a *child.* How much good would it have done to point out to this college president that there never has been any such thing as child races and adult races— and that during the 9th, 10th, and 11th centuries of the Christian era, highly civilized, independent, affluent black kingdoms and empires existed in Africa? How much good would it have done to tell this college president that he— and many other persons who thought as he did—, were rationalizing to justify the degration and exploitation of black Americans?

The black educator, J. C. Price, declared: "Freedom implies manhood." In his 1903 book THE SOULS OF BLACK FOLK, W. E. Du Bois attacked Booker T. Washington's philosophies of education and racial progress, and based his case on Negro manhood. He said that Washington's thinking overlooked the "higher aims of life" in favor of making money. On this, Du Bois declared:

> If we make money the object of man-training, we shall develop money-makers but not necessarily men: if we make technical skill the object of education, we may possess artisans but not, in nature, men. Men we shall have only as we make manhood the object of the work of the schools.

In his last speech in Congress, delivered in 1900, George White, the last Black Reconstruction Congressman, urged his white colleagues to stop maligning the Afro-American and to help him in his efforts to rise. "Treat him as a man," White urged.

Restoring to health the crippled manhood of many Negro males has been a central concern of the so-called Black Muslims and other nationalist-oriented groups. When in his great eulogy at the funeral of Malcolm X, the actor Ossie Davis sought the central meaning of the life of this remarkable man, he found that meaning in Afro-American manhood. Davis declared: "Malcolm was our . . . living, black manhood!" But, as was Marcus Garvey before him, Elijah Muhammed was also a symbol of manhood to thousands of black Americans. In this regard Malcolm and his mentor "made each other." The big objection which many young Blacks had with the non-violent philosophy of Martin Luther King, Jr. was their conviction that not to strike back when hit is unmanly. Even though many felt that Dr. King compromised when he would not strike back, because he fearlessly, willingly, and continuously, offered his body to be bruised, arrested, and murdered, he too, was a true symbol of manhood to millions of Black Americans.

Some persons contend that the young Black male of the ghetto participates in riots because he is not allowed enough other means of asserting his manhood. Consider also the "Deacons" of the South, and the Black Panthers, and their concern with Black manhood. Also, read Eldridge Cleaver's book, *Soul on Ice*, and notice his great concern with Black manhood.

Even a superficial reading of the documents of Afro-American history reveals that the central theme of Black history is the quest of Black Americans for freedom, equality, and manhood. This can be further seen when one surveys the development and philosophy of Negro history.

Because of the experience of slavery, when George Washington Williams, the first serious student of Negro history appeared in the early 1880s, white America already had produced such eminent historians as Francis Parkman, William H. Prescott, both Bancrofts, and Charles Gayarré. Among earlier Blacks who wrote history, such as William Cooper Nell, James W. C. Pennington, Robert Benjamin Lewis, James Theodore Holly, Joseph T. Wilson, and William Wells Brown, the latter had the greatest success.

Carter G. Woodson is often called the Father of Negro History. Woodson was born in Virginia, December 19, 1875. In 1912 he received the Ph.D. in history from Harvard University. Three years later, in Chicago, he started the Association for the Study of Negro Life and History. In 1916 he founded the *Journal of Negro History*. Later he started the *Negro History Bulletin* and the Associated Publishers. The latter firm published all of the many books written by Dr. Woodson, as well as numerous books on Negro history written by others. After a long life devoted almost exclusively to studying and popularizing Afro-American history, Dr. Woodson died in 1950. When Dr. Woodson launched the Negro History Movement one of his chief aims was to use history to replace ethnic shame with pride of race. By reminding young Blacks of men and women of their race who had made notable contributions,

Dr. Woodson hoped to inspire them to high achievement. In 1923 he published a book entitled, The *Mis-Education of the Negro*, in which he pointed out that modern culture has systematically exalted the white race and denigrated the colored races. Later W. E. B. Du Bois echoed this theme in a book entitled, *Color and Democracy*; and still more recently this was the theme of E. Franklin Frazier's book, *Black Bourgeoisie*, and Nathan Hare's book entitled, *The Black Anglo-Saxons*. All of these scholars contend that their race has been brain-washed into a blind glorification of whiteness and European values, and that, as a consequence, Negroes not only lack sufficient pride in their own identity and potentialities, but they are overly imitative rather than creative. These scholars contend that there can be no fullness of maturity where there is insufficient self-acceptance.

In 1915 Dr. Woodson launched the modern Negro History Movement to correct the thinking of both races. Although over fifty years had passed since he began this great work, 1969 found the nation in the throes of a mighty effort to complete the task which he began.

In 1969 the movement of black consciousness or black awareness or black affirmation was one of the dominant concerns of colleges and universities, and this movement affected the materials and methods and other aspects of education in the elementary and high schools. Through painfully slow growth many Black Americans had acquired such a high level of pride and self-respect that they could no longer tolerate age-old indignities, insults, and obstacles to opportunity and achievement. As the nation learned during the 1960s in such places as Watts, Detroit, Newark, Orangeburg, and Memphis, involved here is considerable pain and agony for the total population. A central concern was the task of ending racism in the nation, and despite the danger of the assassin's bullet, no American could escape involvement in this task.

There are at least three basic reasons why the Negro History Movement began and continues to exist. The first is related to the fact that historical writing has been slow to shed its aristocratic tradition and bias of being almost exclusively concerned with the affairs of the ruling class or elite. Even after written history shifted from its aristocratic-political emphasis, it long neglected numerous segments of society. Thus it is that even today there is too little writing on the role of women in history. Thus it is, too, that the Negro History Movement came into being because Blacks, as human beings, had been left out of history. Dr. Woodson called the Association for the Study of Negro Life and History "the first systematic effort . . . to treat the records of the race scientifically and to publish the findings to the world." He gave this same justification for the founding of the *Journal of Negro History*, but, to this he added that the *Journal* was also dedicated to "the promotion of harmony between the races by acquainting the one with the other."

A second reason that the Negro History Movement came into being was the prominence of racial prejudice and stereotypes. To justify slavery and the system of degradation which followed emancipation, many people found it convenient to argue that Blacks belonged in a degraded social position because they were biologically inferior. A highly articulate and influential segment of Occidental civilization long has depicted Blacks as being emotional, impulsive, nonrational, childish creatures. This, of course, was the judgment which was pronounced by the ante-bellum slave owners and their apologists, and it has been the judgment of numerous racist social scientists who have written in more recent times. James Schouler, a noted American historian of the Nationalist School, described Negroes as being "a black servile race, sensuous, stupid, brutish, obedient . . . and childish." Ulrich Bonnell Phillips described the Negro as being innately stupid, docile, submissive, unstable, and negligent. William A. Dunning, John Fiske, J. G. Randall, and Claude H. Van Tyne are also among the sizeable number of American historians who have depicted Blacks in this vein. Well-known is the manner in which such European writers as Houston Stewart Chamberlain and Count de Gobineau told the world that such was indeed the scientifically verified picture of the mentality, personality, and character of Blacks.

The Negro History Movement came into being to combat this image and to correct a serious sin of omission made by Caucasian historians. Disbelief of this so-called science, plus a desire to round out and complete the record, and to set the record straight, caused Drs. Woodson, Du Bois, and other scholars to concentrate on studying and popularizing the truth about the Afro-American past.

In a multi-ethnic society like the United States of America, every public school and college graduate should know that when white Christian Europe was living in her Dark Ages, there were great Black kingdoms and empires and high civilizations in Sub-Sahara Africa; that the successful revolt of black people led by Toussaint l'Ouverture was a major reason why Napoleon I sold the Louisiana Territory to the United States. They should know that this nation probably would have lost its War for Independence if George Washington had stuck to his early decision not to use Black soldiers; that Andrew Jackson praised the service of the Black troops who fought in the battle of New Orleans; and that Abraham Lincoln admitted that the Union could not have been preserved without the service of the Black soldier. They should know that Black men and women have made outstanding contributions not only in music, entertainment, and sports, but in such fields as scholarship, literature, medicine, invention, and science—and they should know the names and achievements of some of these men and women.

They should know that in recent years a number of

books have been published which not only revise old views and attitudes, but fill gaps in our knowledge of the history of this nation. Thus it is, for example, that there now exists a book on the Negro cowboy, and a volume on slavery in the cities. Thus it is, too, that there is, in Kenneth Stampp's book *The Peculiar Institution,* a more favorable view of the slave than that given in the books of Ulrich Bonnell Phillips. Also, Stampp, John Hope Franklin, and others, have caught the spirit of W. E. B. Du Bois's book, *Black Reconstruction,* and have assaulted the old myth that black people and so-called Radical Republicans were responsible for all of the evils of a supposedly bleak and barren Reconstruction period.

History is the memory of mankind and all men need and use it. The question is not whether men know some history and use it, but rather how well they understand and use history. Especially are professional historians aware that, because everyone needs and uses history, everyone should not only seek a fuller understanding of it, but should be concerned that the history he knows is as free as possible from class, racial, religious, or national bias.

A third reason why the Negro History Movement came into being was to inspire Blacks to high achievement. People always have sought to inspire the young by telling them of the outstanding achievements of their ancestors. Evidence that leaders of the Negro History Movement hoped and sought to use history to bolster the race's self-esteem and self-confidence is abundant. This is seen in the fact that until around 1920, many histories of the race were largely biographies of outstanding Blacks. Writing in the year 1931, in a volume entitled, *The Negro Author,* Vernon Loggins observed this tendency. "A characteristic of much Negro history," he wrote, "is that the historian seems to arrive at a point beyond which he cannot go without bringing before us, in catalogue order, the main facts in the careers of illustrious members of his race." In the preface to his *His-*

tory of the Negro Race in America, George Washington Williams stated that one of his reasons for writing the book was to "incite the Negro people to greater effort in the struggle of citizenship and manhood." W. E. B. Du Bois states that he studied and wrote history, in large part because he felt that to do so would help elevate the race through re-educating both black and white Americans toward a greater respect for the Black race. "The world was thinking wrong about race," he wrote, "because it did not know. The ultimate evil was stupidity. The cure for it was knowledge based on scientific investigation." While he is not generally known as an historian, Booker T. Washington produced a two-volume history of the race which has been widely read. In the preface, Washington expressed the hope that the book would "inspire" some Negro "to make himself useful and successful in the world."

Carter G. Woodson's life was devoted to correcting the false image of Blacks so that, as he put it, his race might "escape the awful fate of becoming a negligible factor in the thought of the world." In the introduction to his little book entitled *The Mis-Education of the Negro,* Dr. Woodson said: "When you control a man's thinking you do not have to worry about his actions." One of Dr. Woodson's often-repeated themes was the power and importance of faith and self-affirmation. In effect, he said to his race: "Yes, your ancestors were slaves, but they had a distinguished history *before America was discovered,* and even as slaves, they never stopped loving freedom!" And in spite of the long dark night of bondage, they still produced the poetry of Phyllis Wheatley, Paul Laurence Dunbar, James Weldon Johnson, Margaret Walker, Gwendolyn Brooks, and Langston Hughes; the scientific genius of Benjamin Banneker, George Washington Carver, Daniel Hale Williams, Ernest Just, and Charles Drew; the novels of Richard Wright, Ralph Ellison, Ann Petry, and James Baldwin; and the eloquence and saintliness of Frederick Douglass, Medgar

Evers, and Martin Luther King, Jr. Dr. Woodson reminded men that the Afro-American has been much more in history than a hewer of wood and drawer of water, and that there is nothing wrong with Black affirmation.

The popularity of certain aspects of history has some relationship to social conditions and usefulness. When it was true that the sun never went down on British soil, the history of England was more popular than it is now. When President Franklin D. Roosevelt was promoting the "Good Neighbor" policy, the history of Latin America acquired greater popularity. In 1969 the fact that the so-called Black Revolution was one of the nation's major domestic issues presented an added reason why both white and black Americans should look to Afro-American history for whatever inspiration, mutual respect, and sense of direction they can acquire from this history.

During the summer of 1967 Martin Luther King, Jr. announced that his organization was newly committed to the Black History Movement. Such organizations and groups as the Congress of Racial Equality, National Association for the Advancement of Colored People, municipal and state boards of education, and colleges and universities made similar commitments during that and subsequent years. These people knew that history inspired such men as Winston Churchill, and that history may be used to liberate as well as to oppress. These people knew that many Blacks have been ashamed of their history—and of themselves—only because degrading propaganda and mythology have been fed to them as scientific truth, and they knew that even if accentuating the positive also is sometimes myth and propaganda, it is better to inspire than to discourage.

Both black and white Americans need an acquaintance with Black history. Unless they, too, can endorse the Black History Movement, white Americans of this generation cannot have respect for black Americans of this generation. It is impossible to think positively about any group whose past you view negatively. The negative view can never predominate if we will always keep in mind that the central theme of Black history is the Afro-American's quest for freedom, equality, and manhood.

CHAPTER II

THE WHY AND WHAT OF AFRO-AMERICAN HISTORIOGRAPHY

Afro-American historiography has come a long way in the twentieth century. After perusing the field to the turn of the present century, Vernon Loggins concluded: "The long line of Negro autobiographies . . . gives undoubtedly a better understanding of the progress of the American Negro than the writings of the avowed historians."[1] Such a situation no longer exists.

Just as the history of the South had its inception only a few years ago as a distinct field for specialization and intensive study,[2] so also the field of Afro-American or Black History is largely a product of the twentieth century.[3] This chapter is a further elaboration of the "why and what" of Afro-American historiography.[4]

Why Afro-American History?

Upon posing the question, "Why Afro-American History?" one finds that many historians have felt the urge to justify their concentration in this field. George Washington Williams is generally regarded as the first serious student of Negro history.[5] Williams states his reasons for studying and writing his celebrated work in this area thus:

> . . . because Negroes had been the most vexatious problem in North America from the time of its discovery down to the present day; because that in every attempt upon the life of the nation . . . the Colored people had always displayed a matchless patriotism and an incomparable heroism in the cause

of Americans; because such a history would give the world more correct ideas of the Colored people, and incite the latter to greater effort in the struggle of citizenship and manhood. The single reason that there was no history of the Negro race would have been a sufficient reason for writing one.[6]

Williams further indicated that one of his reasons for writing Black history was his love for truth, which he felt had not been told in this respect. "Not as a blind panegyrist of my race," he wrote, "nor as a partisan apologist, but from a love for *'the truth of history,'* I have striven to record the truth, the whole truth, and nothing but the truth." "I have not striven to revive sectional animosities or race prejudices," he added.[7] Williams felt that the writing of his race's history would serve to elevate the position of the group in American society by educating the majority of the population to the former's true value. Similarly, he felt that history would stimulate the race to greater achievement. "Race prejudice is bound to give way," he wrote, "before the potent influence of character, education and wealth."[8] Upon completion of his account of the services of Negro troops in the Civil War, Williams expressed his faith in the power of history to stimulate Negroes to greater effort. "The masses of Negroes in the United States are ignorant," he stated, "but from their loins will spring only a race of patriots so long as a monument exists which records the magnificent military achievements of the Negro soldier."[9]

Not until the appearance of W. E. B. Du Bois's *Suppression of the African Slave Trade* in 1896[10] was any other Colored historian to produce works of such substantial magnitude as those of Williams. Du Bois was the first member of his race to receive a Ph.D. in any of the social sciences,[11] and he inaugurated a new era in Negro scholarship in general.[12] Together with Carter G. Woodson, Du Bois deserves rank as a leader and maker of the field of Negro history.[13] Dr. Du Bois studied and wrote history, in part because he felt that to do so would help elevate the position of the race through re-educating both Black and White Americans toward a greater respect for the nation's largest minority. Moreover, it would, he felt, inspire the latter to greater achievement. "The world was thinking wrong about race," he thought, "because it did not know. The ultimate evil was stupidity. The cure for it was knowledge based on scientific investigation."[14] Again he wrote that he held a "firm belief that race prejudice was based on wide-spread ignorance. My long-term remedy was truth: carefully gathered scientific proof that neither color nor race determined the limits of a man's capacity or desert."[15]

Upon completion of his pioneer study, *The Philadelphia Negro*,[16] Dr. Du Bois recommended that such studies be made of other leading American cities with large Black populations. Such studies, he asserted, are a prerequisite for the education of the races. "Until he [The Scholar] has prepared the ground by intelligent and discriminating research, the labors of philanthropist and statesman must continue to be, to a large extent barren and unfruitful," he contended."[17]

Only a few years lapsed between the time when Du Bois first catapulted into the limelight of the scholarly world and the appearance of Carter G. Woodson, another Harvard University Ph.D. in history. Dr. Du Bois, for the time being, had continued his work in the field of sociology, and it was Dr. Woodson who was to get Afro-American history generally recognized as an area for serious study. The latter gave up the classroom after a short period and became the first member of his race to devote his full time to collecting and publicizing the history of the race. This activity is reflected in his many books, articles, and lectures. In 1915 he founded the Association for the Study of Negro Life and History, and in 1916 he began issuing the *Journal of Negro History*. In 1926 he inaugurated Negro History Week which quickly became a national success.

Dr. Woodson, like Williams and Du Bois, wrote history in part because he believed it would elevate the position of his race in American society by re-educating both Caucasians and Blacks to a greater appreciation of the black race, and through inspiring the latter to greater achievement.[18] It was, he believed, the job of the historian of the Afro-American to prove that the race had a creditable past. On this point, he wrote:

> If a race has no history, if it has no worthwhile tradition, it becomes a negligible factor in the thought of the world, and it stands in danger of being exterminated. The American Indian left no continuous record. He did not appreciate the value of tradition; and where is he today? The Hebrew keenly appreciated the value of tradition, as is attested by the Bible itself. In spite of worldwide persecution, therefore, he is still a great factor in civilization.[19]

Dr. Woodson is equally clear in the expression of his belief that race prejudice in America was the result of miseducation of both races. He, too, felt that a different type of education which presented the black race in a more favorable light was the basic solution to the so-called color problem. Race prejudice, he argued, "is not something inherent in human nature. It is merely the logical result of tradition, the inevitable outcome of thorough instruction to the effect that the Negro has never contributed anything to the progress of mankind. The doctrine has been thoroughly drilled into the whites and the Negroes have learned well the lesson themselves."[20] Woodson denied the validity of the doctrine of white supremacy. "One race has not accomplished any more good than any other race," he wrote, "for God could not be just and at the same time make one race the inferior of the other."[21] Emphasizing his faith in education as the proper solution, he wrote, that "just as thorough education in the belief in the inequality of races

brought the world to the cat-and-dog stage of religious and
racial strife, so may thorough instruction in the equality of
races bring about a reign of brotherhood through an appreciation of the virtues of all races, creeds and colors."[22]

Throughout his life, Woodson continuously reaffirmed
his convictions that (1) race prejudice was the result of
historical writing and teaching which either ignored the
Afro-American's achievements or said they were nonexistent,
(2) the Afro-American must be shown that he does have a
creditable past or he will lack "inspiration" and (3) Caucasians must be educated to this conclusion or they will lack
respect for the Black race. Woodson's entire life became
devoted to accomplishing these ends that his race might
"escape the awful fate of becoming a negligible factor in the
thought of the world."[23] In his book, *Mis-Education of the
Negro*, Woodson said, "when you control a man's thinking
you do not have to worry about his actions."[24] Though
Dr. Du Bois later embraced a Marxist outlook and decided
that race prejudice did not spring nearly so much from
mis-education of the two races as it did from actual economic, political and social organization, Carter G. Woodson apparently never experienced this change of conviction.[25]

Black historians who have become prominent since
Woodson launched his great work, in general, have never
substantially differed with his interpretation of the efficacy
of Afro-American history (and its need) in effecting a great
change for good in the thinking and acting of black and
white Americans. On the contrary, many have agreed with
Dr. Woodson and have been inspired and directed by these
convictions. These convictions have played a prominent
role in determining historians of the race to re-interpret the
topics of slavery, Civil War and Reconstruction in American
history just as the desire of southerners to seek for themselves a more creditable presentation inspired their pre-
occupation with these themes. Breaking with this tradition,
as Du Bois also did, L. D. Reddick issued in 1937 a call for

a new interpretation for Negro history and scored the pre-occupation with the "slavery theme."[26]

While he is not generally known as an historian, Booker T. Washington produced a history of the race which has been called the most widely read of all such works.[27] Not undertaking to write a formal or detailed history, Washington had a limited and positive objective in mind. "It has been my object," he wrote, "to show what the Negro himself has accomplished in constructive directness."[28] Washington stated:

> If the reading of these chapters shall in any degree inspire any Negro to make himself useful and successful in the world, and if in any degree what I have written will cause any individuals, not members of my own race, to take a more generous and hopeful view of the condition and prospects of the Negro, I shall feel that I have accomplished what I started out to do in writing these pages.[29]

Dr. Charles H. Wesley, successor to Woodson as Director of the Association for the Study of Negro Life and History, also expressed his convictions on the efficacy of history in bringing about an elevation of the position of this minority in American society. In 1935, Wesley pleaded for a reconstruction of history along the lines laid down by Woodson.[30] He reechoed this position a decade later. Writing under the title, "The Concept of the Inferiority of the Negro in American Thought," Wesley blamed this concept on the mis-education of both groups and concluded: "Here, then, is the challenge to American scholars, Negro and white, for the days of race propaganda continue. . . . It is imperative that we study again the capacity of races."[31] It is difficult to understand the need for such a study if one accepts the premise of Du Bois that the Afro-American "is an average and ordinary human being, who under given environment develops like other human beings,"[32] or Woodson's statement that "God could not be just and at the same time make one race the inferior of the other."

Another teacher opined that "The teaching of Negro history will serve the two-fold purpose of informing the white man and inspiring the Negro . . . [and] contribute much to the solution of [the] complicated race problem."[33] "By contemplating the deeds of the worthy members of his own race," this writer opines, "the Negro youth will have his aspirations raised to attain the highest objective of life."[34]

Very few Black historians have written general histories of the United States. One such effort, written for the elementary school level, was produced as "an attempt to help America solve one of her most complex problems—the relation between the white race and the Negro race."[35] This work was written because, "Studies of the many books used in our schools show that much has been emphasized which does not give the child the right ideas about the social order in which he now lives. In other instances, much has been deleted with the result that one who studies them gains a biased view of our great country and its people."[36]

There are other motivating factors responsible for Afro-American historiography which are not so obvious from reasons stated by these writers. Concomitant with the New Colonialism of the second half of the late nineteenth century was a swelling tide of nationalism and humanitarianism, which affected people in all quarters of the globe. Everywhere racial and cultural groups became intensely interested in their pasts. Many sought a folk genius of some kind which would explain their achievements or promises of achievement and serve as a stimulus to group pride. Well does the twentieth century know how, in some quarters, this absorbing interest was perverted into master race theories.

Too, as the number of Black college graduates swelled, colored scholars became aware of work by archaeologists, anthropologists, and artists in their discovery and re-evaluation of the pottery, vases, metal arts, and other artifacts of primitive African peoples. These latter scholars, largely Europeans, were proving what the Black historian had long contended, —namely, that Africans have made a substantial contribution to cultural progress and civilization. While a student, Carter Woodson had sensed this fact. Franz Boaz was to bring it to the attention of W. E. B. Du Bois.

Writing in *The New Negro*, published in 1925 by Albert and Charles Boni, the volume's editor, Alain Locke, showed a keen awareness of these developments. The same may be said for Arthur A. Schomburg, who wrote an article for this volume entitled, "The Negro Digs Up His Past." Thus, for a number of reasons, the Black historian came to insist that the history of the United States be re-written so as to include the positive contributions of his race, and that world history be re-written so as to give recognition to black Africa's gift to civilization.

This summary of the views herein included shows that some of the most outstanding of these historians have been influenced by the conception of Black history as *a weapon in the fight for racial equality*. This orientation has been, in some respects, detrimental to their historiography. An analysis of the reasons why Black historians have believed history to be an essential weapon in the fight for racial equality will show some of the strengths and weaknesses of their thinking. A consideration of these ideas follows.

1. *The Idea that a Glorious and Wonderful Past is Necessary for Racial Achievement*

From the foregoing it is clear that several Black historians of prominence have felt that a glorious and wonderful past is a prerequisite stimulus for racial achievement, and that such a past would produce greater achievement. As Dr. Woodson puts it, the race "that has no history . . . becomes a negligible factor in the thought of the world, and it stands in danger of being exterminated."[37]

This motivating idea is suspect because there is no convincing proof of its truthfulness. There is much to deny such an assertion. In contradistinction to the Woodson view, the American Indian was not vanquished because "he did not appreciate the value of tradition," but rather because the technological and cultural levels of development of the Indian were below that possessed by Europeans. And, despite persistent statements to the contrary, there is no general agreement that the explanation for survival ability of the Hebrew is due to the fact that he "keenly appreciated the value of tradition." Similarly, the remarkable rise of western Europeans to world domination, and their attainment of a high level of culture despite the fact that they had no glorious past (as Dr. Woodson and others constantly point out in their efforts to show African superiority to Europeans during the Middle Ages) belies the contention that the race "that has no history . . . becomes a negligible factor in the thought of the world, and . . . stands in danger of being exterminated." The same might be said for the barbaric Greek invaders of the Aegean, or any other group which is "on the make" for the first time. Although Afro-Americans had the great achievements of black Africa's remarkable medieval kingdoms and empires,—such as Old Ghana and Songhay,—in their past, the first rise to prominence of any race or peoples must of necessity take place without a prior "history."[38]

There is even evidence that the reverse position from that taken by Woodson and others is true, that is, that the possession of a "history" negates the possibility of future achievement and survival of a race or peoples by causing them to "rest on their oars."[39] And it is a fact of common observation that many individuals strive all the more to create a present because they have no past. Still, Woodson's insistence that a race's self-esteem is of crucial importance is beyond question. And, although it sometimes seemed that early Negro historians were interested in manufacturing

a great and glorious African past, scholarship of recent decades has confirmed their claim that Black Africa's cultural
contribution is rich, praiseworthy, and not at all inferior.

2. *The Idea that the Doctrine of White Supremacy Draws
   Its Main Inspiration from Over-Emphasis of Achieve-
   ments of Europeans and Under-Emphasis of
   Achievements of Non-Europeans*

The above summary of the *raison d'être* of Black history,
as given by Colored historians themselves, shows that many
have believed that race prejudice springs primarily from
historical writing and teaching which depicts the Black as
an inferior being, or ignores him entirely. This belief has
stimulated many of these scholars to present the story of
the Afro-American as a teaching device for the improvement of race relations.

While there is little doubt that a "filio-pietistic bias"[40]
contributes to the tenacity of the doctrine of white supremacy, it seems clear that, as Dr. Du Bois came to see, this
doctrine has been primarily a rationalization of an actual
de jure and de facto situation. Since the sixteenth century,
Europeans have held actual economic, political and military
superiority or supremacy in almost every quarter of the
globe. Thus the doctrine of supremacy of Caucasians grows
from no mere verbalization or educational system, but
springs primarily from the existence of a concrete situation.
And, it is perhaps accurate to say that in-roads made on
this doctrine owe the greater part of their success to in-
roads made on European hegemony of the world.[41] Some
Black historians have indicated little appreciation of the
true basis for the doctrine in question. These have generally
shown, as Dr. Reddick states, too little awareness of economic forces in history.[42] Their philosophy of history has
been too largely a moral one. Thus, too frequently such institutions as slavery and colonialism disappear simply because they were sinful and immoral, and wars are explained

as God's punishment for wrong-doing. It is this type of thinking which explains the general failure of some historians of color to see that the concept of racial inferiority stems primarily from and feeds on the actual economic, political, and social inferiority of the masses in their race.

Along the way to this realization, Du Bois wrote: "My own panacea in earlier days was flight of class from mass through the development of a Talented Tenth, but the power of this aristocracy of talent was to lie in its knowledge and character and not in its wealth."[43] After his change of outlook, Du Bois placed the emphasis on race consumer and producer cooperatives and the utilization of improved means of organization to advance directly the *economic* position of the Negro.[44] "My whole attitude toward the social sciences began to change," he wrote, "The studies which I had been conducting . . . I saw as fatally handicapped because they represented so small a part of the total sum of occurrences; were so removed in time and space as to lose the hot reality of real life. . . . I saw before me a problem that could not and would not await the last word of science."[45]

3. *The Idea that Scientific Studies Were Essential to Racial Progress*

As shown, several of these historians have been imbued with the idea that the prerequisite to an elevation of the position of the race in America was studies designed to show the "scientific" position and condition of the race. The famed Atlanta University Studies which were inaugurated and carried out by Du Bois, and many of those conducted by the Association for the Study of Negro Life and History were made specifically to provide such data.[46] This belief has provided a powerful stimulus to this historiography.

It would seem that in their earnest desire to serve the cause of advancement of the race, and their effort to serve the cause of knowledge for which their training and scholar-

ly proclivities fitted them, several of these men have succeeded in convincing themselves that their training and abilities were *sine qua non* for the advancement of the race. As
Du Bois first believed: "Until he [the scholar] has prepared
the ground by intelligent and discriminating research, the labors of philanthropist and statesman must continue to be,
to a large extent, barren and unfruitful."[47]

It is not this writer's purpose to contend that Afro-American history as an educational device has not contributed
at all to better race relations, or that scientific studies have
not so contributed, or that the doctrine of white supremacy
has not been augmented by filio-pietistic history. The position here is simply that several of the foremost of these
historians have misconstrued the significance of these things
as justifications for Black history, and, that even if these
motivating ideas were completely sound, they do not constitute the total justification for the field.[48]

Probably it is a normal trait for civilized individuals and
groups to desire to discover and publish, with the emphasis
on favorable aspects, the facts about their racial and cultural backgrounds; especially so, when there is some reason
for either being especially proud or not-so-proud of that
background. Also, as earlier stated, as Southern historiography drew its primary inspiration from the desire to re-
draw the unfavorable picture given of that section's role
in the Civil War and Reconstruction periods, so Afro-American historiography drew its primary inspiration out of the
desire to re-draw the unfavorable picture which many
scholars have presented of this American minority. Still of
all forces which combined to give rise to this body of literature, the racial uplift theme stands out prominently
among those given by most black historians.

Another Justification for Black History

This leads to the question of what is another justification for Black history? It does not need to seek its jus-

tification alone in the contribution it has made to the advancement of the race (and undoubtedly it has made some contribution to this cause). It may well be that it is not necessary, as herein indicated, that a race, or other group have a creditable past for achievement, despite the fact that the ability to make such a boast swells the pride and inflates the ego. It may well be that the scientific studies carried out by these scholars were not an essential prerequisite to progress of the race. Another justification for Black history, as with any other work of scholarly endeavor, is that *it constitutes a contribution to the knowledge and understanding of mankind.* An important inspiration necessary for the scholar is that he, through his researches and writings, is giving to his generation and to posterity knowledge and understanding. Any other outlook may be detrimental to scholarship. What more extreme forms of "filio-pietism" can produce is evident in German Historiography of the late nineteenth century Nationalist School and in National Socialist and Fascist and Bolshevik propaganda.

Is this merely the "bourgeois doctrine" of knowledge for the sake of knowledge? Does not this view run counter to the idea that, in time of revolution, all men and all disciplines must be revolution-oriented? Objectivity to the Black historian has never meant an endorsement of the *status quo.* From its inception to the present, central to all Afro-American historiography is an attack on the racial *status quo.* The central theme of Black history is the quest of Afro-Americans for freedom, equality, and manhood. Considered from this frame of reference, Afro-American History is not simply biography of great men and the chronicling of noble achievements. It becomes a record, viewed in the light of conditioning circumstances, of the race's achievements and failures, dreams *and* lack of dreams. While cause-serving on the part of the scholar has some merits, it also rings up a score of demerits. Perhaps the large and creditable body of literature produced by Black

historians would be more convincing (hence a greater contribution), had the work been conceived in an outlook farther removed from cause-serving of a racial nature. In his
"A New Interpretation for Negro History," Reddick pleaded
for this type of outlook, as he denounced the posture of
"liberalism."[49] Vernon Loggins, the historian of Negro literature, attests to the negative influence of "filio-pietism"
on Black historiography. He writes:

> A characteristic of much Negro history . . . is that
> the historian seems to arrive at a point beyond which
> he cannot go without bringing before us in catalogue
> order the main facts in the careers of illustrious mem-
> bers of his race.[50]

Du Bois admitted that writings by Colored Americans
on the Reconstruction Period are too one-sided and suffer
from an attitude of "striking back."[51] His own historical
writings have been criticized for this same reason, and for
the bitterness which they so poignantly reveal. A leading
liberal called this "his strength . . . and also his chief weakness."[52] Though Woodson launched the *Journal of Negro
History* with the belief "that facts properly set forth will
speak for themselves,"[53] one only has to read many of the
reviews written by Dr. Woodson for this organ to wish that
he had not insisted so often on using a review to proselytize.
His more lengthy writings have also been criticized to some
extent, because of this fault.[54]

Still, it is understandable, that the Black historian, like
members of his race in other pursuits, also has been unable
to escape completely the intense urge to use every available
opportunity to wage unrelenting warfare against the inferior
position accorded his race in the United States. That he has
wrought so well as he has, is the thing to be marvelled at.
All America owes these historians great homage and respect for the splendid manner in which they have uncovered
and ordered the facts of their group's past and published

them to the eternal edification and enlightenment of all mankind. This has been a "solid service . . . rendered not merely to the Negro race, but to historical scholarship generally . . . in a difficult and still largely unworked field."[55] *This is another well-earned justification for Black history.*[56]

CHAPTER III

THE PHILOSOPHY OF BLACK HISTORY

Objectives of Negro History

An examination of the writings of such nineteenth century Black historians as William Cooper Nell, James W. C. Pennington, Robert Benjamin Lewis, James Theodore Holly, Joseph T. Wilson, William Wells Brown, and George Washington Williams reveals that written Negro History had its beginnings in America primarily as an attempt to justify emancipation.[1] Here it is of interest to compare the purposes which motivated the earliest Black historians with those of their white contemporaries. Posing recently the question, "What is written history good for?", Henry Steele Commager informs us that:

> The generation that had rejoiced in the stately histories by Bancroft, Motley, Prescott, and Parkman had not been troubled by this question. It had been content with the richness of the narrative, the symmetry of the pattern, the felicity of the style that was to be found in these magisterial volumes.[2]

As indicated, such was not the case with the Beginning School of Black Historians, who were as much interested in the uses of their history as they were in its discovery. Here it can be seen that Afro-American History originated from an urge to social reform as well as the urge to scholarship. The conception of its nature, purposes or goals, and of values to be derived from the study and teaching of this discipline have been shaped, to a large extent, by this duality of urges. If one follows the practice of the many modern educators who "divide subjects or areas into two kinds called 'tool studies' and 'content studies,'"[3] he finds that always Afro-American History has been viewed as both a "content study" and a "tool study."

Of the scholarship goal, George Washington Williams declared in his celebrated study—"Not as a blind panegyrist of my race, nor as a partisan apologist, but from a love for 'the truth of history,' I have striven to record the truth, the whole truth, and nothing but the truth."[4] Similarly, Article II of the Constitution of the Association for the Study of Negro Life and History, published when this organization had been in existence only two years, gave as the Association's object, "The collection of sociological and historical documents and the promotion of studies bearing on the Negro."[5] Of the social reform goal, in 1841 James W. C. Pennington voiced a sentiment which practically every Black historian has echoed. Giving the purpose of his *Textbook of the Origin and History of the Colored People,*[6] Pennington declared in his Preface, "Prejudices are to be uprooted, false views are to be corrected." In 1936 L. D. Reddick stated before the annual meeting of the Association for the Study of Negro Life and History, in Richmond, Virginia that one of the purposes of Negro History is to "inculcate a dynamic pride in . . . Negroes."[7] "It is clear," Reddick continued, "that Negro History has the generalized objective which it shares with all scholarship of seeking the advancement of knowledge plus the specific design as a lever of what might be termed 'racial progress.' "[8] In 1940 Professor W. B. Hesseltine stated that this Association "has assumed the task of inspiring pride in the achievements of the [Negro] race,"[9] and in 1957 John Hope Franklin wrote that "Negro history . . . can and, in time, will provide all America with a lesson in the wastefulness, nay, the wickedness of human exploitation and injustice that have characterized too much of this nation's past."[10] There may be no better evidence of the social reform goal of Negro History than the language of the section entitled, "Why the Negro in History," which Carter Woodson penned for the 1926 brochure on Negro History Week. Here Dr. Woodson wrote:

> Let truth destroy the dividing prejudices of national-
> ity and teach universal love without distinction of
> race, merit or rank. With the sublime enthusiasm
> and heavenly vision of the Great Teacher let us help
> men to rise above the race hate of this age unto the
> altruism of a rejuvenated universe.[11]

In its social uplift role the Association for the Study of Negro Life and History has followed the pattern of practically all organizations in the Afro-American or any other minority group which is segregated and discriminated against. The organizations of oppressed groups are not usually at liberty to have singularity of purpose, and it is to the credit of this Association that, with the primary and permanent role of promoting scholarship, it has mixed the social protest role.

In writings of the past the present writer has suggested that the Beginning School of Black Historians had an inordinate faith in the role of education, both as a cause of race prejudice when misused, and as a corrective of this prejudice when correctly applied. Yet, this prejudice was rooted in an actual de facto and de jure situation. Furthermore, the 1876-1912 bias against the Black man which American historiography displayed was not due solely to the romanticist leanings of the new Southern historiography, nor to the writings of such Europeans as Houston Stewart Chamberlain and Count Joseph Arthur de Gobineau. This bias drew considerable sustenance from the urban-Eastern-inspired aristocratic tone which dominated American historiography from 1865-1893. The twentieth century shift to a more favorable view of the Black man in history is in part the result of a general shift in American historiography from an aristocratic to a democratic bias. Further, the present writer has averred that an "improper mixing" of the scholarship and social protest urges, may be detrimental to Black historiography. There can be no quarrel with using Afro-American History to teach Black youths to respect themselves and their race, or to instill in American whites a greater respect for this nation's largest ethnic minority. This might well be called "applied Black History" and is a valid endeavor. However, while the scholar may be inspired to do research on a topic in this area by many motives, social uplift among them, once he begins his research and writing he is the pure scientist who should be guided by only the desire to discover, understand, and relate the truth as objectively and fully as he can. Ideal historical writing is not tendential and polemical, and only when his task of finding and relating the truth about the Black man in history is completed is the scholar free to enter upon the role of the applied social scientist, who brings the truth to bear on whatever problems may need resolution. Chattel slavery and racial segregation and discrimination have caused the Black historian periodically to lay down his scholar's mantle for that of the applied social scientist much more than has been the case with the American historian of the majority group.

The present writer has differed with some noted scholars regarding some of the reasons they assigned as primary justifications for Black History. Spinoza insisted that the philosopher must try to see things "under the aspect of eternity" and, in this view, the main end to which Negro History is absolutely necessary is to the fullest knowledge and understanding of human history. In the final analysis the cause of Black History is circumscribed by neither time nor circumstance, for it is the cause of knowledge and truth. Although it is understandable that the early makers of Afro-American historiography saw its meaning, significance, and value largely in terms of social usefulness, never should it be forgotten that when all present social problems are solved, Black History still will have all of the uses peculiar to any other body of knowledge. By 1969 it did not appear that the purpose or objectives of Black History had changed much since the Association was organized in 1915. While the scholarship goal is permanent, the social uplift goal remained because race prejudice, segregation, and discrimination remained. Yet, where other aspects of this discipline are concerned, it would seem that at least two important changes had occurred since 1915 which should be reflected in the philosophy of Afro-American History. These changes affect its nature and scope as well as interpretation. By reference to two other areas of historical specialization this may be illustrated.

Evaluating the present state of Occidental research into Chinese history, one critic stated recently that "the field is characterized more by basic 'factual' research than by sweeping interpretive writing."[12] On this, the critic continued:

> This is largely due to the recency of the assault on Chinese history by the American and European academic communities. Confronted with a vast and virgin field of investigation, many scholars have naturally been inclined to concentrate on particularities rather than generalities.[13]

Scientific Afro-American historiography is also of rather recent origin, and has been characterized more by "basic 'factual' research than by sweeping interpretative writing." Carter Woodson often said that in his day the great need of the area was for basic factual research. By 1969, however, the time had probably come when Afro-American History should be subjected to more comparative studies and to broader interpretive emphases.

Germaine to the second point is the comment which another scholar made recently about research and writing in state and local history. "Local history," he said, "has altered with the times, but the change has been so gradual and imperceptible that it seems not to have been noticed even by its practitioners."[14] Continuing, this scholar stated:

Crisply put, the change is this: local history is becoming less localized. It is widening out, extending its horizons, reaching for far-flung comparisons and points of reference. It is looking toward regional and interregional areas of interest.

.   .   .   .

The truth is, the world has shrunk, and in shrinking, the local at times . . . becomes even more significant.[15]

Have not these same developments implications for the present philosophy of Afro-American History? Does not the rise to world power of the U.S.A., the shrinking of the globe, and the increased internationalism have implications where today's philosophy of Afro-American History is concerned? Do not these developments mean, in part, that Afro-American History is perhaps more important than ever, and where interpretation is concerned, do not these developments call for a "widening out" of this history, and extending of its horizons, and reaching for far-flung comparisons and points of reference?

Today's student of Afro-American History has been well prepared for these emphases. Carter Woodson, W. E. B. Du Bois, Charles H. Wesley and other makers of modern Afro-American historiography have long contended that the approach to history should be broad. Dr. Woodson often declared that "Negro History Week" was more properly a "History Week," for, he stated, "there is no such thing as Negro History or Jewish History or Chinese History in the sense of isolated contributions."[16] The relations and interrelations of races, he declared, "the close communication of peoples, and the wide-spread diffusion of ideas have made it necessary for one group so to depend upon the other and so to profit by the achievements of the other that

it is difficult to have any particular culture ear-marked."[17]
"History, then," he concluded, "is the progress of mankind
rather than of racial or national achievement."[18]

The Problem of Interpretation

In the matter of interpretation, probably the biggest
pitfalls for the student of Afro-American History have been
the moral, Great Man, and economic emphases. The Beginning School, comprised of such men as Nell, Pennington,
Lewis, Holly, Wilson, Brown, and Williams, viewed history
almost exclusively as an affair in which, using individuals
as tools, the forces of God and the Devil were in conflict,
with the latter inexorably doomed. In this view the Civil
War came as God's way of ending slavery and as punishment to the nation because of its wrong-doing. This interpretation, even if related to the tone of Abraham Lincoln's
Second Inaugural Address, is erroneous in its simplicity.
The same is true of that view which makes personalities always the prime determinants of events.

Frederick Jackson Turner's epic 1893 paper read before
the American Historical Association has been taken as the
event which signalled a "massive shift of American historiography" from an urban-Eastern-inspired aristocratic
bias "to a pro-democratic orientation."[19] Yet, because the
nineteenth century Black historian had generally been out
of step with the "patrician liberalism" of the 1865-1893 period, the shift for Afro-American historiography was not
nearly so massive as it was for American historiography in
general. Still, the appearance in 1896 of W. E. B. Du Bois'
book on the suppression of the African slave trade, and the
beginning of Dr. Woodson's work a few years later, ushered
in a new Afro-American historiography which was not only
superior in literary presentation, but in interpretation as
well. In spite of this, however, there was to begin in the
1930's a searching re-appraisal which appears to have been
triggered by the appearance in 1935 of W. E. B. Du Bois'

book, *Black Reconstruction,* the Marxian thesis of which several able scholars would emphatically hail as a highly welcome and long-overdue fresh frame of reference for Afro-American History. When this book appeared, Rayford W. Logan wrote that its "fresh interpretation" is "as significant as was Charles A. Beard's *Economic Interpretation of the Constitution of the United States.*"[21] A few other persons were similarly impressed, but the fact was soon to be grasped by most scholars that the Marxian thesis therein was not the greatest contribution of the book *Black Reconstruction.*

The Revolt against Classical Liberalism

One year after the appearance of this book, Dr. L. D. Reddick, at the twenty-first annual meeting of the Association for the Study of Negro Life and History, issued a call for "A New Interpretation for Negro History."[22] This history, he stated, "is quite different from the study of the Negro in that Negro History has a purpose which is built upon a faith."[23] Elaborating on this position, Dr. Reddick continued:

> At the sound of such words—purpose, faith—our theoretical objector may again rush forward to protest that the validity of history as history is destroyed if it is urged forward by any purpose other than the search for truth or sustained by any faith save that invested in the methods and procedures. This objection, quite fortunately, is over-ruled by the evidence that despite what the authors themselves may say, all history has been written with an 'other' purpose. . . . In the better works, the thesis is implied more often than stated; still it is never absent. It seems humanly impossible to escape point of view.[24]

Holding that there was in 1936 little difference between the philosophy of Black historians before or since Dr. Woodson's work, Reddick declared that these historians should end their preoccupation with the "slavery theme" and with the Black man in the U.S.A. and turn more to Africa and South America as they were beginning to do. Also, he said, they should end their bondage to the "philosophy of liberalism" which emphasized individualism, rationalism, tolerance, laissez-faire, and progress. This philosophy, he declared, "has included many of the true factors" in the nation's historical development, but "has been superficial in relating these factors and in determining the forces which have been influential."[25] In giving his own preferred frame of reference and interpretation, this scholar, obviously influenced by Charles A. Beard and W. E. B. Du Bois,[26] gave great stress to the role of economic factors. Reddick had considerable to say about the Civil War as essentially a "conflict of economic systems," the role of "economic interests" on Reconstruction and the effects of a "rather blatantly aggressive industrialism" on events since 1865. He contended that while up to 1936 the "social philosophy of the Negro historians" had been "sadly lacking in a grasp of the dynamic forces" hence had turned out to be "the rather naive Emersonian gospel of self-reliance, simple optimism and patient regard for destiny," when his own economic perspective is taken American history begins "to assume a pattern astonishingly intelligible."[27] In continuation he urged young scholars not to "fall into the errors of their literary fathers." In conclusion, he stated:

> Since point of view is inescapable, it is . . . essential that the frame of reference should be large, generous, and socially intelligent; that the developments in Negro life be seen in connection with those of the general pattern of other racial, minority and laboring groups.[29]

And:

> If Negro History is to escape the provincial nature of its first phase, it will surely re-define the area of

subject matter in terms of a larger focus; recast its
catalog of determinative influences affecting Negro
life and re-examine the social philosophy implicit
throughout the work.[30]

Two years after this call was issued for a new interpretation for Afro-American history, an academic colleague,
who was teaching less than one hundred miles from where
Dr. Reddick was employed,[31] read a paper at the annual
meeting of the same Association which revealed a major
source of the Reddick proposals. In a discourse entitled,
"The Interpretation of the Thought of the Contemporary
Negro from the Standpoint of the Theory of the Sociology
of Knowledge," Dr. W. T. Fontaine referred glowingly to
Professor Reddick's "new interpretation" and declared that
this was part of a new "toughmindedness" in Negro thought
which showed "an opposition to the thought patterns, concepts and techniques of the democratic-liberal-scientific
Weltanschauung."[32] Like Dr. Reddick, Professor Fontaine
had nothing but praise for the Marxist thesis of Du Bois's
Black Reconstruction. Fontaine mentioned with apparent
favor the "agnosticism of the late Weldon Johnson, Du Bois
and Just, the atheism of Schuyler and Hughes, and the con-
tra-acculturative 'black God' religion of Father Divine," as
well as new departures in thought among certain distinguished Negro scholars,[33] and took polite jibes at the sometimes "conservatism" of Alain Locke[34] and Charles S. Johnson.[35] Again like Dr. Reddick, Fontaine deplored "the
uncritical acceptance of the liberal-democratic Weltanschauung by the American Negro," which he called "a supreme example of a situationally determined knowledge."[36]
Fontaine made it clear that he preferred that the Black man
reject the liberal-democratic view in favor of a militant
rationally determined outlook and, several times, he expressed the conviction that the new trend in Afro-American
thought which he favored was largely the product of "a defense psychology thrust upon it by social conditions."

It is fairly clear by now that in some of its aspects the revolt against moderation, objectivity, and faith in progress which Reddick and Fontaine evidenced in the thirties was itself a temporary phenomenon. This radicalism in historical interpretation was part and parcel of the radicalism which saw a number of black and white intellectuals flirt with Communism, and a general pushing to the fore of pessimism, iconoclasm and nihilism in the thought and actions of Occidental man. Much of this had too much of the heavy hand of prevailing but temporary social conditions upon it. Yet, in numerous ways, by 1969 the wheel had turned full circle again.

Although the rejection-without-qualification of the liberal philosophy mentioned above was extreme in some respects, it was far from being completely in error. Not only was this rejection in line with a larger movement among Afro-American scholars, but the reading of such a discourse as R. R. Palmer's "The Waning of Classical Liberalism," shows that this thinking was in line with a movement which was affecting the whole of Occidental culture.[39] As Professor Palmer shows, Classical Liberalism had been visibly on the wane since about 1880 and in many ways this philosophy was given the COUP DE GRACE by World War I and the Great Depression. By the time Dr. Reddick read his paper before the Association the mighty weight of social circumstances had demonstrated clearly that some elements of the old liberalism had become antiquated and harmful. Of these no-longer-useful elements the most pronounced were probably the faith in automatic progress and the faith that science and knowledge are inherently benign. When these faults of the liberal philosophy are considered, it can be seen that Professor Reddick's judgment that not only was a revised or enlarged interpretation for Negro History in order, but that the same need existed for the whole of American and Occidental historiography, was essentially correct. Yet, reacting against malevolent factors and trends in modern technology, corporateness, war, depressions, and poverty, and against certain ideas implicit or explicit in Social Darwinism, Freudianism, and Behavioristic Psychology, the opponents of Classical Liberalism sometimes went too far. The old liberalism contained many elements which were not just "situationally determined," as Dr. Fontaine would say, but which are or ought to be of value as long as men claim to be civilized.

In their insistence that in nineteenth century Afro-American historiography the list of determinative influences was too narrow, and that point of view is inescapable, Drs. Reddick and Fontaine were correct. But too much easily can be made of this latter point. That Edward Gibbon was a rationalist, Leopold Von Ranke a conservative, and Heinrich Von Treitschke a nationalist, as Reddick points out, does not legislate these faults into any general acceptance. Productions as complete, objective, and free from bias as is humanly possible ever must be the scholar's goal, and Afro-American History possesses no exception to this.

By 1969 it was clear that the list of determinative influences on Afro-American history should be expanded to accommodate a new uncompromising militancy of black Americans which was best symbolized by the term "black revolution." Central to this mood were a heightened appreciation for the role and significance of the least-privileged segments of black society, acceptance of some racial segregation, unity of purpose and action for the total black community, greater acceptance of Africa and the culture of Afro-Americans, and a sense of racial mission that was unique in scope if not in aim. Although these notes were most-often sounded in the utterances of such persons as James Baldwin, Martin Luther King, Jr., Malcolm X, Elijah Muhammed, Adam Clayton Powell, Jr., Stokely Carmichael, Floyd McKissick, Ron Karenga, and Eldridge Cleaver, the black professional historian was compelled to react. Since explicit here was an attack on the Negro in-

tellectual reminiscent of the earlier Marcus Garvey movement, a few Negro historians felt menaced by this movement that was often popularly-labelled "Black Power." If it
frightened some white Americans, still more of them ob-
jected to Black Nationalism. The latter may be defined as
any philosophy, program, or movement by Afro-Americans
which directly and importantly connects their efforts to
acquire freedom, equality, and manhood to the concept or
reality of the nation; which accepts and exalts the African
past; and, which exalts the Black masses as the focal point
of the philosophy and program. Here the *scope* of the specific philosophy or program is of central importance. A philosophy or program of black nationalism does not necessarily
require an increase in racial segregation,—nor a separate
nation—, but it must call for making the best possible use
of that racial separatism which exists.

Black nationalism has been a chief means by which Afro-
Americans have sought to raise their philosophies and pro-
grams for liberation above the level of the trivial; to expand
the scope of their planning and efforts beyond the level of
the municipal, state, or regional levels. By 1969 the Black
historian knew that, except in its most extreme forms, black
nationalism raises instead of lowers the quality of Afro-
American citizenship, hence black nationalism ought to be
encouraged and supported, even and especially by white
America.

Doubtless some Afro-American historians were guilty of
having over-valued Europe, middle class values, and whiteness, and having denigrated blackness, the lower classes and
Africa. Still to the Afro-American historian "Black Power"
was less traumatic than perhaps for any other group of
Americans. Indeed, the black historian found some aspects
of this movement flattering, for to him they were somewhat
ancient notes, a terminus rather than a beginning. Because
he sees better than most people the old in the new, the historian is likely to feel less menaced by the "new." But

there is more here. Carter Woodson, W. E. B. Du Bois, Charles Wesley, and numerous other Black historians long had urged that Africa and the black man's history and culture should be appreciated and disseminated, and that snobbishness should be eliminated not only from historiography but from culture and society in general. Almost a half century had passed since Woodson in, *The Mis-Education of the Negro,* urged a reconstruction of curricular offerings for the black student, and during the 1930's Du Bois had urged his race to embrace and make positive use of the racial segregation that was imposed upon them.

There was little in the thought and writings of the professional Black historians which pointed to the sense of mission which by 1969 was a prominent element in the thought of Afro-Americans. But by this date, the professional Black historian, more likely to hold the Ph.D. degree, was more likely to be literate enough to see that the views of Occidental culture which such persons as Malcolm X or Eldridge Cleaver were projecting were supported by such works as Frederick Nietzsche's, *Thus Spoke Zarathustra,* Sigmund Freud's, *Civilization and Its Discontents,* Oswald Spengler's, *Decline of the West,* Pitirim A. Sorokin's, *Social and Cultural Dynamics,* Arnold J. Toynbee's, *A Study of History,* Norman O. Brown's, *Life Against Death* and *Love's Body,* Thomas J. Altizer's, *Mircea Eliade and the Dialectic of the Sacred,* Marshall McLuhan's, *Understanding Media* and *War and Peace in the Global Village,* and many other volumes and articles. These scholars depicted an obsolescent Occidental culture and man, both overly-repressed, fragmented, specialized, calculating, cold, cruel, alienated, inhuman, and doomed. These scholars differed on the cause but not on the description of the disease. As to cause, Karl Marx blamed the workings of classes and the dialectic and the natural tendencies of the Bourgeoisie, Nitezsche stressed conscience and guilt, Norman O. Brown blamed an unnatural ending of the harmony between the life and death instincts, Sorokin blamed the natural tendencies of a Sensate culture, Altizer blamed the workings of the dialectic and the death of God, McLuhan saw the Gutenberg visual-linear culture of the mechanical age as the villain and the inauguration of the electric technology as the key to the new image and destiny of the Afro-American and all Occidentals.

The emergent new culture depicted by such thinkers as Norman O. Brown, Thomas J. Altizer, or Marshall McLuhan is to be a healthier one in which there will be more play and less poverty, repression, alienation, hatred, and war. Yet, denied access to the mainstream, most black people have been less contaminated by the old culture. The age-old laughter, song, dance, friendliness, and humanism of black people provide a key pattern and prototype (along with the Orient, or many folk-level cultures) for those Occidentals who are ill to use in finding their way to wholeness and sanity. In 1969 some of this scholarship was still too-recent for definitive evaluation, but enough had been said, often enough and long enough, to let the black professional historian know that, properly viewed, he could take serious-ly much of the thinking of such writers as James Baldwin, Malcolm X, and Eldridge Cleaver.

By 1969 the Black historian had to fit his discipline into the rising demand on college, university, and high school campuses for a curriculum in Black Studies. Black students in particular declared that curricular offerings long had been too-European or White-oriented, and they demanded that Africa and the Black experience be given an equal place in curricular offerings. Some persons agreed with the aims of the Black students, but disagreed with the methods and tactics which were used in their efforts to achieve these goals. Most of the persons who opposed Black Studies pro-grams appeared to commit the fallacy of presenting an ei-ther—or situation. They seemed to feel that Black students had to make a choice between Black Studies and "White

Studies," and that to choose the former was simply a way of "copping out." Black Studies, these critics held, were nothing but easy courses for the lazy student, and these courses had little or nothing to do with the "real world." While white students need the Black Studies curriculum, it was argued, for effective participation in the "real world" Black students needed only plenty of "White Studies" such as chemistry, physics, biology, mathematics, and engineering. Yet, by 1969 it was so clear that Black students needed *both* Black and White Studies until it was difficult to understand why some persons felt that here an either—or situation existed.

There long has been a debate as to whether the Historian should be a moral critic. In an article entitled, "The Historian as Psychiatrist," in the November 24, 1962 issue of *The Nation,* Theodore Roszak held that unless the Historian serves as a moral critic he appears to condone everything that he reports. To this might be added that, unless he serves as a moral critic, the Historian's role is artificial and non-human. To write history in which the author shows no joy or sorrow, pride or shame, approval or disapproval is to write as though the Historian is not a human being. By 1969 some Black students, at least, were objecting to Black historiography which simply reported the events of Black history. These students insisted that in historical writing goodness should be praised and evil condemned.

The Black historian of the era of Carter G. Woodson (1915-1950) championed the cause of the Black masses because he believed in political, economic, and social democracy. The Black historian of the late 1960s had the additional reason that the culture of the Black masses was winning recognition as an authentic, distinct culture—which should be preserved, and—, whose richness and dynamism had therapeutic values for not only the youth of all races and nations, but also for jaded, overly-sophisticated members of the middle and upper classes.

CHAPTER IV

THE FATHER OF NEGRO HISTORY

Carter Godwin Woodson was born of ex-slave parentage in Virginia, December 19, 1875. He was one of nine children. When young Woodson was seventeen years of age, he moved with his family to Huntington, West Virgina. With only the barest rudiments of an education, like Booker T. Washington before him, he worked several years in the coal mines of West Virginia.[1]

In 1895 this young man entered Douglass High School in Huntington. He had mastered the fundamentals of common school subjects largely from self-instruction and soon graduated from this high school. The first two years after graduation he taught in the public schools of West Virginia, and was then given the honor of serving as Principal of the high school from which he had graduated. Keenly ambitious, Woodson studied at Berea College in Kentucky and several summers at the University of Chicago until, in 1907, he received the bachelor's degree from the latter institution.

From 1903-1906 Woodson was a supervisor of schools in the Philippine Islands. This experience gave him a facility with the Spanish language which was to stand him in good stead during later researches. This experience was followed by a year of travel in Asia and Europe, during which time he spent one semester at the Sorbonne in Paris. He became a fluent user of the French language also. Returning home, he continued his studies at the University of Chicago, and received the M.A. degree from that institution in 1908. The next year found Woodson working on a doctorate degree at Harvard University. There he studied un-

der such outstanding teachers as Professors W. B. Munro
and Edward Channing.

In order to do research on his dissertation at the Library
of Congress, Washington, D. C. Woodson took a job teaching
Romance languages in a high school in Washington. His dissertation topic was "The Disruption of Virginia," and he received the Ph.D. degree from Harvard in 1912—only the second Negro ever to receive the degree in History from that institution. Woodson's dissertation was never published because Charles W. Ambler had brought out his *Sectionalism
in Virginia, 1776-1861.*[2]

The years 1919-1920 found Woodson serving as Dean
of the Howard University (Washington, D. C.) School of
Liberal Arts, but he resigned after one year because he
disagreed with the educational policies of the school. From
1920-1922 he was Dean of West Virginia Institute (later
West Virginia State College). Apparently for the same
reason that he resigned from Howard University, plus his
desire to live in Washington so as to be able to continue his
researches, he resigned from West Virginia Institute and
gave up classroom teaching as a major interest. His dominant purpose, according to Kelly Miller, was to "turn his
historical training and preparation to the best racial account.[3]
Thus Woodson turned to what was to become his life work.
At Chicago, on September 9, 1915, he had organized the
Association for the Study of Negro Life and History. This
organization was incorporated in Washington, D. C. the
next year.

*The Association for the Study of Negro Life and History
and Its Organs*

The Association for the Study of Negro Life and History
was organized in a brief meeting in Chicago by Carter G.
Woodson, with the assistance of four other persons. The organization was to have an Executive Council, Editor and
Editorial Staff of eight persons.[4] It was the "first sys-

tematic effort of the Negro to treat the records of the race scientifically and to publish the findings to the world."[5] The next year Woodson brought out, on January 1, the first issue of the Association's quarterly, the *Journal of Negro History*. For this initial issue, he used largely his own funds, and published it without consulting the Executive Council. One member of the Council resigned in anger and disgust.[6] Modelled after the *American Historical Review*, the purposes of the *Journal of Negro History* were "the collection of sociological and historical data on the Negro, the study of peoples of African blood, the publishing of books in this field, and the promotion of harmony between the races by acquainting the one with the other."[7]

Despite the fact that during its first three years annual deficits had to be made up from Dr. Woodson's small salary as a teacher at the Armstrong High School in Washington, D. C., in 1969 the *Journal* had never missed an issue. It soon became practically self-supporting. Included among the scholars who praised the appearance and quality of this new organ, and wished it well, were A. H. Buffington, Charles H. Haskins, A. C. McLaughlin, Ferdinand Schevill and Frederick Jackson Turner.[8] Professor Buffington wrote: "The more I think of the matter, the more I do believe there is a place for such a publication. The history of the Negro in Africa, in the West Indies, in Spanish America and in the United States offers a large field in which little appears to have been done."[9]

Woodson remained editor of the *Journal* throughout his life and wrote many of the articles which appeared in it. He was the largest single contributor of book reviews to this publication. The Association hired many young historians to work with him on topics in which the editor was interested. Money received from this work was of importance to some of the young scholars in enabling them to complete their doctoral studies. Among these investigators were Drs. Alreuthus A. Taylor, Lorenzo J. Greene, Rayford

Logan and Florence Beatty Brown, all of whom came to rank among the best of Black historians and teachers.[10]

Upon the inception of the *Journal of Negro History*, Frederick L. Hoffman, statistician of the Prudential Life Insurance Company, "likened the movement unto the important work started by John R. Green, in popularizing the history of England."[11] According to Woodson, the public immediately began to see that "the need of the hour was not to write books from the scant materials available, but to collect and preserve sufficient data of all sorts on the Negro to enable scientifically trained men to produce treatises based upon the whole truth."[12] Ferdinand Schevill stated that the first issue of the *Journal* bore "every evidence of a scientific disposition on the part of the editor and his board."[13]

The first substantial support for the *Journal of Negro History*[14] came from Julius Rosenwald, who for years gave $100.00 a quarter for the support of the Association and its publication.[15] It was not until after 1919 that this publication was self-supporting. However, rising costs of printing changed this favorable situation the very next year. The financial worries of this organization and its journal ended temporarily when the Carnegie Corporation, in 1921, appropriated $25,000 to the Association. This amount was to be paid at the rate of $5,000.00 per year. It is at this point that Woodson was able to give up teaching school and become full-time director of the Association.[16]

Also in 1921 the Laura Spelman Rockefeller Memorial appropriated a like sum of $25,000 to be paid to the Association in a similar manner. This fund was to be used for studying "the free Negro prior to the Civil War," and "the Negro in the Reconstruction of the Southern States."[17] In addition to Dr. Woodson, the Association was now able to hire other investigators to work in the United States and other parts of the world, collecting documents and facts on black people. Also, Woodson was then able to devote part of his time to field work with clubs and schools in his effort to popularize the teaching and studying of Black history, and the Association was serving as a reference bureau for information respecting the Black race.

Luther Porter Jackson pointed out in 1940 that the early volumes of the *Journal of Negro History* "show a low standard of documentation," while the later volumes show "a high standard of documentation."[18] This, he thinks, was due to the fact that few sources on the Black man had been collected during the early years of the existence of the *Journal*, and that the earlier Black historians mostly held only the master's degree. Of the documents which had been published in the *Journal* by 1968, almost all of them are found in volumes one through fourteen.[19] Jackson attributes the failure of the Association to continue the publication of as many documents as were published during these early years to the lack of funds for the expensive task of locating them.[20] He also points out that the first twelve volumes of the *Journal* carried sixteen book reviews each. Volume twenty jumped to twenty-six reviews, and volume twenty-two carried fifty-one.[21] The growing number of reviews reveals, perhaps, the growing interest in Afro-American history, as well as the growing number of Afro-American and other scholars who could be called on to prepare reviews.

Shortly after founding the Association for the Study of Negro Life and History, Dr. Woodson organized the Associated Publishers to handle both the publication and sale of books. This was a private corporation, in which he held over ninety per cent of the stock, organized because he felt that white publishers were not interested in bringing out scholarly works by American Blacks. In addition to publishing his own numerous volumes, the Association sponsored and published the researches of other scholars. On this point Woodson wrote:

> The Negro faces another stone wall when he presents . . . scientific productions to the publishing

houses. They may not be prejudiced, but they are not interested in the Negro. We understand that the more serious the work is the less chance it has for reaching a large reading public. Yet scholarship must be advanced by these strictly scientific works. This represents a very dark prospect for the rapidly increasing number of young men and women who are prepared for creative work but receive no encouragement whatever. In this way the cause of Negro scholarship has dreadfully suffered in spite of the one-sided method of the foundations in trying to broaden the minds of Negroes teaching in their own schools. What is the use of knowing things if they cannot be published to the world? If the Negro is to settle down to publishing merely what others permit him to bring out, the world will never know what the race has thought and felt and attempted and accomplished and the story of the Negro will perish with him.[22]

At the end of The Associated Publisher's first ten years of existence, Woodson had published ten monographs, and "stimulated and trained young men with the capacity for research according to the methods of modern historiography."[23] He regarded as the crowning achievement of this first decade of the Association's existence, that it had "made the world see the Negro as a participant rather than as a lay figure in history."[24] By this time the *Journal* was a great success, circulating among libraries and scholars all over the world. This scholar always emphasized that his work was the beginning of a crusading movement to establish Afro-American history as a recognized and respected field. This attitude caused him to make repeated mention of the stimulation and training of "young men with the capacity for research according to the methods of modern historiography." And near the conclusion of his life's work, he stated, "The stimulation and training of young men for historical research may be regarded as the outstanding achievement of the Association."[25]

By 1930 the contributions to the Association by wealthy white Americans and foundations had begun to fall off. Woodson always believed that this was due to people growing dissatisfied with his attacks on the "white supremacy" doctrine—his policy of "telling the whole truth and nothing but the truth regardless of whom it affected."[26] He turned to trying to organize the Black population of the United States to obtain the needed support from them, and by 1940 the income of the Association had risen to about two-thirds of what it was during its most prosperous years.[27]

In its first twenty-five years of existence, the Association received and spent $337,926.24, and published over thirty volumes.[28] By 1940 the Association was publishing not only its own organs but directing studies in Afro-American history in clubs and schools, promoting the home study of the race by mail, producing textbooks, collecting and preserving documents, and subsidizing young scholars in their historical studies. It had sent investigators to work in the Archives of the Indies, in Seville, Spain, the British Museum and the Public Record Office of London, and had sent one person to study folklore in Haiti. In addition, by this date the Association had purchased the collection of 4,000 books on the race known as the A. A. Schomburg Collection and presented this collection to the New York Public Library. Funds for this latter purchase were granted by the Carnegie Corporation.[29]

By 1935 at least 350 articles and series of documents had appeared in the *Journal of Negro History*, of which 241 were devoted either wholly or primarily to the Afro-American in the United States. Thus, about one-third of the material had dealt with the race outside the United States of America. Of this one-third, most of the articles and series of documents had dealt with Africa, an almost equal number with Great Britain and Europe, and the remainder with

Latin America, Canada, the West Indies other than Haiti
and Cuba, and an almost negligible number with the Pa-
cific Area and Near East.[30] Of these articles Rayford W.
Logan wrote:

> Some of the articles have been excellent, a few
> mediocre, but the general average has been entire-
> ly creditable. A large number of these articles
> utilized primary sources not only in English, but in
> French, German and Spanish. It is gratifying to find
> a growing number of Negro scholars able to read
> easily French. All too small a number, however, have
> mastered German. Some have used the rich store of
> Spanish resources. But the great mine of Brazilian
> sources in the Portuguese language has been left al-
> most totally unexplored.[31]

Dr. Logan failed to mention the great neglect by Afro-
American scholars of the ancient and medieval periods. Few
have chosen these areas, and the American Negro researcher
has made almost no contribution to them. Almost all have
received their formal training with a concentration in American history. Thus, almost completely, they have failed to
develop facility in some languages, such as Greek, Latin,
Arabic, Spanish, and Portuguese, which is necessary for complete coverage of the field of Afro-American studies. Especially are the first three languages necessary for study
of some important segments of the African background of
the Afro-American. Dr. Logan ended his summation with
an interesting prediction. "When the *Journal* has had an
existence as long as has the *American Historical Review*, it
is confidently expected that the *Journal* will not suffer by
comparison with the best in the world."[32]

The *Journal of Negro History* gave tremendous impetus
to scholarship in history by Blacks by providing them with
a Journal which they felt would receive their articles with
friendliness, and by giving them a living example of the

level of scholarship that could be reached within the field of racial history. Among early subscribers to the *Journal* were Oswald Garrison Villard, Helen Keller, J. E. Spingarn, Julius Rosenwald, Edward Channing and other outstanding Americans. Among the early contributors of articles and reviews were Marcus W. Jernegan, Jerome Dowd, W. E. B. Du Bois, A. E. Jenks, J. S. Bassett, A. B. Hart, and other top scholars. During its first year, the *Journal* had circulated on all five continents and it had begun its second year with a circulation of 4,000.[33]

Negro History Week and the Negro History Bulletin

"Negro History Week" grew out of an effort to celebrate annually the literary achievements of the race begun by the Omega Psi Phi Fraternity, the oldest of fraternities to be established on a colored college campus.[34] Carter G. Woodson, an honorary member of this fraternity, convinced its leaders that he could make the celebration more effective by sponsoring it as an activity of the Association for the Study of Negro Life and History. Thus, in 1926, Woodson took over the celebration and gave it the name of "Negro History Week." The celebration immediately became a national success. This annual event, said Woodson, "taught Negroes not to play up their grievances but to demonstrate what Negroes have actually achieved in spite of their handicaps," and "stimulated other efforts of the Association and of other organizations for the improvement of Negroes."[35] Again, calling the observance of Negro History Week one of the "most fortunate steps ever taken by the Association," Woodson pointed out that this event, "Easily understood, . . . was readily taken up by ministers, teachers, social workers, and businessmen and several state departments of education," which rallied to the support of the movement.[36]

Woodson states that the success of Negro History Week led to a demand for a simplified organ which would regularly publish the many little-known facts such as those which he had sent to schools as brochures as a part of the annual celebration of Negro History Week.[37] The result was the *Negro History Bulletin*, first published in October, 1937. The *Bulletin*, a monthly publication, appears only during the nine months of the regular school year, and is especially aimed at meeting the needs which grade school teachers and pupils, and the general public have for heavily illustrated literature and unique and little-known facts about Black people. By 1940 the circulation of the *Bulletin* was 5,000 and it was increasing annually.[38]

Negro History Week and other activities of the Association designed to popularize Afro-American history could not have met with the great success which they did without the cooperation of many persons in many locales. Though these persons were not always professional historians or writers, they made a very significant contribution to the effort to let the world know that Afro-Americans have been more than criminals or hewers of wood and drawers of water. Businessmen, ministers of the gospel, housewives, lawyers, doctors, school presidents or principals or grade school teachers, they came from all walks of life and made some aspects of the work of the Association a middle-class "mass movement." A few non-professional historians who played such a role are: Dr. H. Councill Trenholm, long-time president of Alabama State College; Mrs. Mary McCloud Bethune, late President of Bethune-Cookman College; Dr. Albert N. D. Brooks, long-time editor of *The Negro History Bulletin*; Mrs. Geneva C. Turner, Nerissa L. Milton, and Jessie H. Roy of Washington, D. C.; Jane Shackleford, Helen Adele Whiting, the latter of Atlanta, Georgia; Mrs. Irene M. Gaines, Chicago, Illinois; Mr. O. A. Jackson, Okmulgee, Oklahoma; Mr. Louis R. Mehlinger, Washington, D. C.; Mr. H. A. Tynes and Dr. Marguerite Cartwright of New York; Dr. Benjamin E. Mays, Atlanta, Georgia; Mrs. Jessie P. Guzman, Tuskegee, Alabama; Mrs. Vernell M. Oliver, Wilberforce, Ohio; Mr. Harvey C. Jackson, Detroit, Michigan; Mr.

Arnett G. Lindsey, Washington, D. C.; Mr. J. Rupert Picott, Richmond, Virginia; Mrs. Irene M. Gaines and Messrs. John H. Johnson and James H. Jackson of Chicago, Illinois; and Mrs. Vassie D. Wright of Los Angeles, California.

Some of the professional historians, social scientists, and others who played important roles in getting Afro-American history established as an accepted area of specialization are: Herbert Aptheker, Clarence Bacote, William Brewer, Herman Dreer, Merl R. Eppse, Helen G. Edmonds, John Hope Franklin, Lorenzo Green, Joseph Grimes, Leo Hansberry, Melville J. Herskovits, Luther Porter Jackson, Caulbert A. Jones, Rayford W. Logan, Augustus Low, Louis R. Mehlinger, Dorothy Porter, Benjamin Quarles, Lawrence D. Reddick, James H. Brewer, J. Reuben Sheeler, J. A. Rogers, William T. Savage, A. A. Schomburg, Alrutheus A. Taylor, Joseph H. Taylor, Monroe Work, Charles Wesley, and Prince Wilson.

Woodson's Books

Woodson's first work of significance was his dissertation, completed in 1912 for Harvard University. The title of Woodson's dissertation was "The Disruption of Virginia," and as it covered the same general information as Charles W. Ambler's "Sectionalism in Virginia, 1776-1861" which appeared in 1910, Woodson's dissertation, as previously stated, was never published.

Education of the Negro Prior to 1861

This work appeared in 1915,[39] bearing the sub-title, "A History of the Education of the Colored People of the United States from the beginning of Slavery to the Civil War." Woodson had begun the research for this volume with the idea of writing a complete coverage of the field of Negro education up to 1915. He Believed that there would be so little material on the ante-bellum period that the bulk of his volume would concern itself with post-bellum events. However, he was surprised to find a great amount of material on the earlier period, and decided to cover only pre-war years, since it would make "a much more interesting book."[40] "In fact," he stated, "the accounts of the successful strivings of Negroes for enlightenment under most adverse circumstances reads like beautiful romances of a people in an heroic age."[41]

The author divided the history of Negro education before the Civil War into two periods. The first division ends with the year 1835. During this period, he found that many slaves were given education on the plantations. During the years from 1836-1861 he found that this patriarchal education disappeared, due largely to fear of insurrection which was aroused by such rebellions as those of Denmark Vesey and Nat Turner. During these latter years, the slave received only an industrial-type education.

Woodson found agreement on the high degree of interest which this topic would arouse. Reviewing the volume for the *American Journal of Sociology*, R. E. Park wrote: "Aside from the light which this book throws upon the rather obscure subjects, there is something at once touching and romantic in the story which its record of fact reveals."[42] The book was praised for the high standard of scholarship which it met. One reviewer, calling it "a model of scholarship," added that "Every available fact has been garnered and is made accessible to the reader by a painstaking index, while a scholarly bibliography gives the original sources. A valuable set of documents is appended, including many not hitherto laid open to the general public."[43] Another reviewer wrote, "The author has taken pains to substantiate every fact that he presents . . . This is a work of profound historical research, full of interesting data on a most important phase of race life which has hitherto remained unexplored and neglected."[44] Woodson did not usually take the trouble to document so thoroughly in most of his future writings. Like his distinguished contemporary, Du Bois, his first two serious works were his most scholarly from the standpoint of documentation and general objectivity.

The Negro in Our History

This scholar's textbook for the upper grades, high school and the general reader, *The Negro in Our History,* went through nineteen editions during his lifetime. First published in 1922, the work was in its fourth edition by 1927.[45] Until his death, it was constantly revised and enlarged to keep it up to date and was unquestionably the best textbook on the subject until the appearance in 1947 of John Hope Franklin's *From Slavery to Freedom.*[46] Since Dr. Woodson's death his volume has been revised by Charles H. Wesley.

Woodson's textbook was designed "to present to the average reader in succinct form a history of the United States as it has been influenced by the presence of the Negro in this country."[47] It became the standard text for courses in Afro-American history throughout the United States. One reviewer stated that it bore "the brunt of the movement for the popularization of Negro history," and that "It has actually remolded the attitude of the popular mind, especially among Negroes as to the place and importance of the Negro in American history."[48] This same reviewer criticized the work for being "essentially a compendium of facts," although he admitted that the great influence of the volume might be due to its lack of interpretation. He stated, however, that for the university level a more interpretative text was needed. He concluded that this volume "belongs to that select class of books that have brought about a revolution of mind."[49] Beyong doubt, this book deserves a high place among the forces and events which have won general acceptance for the field of Negro history.

In *The Negro in Our History* Woodson is especially temperate and objective. He was probably aware that, had he given the book an obviously biased nature, it would not have been widely used. While most Black historians severely criticize President Andrew Johnson for opposing Radical Reconstruction, and present the character and personality of Johnson in an unfavorable light, Woodson steers clear of any characterization of this President. Throughout the volume one can observe a similar caution.

The volume gives a brief survey of early Black civilizations in Africa, then discusses the enslavement of the race, early efforts toward emancipation and colonization, the abolition movement, Civil War and Reconstruction, and the freedman's efforts at social justice since the end of Reconstruction. Profusely illustrated, the volume was finished five years before it was published. As World War I was then going on, and the cost of publishing high, publication was delayed.[50] The fifth edition carried 651 pages, 350 illustrations. By then the volume was getting too bulky. Hubert Harrison, reviewing the book for the *New York Tribune*, called it a "primal defect" that Woodson's style was "cramped and slovenly."[51] As is characteristic of Black historians in general, Woodson viewed the issue of slavery as the central cause of the Civil War.[52]

A Century of Negro Migration

In 1918 appeared *A Century of Negro Migration*.[53] This volume reviews movements of Colored Americans from the South to the North and West, both as to the causes and results of the migrations. The chapter on the Civil War period describes the breaking up of northern Black communities when many persons followed the Union Army southward to resettle. Migration westward is also given close attention. The last chapter deals with the exodus during the First World War, which was the greatest voluntary movement of Negroes in the United States to that date. In a lengthy review,[54] the *London Times Literary Supplement* said of the volume: "There is no exuberance of statement, no fervid inaccuracy, no frothy declamation."[55]

The History of the Negro Church

In 1921 appeared his *The History of the Negro Church*,[56] an effort designed to treat the evolution of the Church "from the earliest period to the present time."[57] Woodson admitted that the final product did not represent what he desired to make it. This was because, "many facts of the past could not be obtained for the reason that several denominations have failed to keep records and facts known to persons now active in the church could not be collected because of indifference or the failure to understand the motives of the author."[58]

The History of the Negro Church is one of this historians most scholarly productions. The work is temperate in tone, and almost straight narrative. However, a critical reader would probably regret that this volume is almost completely devoid of documentation, and there is no bibliography or bibliographical notes. Also, Woodson probably generalizes a little too much concerning what Black church leaders have believed about certain political and economic questions during various periods.

In this volume, the church leaders are praised because they have been conservative on racial matters. He praises the traditional conservatism of the church as "fortunate." The statement seems somewhat contradictory to the arguments which Woodson directs at the church leaders in his *Mis-Education of the Negro*. This volume further reveals Woodson as an intellectual with an eighteenth century faith in education. Woodson felt that *the* way to improve race relations was through education of both American whites and blacks. His patience with racial advance probably sprang, in part, from a realization that education is necessarily a slow process.

Early Negro Education in West Virginia, and *Fifty Years of Negro Citizenship as Qualified by the U. S. Supreme Court*

In December, 1921 Woodson published a small booklet entitled *Early Negro Education in West Virginia.*[59] The same year appeared his "Fifty Years of Negro Citizenship as Qualified by the United States Supreme Court," first in the *Journal of Negro History* as an article, and in 1924 in booklet form.[60] In the latter work, the author began with the assertion: "The citizenship of the Negro in this country is a fiction. The Constitution of the United States guarantees to him every right vouchsafed to any individual by the most liberal democracy on the face of the earth, but despite the powers of the Federal Government this agent of the body politic has studiously evaded the duty of safeguarding the rights of the Negro."[61] Although it is a good objective study of Constitutional history of the United States as it affected the freedmen in the period under question, the work fails to give a balanced picture of the reasons why the Supreme Court discriminated against the race in its rulings. By failing to mention that the Court may not have been far behind American public opinion, Woodson makes the Court THE villain.

The Mis-Education of the Negro

Woodson's *The Mis-Education of the Negro* was published in 1923.[62] In this work the author holds that the race has been miseducated because it has not been taught to value itself at its proper worth.[63] Topics handled in this volume are: "Negroes—Education," "Negroes—Moral and Social Conditions," "Negroes—Employment."

Woodson advocated a special type of education for the Colored American. The lack of sufficient race pride on the part of the Afro-American was a matter of serious concern to this scholar. Indeed, it was an obsession which helped move and direct the course of Woodson's life. An un-named reviewer in *Commonweal* reported:

> This is a challenging book. It throws down the gauntlet to those who have had anything to do with Negro education, whether of white or black race, and it bids the Negro to come forward in pride of race and heritage and standing on the basis of his own racial personality, demand an education that will develop that personality and its gifts rather than seek merely to imitate the white man.[64]

In *Mis-Education of the Negro,* Woodson is severe in his criticism of Negro education. "The only question which concerns us here," he wrote, "is whether these 'educated' persons are actually equipped to face the ordeal before them or unconsciously contribute to their own undoing by perpetuating the regime of the oppressor."[65] He believed that the reason Americans of color "accepted" their inferior status was that, for years, they were "daily educated in the tenets of the status quo."[66] Continuing in this same vein, he stated; "The 'educated Negroes' have the attitude of contempt toward their own people because in their own as well as in their mixed schools they are taught to admire the Hebrew, the Greek, the Latin and the Teuton and to despise the African."[67]

Like Du Bois, Woodson had a peculiar faith in the need for scientifically studying the Black race. In this same volume, Woodson wrote:

> We must bear in mind that the Negro has never been educated. He has merely been informed about other things which he has not been permitted to do. . . . The program for the uplift of the Negro in this country must be based upon a scientific study of the Negro from within to develop in him the power to do for himself what his oppressors will never do to elevate him to the level of others. . . . But can you

expect teachers to revolutionize the social order for the good of the community? Indeed we must expect this very thing. The educational system of a country is worthless unless it accomplishes this task. Men of scholarship, and consequently of prophetic insight, must show us the right way and lead us into the light which shines brighter and brighter.[68]

Here Woodson illustrates the manner in which he would reconstruct the curriculum for colored schools.[69] As one would expect, Black history and special problems peculiar to the race are given great prominence in this reconstruction. Such a curriculum would be different from that offered white Americans. Du Bois and Woodson, representing the first group of university trained colored scholars, had an almost inordinate faith in the power and role of the scholar in society. Woodson writes of "Men of scholarship, and consequently of prophetic insight," and states that such men "must show us the right way and lead us into the light." Du Bois expressed a similar view in *The Philadelphia Negro* and other works.

Free Negro Owners of Slaves and Free Negro Heads of Families

In 1924 and 1925 appeared two works which Woodson edited. They bore the titles *Free Negro Owners of Slaves in the United States in 1830*[70] and *Free Negro Heads of Families in the United States in 1830*,[71] respectively. The first was a brief work, which also gave data on absentee ownership of slaves in the United States in 1830. Almost all of the data for both works came from the census reports for 1830. A grant given by the Laura Spelman Rockefeller Memorial in 1921 had made the studies possible, and much of the research had been carried out by employees of the Association. The aim of both publications was "to promote the further study of a neglected aspect of our history,"[72] and both works were largely statistical compilations.

Negro Orators and Their Orations and *The Mind of the Negro As Reflected in Letters Written During the Crisis*

The next year appeared a work on source readings which Woodson compiled, entitled *Negro Orators and Their Orations*.[73] This work was published as a companion volume to another production of source readings entitled *The Mind of the Negro Reflected in Letters Written During the Crisis, 1800-1860*.[74] In *Negro Orators* he found that the "Negro spokesmen were in no sense different from the orators of other groups, although they were not usually so well educated."[75] He concluded that the Black orators should be judged, therefore, not on style, but the effect which they produced in the listeners.[76] In the volume, each speech is prefaced by a brief biographical sketch of the life of the speaker.

Of his *The Mind of the Negro*, the *New York Times* stated; "As a whole the selection presents such an insight into the mentality of the Negro during the period of slavery as can hardly be found anywhere else."[77] The *Catholic World* indicated that the greatest value of such a publication would be for students, to whom it is a "mine of information."[78] Most of the letters included in this volume had already appeared serially in the *Journal of Negro History*. The first section of the volume contains letters to the American Colonization Society regarding the project of emigration to Liberia, and the second contains correspondence on the subject of the anti-slavery movement. The two small concluding sections contain personal, private and miscellaneous correspondence.

Negro Makers of History

In 1928 this work, an adaptation of Woodson's *The Negro in our History* for the elementary school level, appeared.[79] In 1935 he also published a shortened version of *The Negro in our History* especially adapted for high school students.

This latter volume, better documented than its predecessor, bore the title *The Story of the Negro Retold.*[80] Both works were favorably received by critics.[81] Also in 1928, he published *African Myths, together with Proverbs,*[82] as a supplementary reader composed of folk tales from various parts of Africa. This volume was intended for children in the public schools.[83]

In 1929 appeared a work which Woodson co-authored with John H. Harmon, Jr. and Arnett C. Lindsay, entitled *The Negro as a Businessman,*[84] and in 1930 appeared a volume which Woodson co-authored with Lorenzo J. Greene, a young Ph.D. in history just out of Columbia University. This volume was entitled *The Negro Wage Earner,*[85] and was the result of a survey, conducted by Dr. Greene, which considered such topics as occupations engaged in by Negroes, limitations of job opportunities for them, and the increasing proportion of jobs requiring skill. The book began with the jobs handled by Blacks during the period of slavery and showed how members of the race had continued, to a large extent, in these same occupations. The volume is replete with tables and statistical accounts. The authors concluded that it was not until after World War I that more equal distribution of Black labor occurred. This important change, wrought by the needs of American factories in the North and East, introduced Black Americans to new sections of the nation and served, state the authors, to improve race relations in the South.[86]

The Negro Wage Earner, together with *Free Negro Owners of Slaves, Free Negro Heads of Families,* and *The Rural Negro*[87] were all results of a three-year survey of Negro life in America undertaken by the Association beginning in 1926. Woodson's *The Rural Negro* was a treatment of rural persons of the South as to conditions of health, farming, tenancy, peonage, industry, trade, religion, education and recreation. It was well received. One reviewer called it "A first-hand piece of research, well-documented and intimately interpreted."[88] Another criticized Woodson for making the volume, at times, a tract against certain forms of exploitation of the rural Black.[89] This reviewer also criticized the book because of its scanty documentation. The monograph was compiled largely from facts in United States census reports and questionnaires which were sent to rural families.[90]

The Negro Professional Man and the Community

In this volume Woodson gave especial emphasis to the professions of medicine and law.[91] Topics treated were: "Negroes—Employment," Negroes—Moral and Social Conditions," "Negro Physicians," and "Negro Lawyers." The survey on which the volume was based covered almost the whole of the South, and most of the large cities, with considerable coverage of populations outside of the South. For this survey, as with the other topics treated in this series of studies launched in 1926, Woodson had a staff of collaborators who did the bulk of the research, while he served as coordinator, editor and interpreter. *The Negro Professional Man and the Community* possesses almost no documentation. This volume was a companion one to *The Negro Wage Earner.* The entire series of studies were designed, "to portray the social and economic conditions obtaining among Negroes since the Civil War."[92]

The Harvard Law Review praised *The Negro Professional Man and the Community* as being "invaluable and indicating that the colored professional man has the ability to progress if given the opportunity," but added that the abundance of statistical material "may make its reading difficult save to the sociologically-minded reader."[93] *The New York Times* praised the scientific spirit in which the data were collected and the fair-minded manner in which the material was discussed. This review also stated that the study constituted "a valuable sociological contribution to knowledge of the present status of the Negro in the United States."[94]

The African Background Outlined

This excellent volume appeared in 1936,[95] as a syllabus for the study of Afro-American history. This work is misnamed since over one-half of the volume treats the development of the black man in America.[96] In this work, Woodson stated that the history of the black man shows that the race has achieved much in various fields, and "to know the possibilities of the race a scientific appraisal of its past is necessary."[97] Woodson then apparently contradicts himself. He went on to state that, "The author considers the Negro as human—responding very much as others do to the same stimuli, advancing when free to go forward and lagging behind when hindered by obstacles not encountered by others."[98] If the latter statement is true, one wonders, then, why it is not possible to say that "the possibilities of the race" are the same as for any other race without having to go to the trouble of "a scientific appraisal of its past."

This syllabus readily won high praise as "one of the most useful and scholarly works" produced by Woodson.[99] One reviewer felt that the syllabus should "definitely dispel the doubt still held in some quarters whether there is such a thing as Negro history."[100] A unique contribution of the syllabus was the section on Europe-in-Africa, in which Woodson drew on his life-long researches as well as three summers of special research in European libraries and book stores.

African Heroes and Heroines

In 1939 Woodson published this volume as a biographical narrative account of various Africans who had risen to prominence.[101] It was intended primarily for junior and senior high school students. As usual with him when writing on this aspect of African history, this scholar stressed especially the militant resistance of the African nations and tribes to both Arabic and European invaders of the continent. Also included in the volume are a brief survey of the geography and peoples of Africa and the Black states which existed there. A reviewer writing for the *Boston Transcript* criticized the volume for its "strong note of militant vindication that rather mars the strictly expository portions of the book."[102] On a whole, the volume, like most of Woodson's writings, was well received. Even the above reviewer admitted that it filled "a gap in our fund of information."[103] The volume carried a comprehensive bibliography. Of *African Heroes and Heroines*, the author concluded that these "leaders of a despised people measure up to the full stature of the heroic in the histories of other nations."[104] Of the general history of Africa, he wrote:

> The Africans, we ignorantly say, left no history of their entire continent, but no nation has recorded a history of the whole natural division of the universe in which it developed. The ancient history of certain parts of Europe is as obscure, as that of areas in Africa, and the past of Asia is scarcely better known than that of Africa. Much more of the history of Africa is known . . . than we appreciate.[105]

In 1942 appeared four volumes entitled *The Works of Francis J. Grimke* which Woodson had edited.[106] In addition to his monographs, Carter Woodson also wrote numerous articles.[107]

Woodson entered the field of Black history for essentially the same reason as did Du Bois. They were both attacking the neglect of the Black man in the social science volumes most-used in the late nineteenth and early twentieth centuries. Of Woodson, Charles Wesley states:

> Woodson did not set out deliberately to become a scholar. He seems to have been almost pressed into

> scholarship by . . . strivings for explanation in so-
> ciety. . . . He had seen that scholars had selected
> the facts which they desired to include in their pub-
> lished works and had neglected others.
>
> As a result of the omissions and neglect of others,
> he then became a rebel against the learning of the
> scholars in the universities, after having tested this
> knowledge against fundamentally valid truths dis-
> covered through his own life experience. . . .
>
> Woodson insisted upon the discovery of the com-
> plete truth, and when he came upon partial truth,
> he did not hesitate to abandon the false.[108]

As indicated, Woodson believed that a great history would stimulate achievement in the Black race. "If a race has no history," he wrote, "if it has no worth-while tra-dition, it becomes a negligible factor in the thought of the world, and it stands in danger of being exterminated."[109]

Woodson also believed that race prejudice was the re-sult of faulty education, and that if American whites and blacks were told the truth about achievements of the Black man in history, race prejudice would disappear. On this point, he wrote:

> Race prejudice . . . is not something inherent in
> human nature. It is merely the logical result of tradi-
> tion, the inevitable outcome of thorough instruction
> to the effect that the Negro has never contributed
> anything to progress of mankind.
>
> Just as thorough education in the belief in the
> inequality of races brought the world to the cat-and-
> dog stage of religious and racial strife, so may thor-
> ough instruction in the equality of races bring about
> a reign of brotherhood through an appreciation of
> the virtues of all races, creeds and colors. In such a
> millenium the achievements of the Negro properly
> set forth will crown him as a factor in early human
> progress and a maker of modern civilization.[110]

Woodson was a strong believer in cultural history. No doubt he was influenced in this belief by the so-called New History movement led by James Harvey Robinson and others, which was tending in this general direction. But, it is highly probable that his desire for a greater consideration of the Negro underprivileged minority was a considerable factor in causing him to champion a history which included the story of the masses. On this point, he wrote that history should be broad, social and cultural. He complained that most written history was "that sort . . .which is merely the record of the successes and disappointments, the vices, the follies, and the quarrels of those who engage in the contention for power."[111] "The real makers of history," he wrote, have been "those servants of the truth who have labored to enlighten humanity, to lift it out of drudgery into comfort, out of darkness into light, and out of selfishness into altruism."[112] Du Bois also very frequently stated that most history was little short of "propaganda."

Though the purpose in writing his widely used *The Negro in Our History* was "to present to the average reader in succinct form the history of the United States as it has been influenced by the presence of the Negro in this country," there is in the volume an almost total omission of such bad features as high crime rates, slums, disease, and other undesirable phenomena which "the presence of the Negro in this country" has sometimes meant. When Woodson adapted his *The Negro in Our History* to the capacity of children in the elementary schools, he wrote that "The aim here is to facilitate the teacher's task of preparing children to play their part creditably in this new age. The teacher must hold up before them the examples of their own people, who have done things worth while. Those who have no record of what their forbears have accomplished lose the inspiration which comes from the teaching of biography and history."[113] Dr. Woodson felt keenly that the Afro-American must be re-educated to a greater appreciation of the race's past. He utilized almost every conceivable opportunity for reaching not only scholarly inclined persons, but the elementary and high school populations, teachers of all levels, as well as the laity.

Woodson felt that the historian should strive for maximum objectivity and should be scrupulously exact and honest in presenting facts. He generally succeeded in keeping his history correct, and his writings are usually unimpassioned. Unlike George Washington Williams, William Wells Brown, Du Bois and some others, Woodson's writings seldom read like orations and sermons. He lacks the prolific use of adjectives and elegant phrases which was until recently characteristic of much Black historiography.

Woodson not infrequently interrupts his historical narrative or criticism to moralize. While this tendency is to be noted in many historians, ancient or modern, and is perhaps forgivable when kept to a minimum, this scholar took excessive liberties with the privilege. Still, he does not go to the extent in this regard to which many of his predecessors did, and as did his contemporary, W. E. Du Bois. However, this tendency on the part of Woodson, and others, shows that they have sought to utilize historical writings as a weapon in the race "cause." Woodson's greatest fear for the Black race was that "awful fate of becoming a negligible factor in the thought of the world."[114]

One writer referred to Woodson's style as "cramped and slovenly."[115] It is highly probable that some of the "faults" of his style are attributable to the speed with which he wrote, as well as to the unsophisticated audiences for which he wrote numerous of his books. Along with Du Bois, he was by far the most prolific historian of color which this country had produced. At his death in 1950, he was endeavoring to write a six volume comprehensive history of the race. This, and an encyclopedia of the Black race, he hoped to make the crowning achievements of his life.[116] Neither was finished. Woodson constantly mentioned the need for an Encyclopedia Africana. His greatest contribution to historiography lies not so much in his writings, as effective as they were, but in the fact that he launched and popularized a successful movement. He had great organizational abilities and an eye for the future. Thus he founded the Association, the *Journal*, the *Bulletin*, the Associated Publishers, launched Negro History Week, and interested promising young historians in his cause and aided them in the securing of their training. On this aspect of Woodson's life, Wesley writes:

> His successful organization of membership campaigns, and the financial appeals, mark him as more than the scholar of the ivory tower. He collected disciples, young men and women who were invited to his meetings and who loved the cause even more than the master, but at the same time they admired him and his abilities. Many became of themselves pioneers in selected areas of Negro scholarship in the social sciences. He gave his movement a philosophy and built an organization for it.[117]

Woodson's pioneer efforts in studying the history of the race contributed tremendously to the coming into being of a new area for historical research and study which, stated M. J. Herskovits in 1951, "did not exist in recognizable form as recently as twenty years ago."[118] "Dr. Woodson," states another writer, "has probably done more than any single person to rescue Negro history from oblivion."[119]

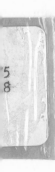

CHAPTER V

MEDIA AND AFRO-AMERICAN HISTORY TO 1930

Since the appearance of his volume, *The Gutenberg Galaxy* in 1962, Marshall McLuhan's name has been very prominent among persons who have an interest in cultural and historical theory. Like Edward Gibbon, Arnold J. Toynbee, Pitirim A. Sorokin, Norman O. Brown, and others among the noted systematic cultural critics, McLuhan has avid supporters and detractors.[1] Without attempting to determine the truth or falsity of his many ideas, what follows is an effort to apply some of these ideas to an interpretation of some aspects of Afro-American history. Although footnote references herein are often to specific pages in McLuhan's writings, frequently he only suggests,—to this writer—, the idea being presented. Hence, no claim is made that Mr. McLuhan would concur with these extensions of his study of "the extensions of man."

McLuhan declares that throughout the centuries media,—extensions of the human body and senses—, have had revolutionary, but usually unrecognized, effects on the human psyche and all institutions and values. What he largely chronicles is the rise and fall of "Gutenberg culture." He writes of the "Gutenberg effect" as an early modern revolution in concepts of time, space, and all elements of culture. The Gutenberg culture, or Age of Print—, dominant from the invention of printing by movable type until past the invention of the telegraph—, was based on rationality, objectivity, explicitness, orderliness, uniformity, fragmentation, separateness, superficiality, specialization, lineality, and continuity. This culture also had an arbitrary sense of time and space which seemed instinctive, stressed detached ob-

serving and studying rather than participation, was individualistic and non-humanistic, and had a fixed point of view.
This culture was "hot," which is to say it was low in individual participation and involvement, whereas the Electric Age
culture of the twentieth century is "cool" or high in participation and involvement.[2] Prior to the invention of the
phonetic alphabet all cultures tended to be cool, tribal, and
aural-oral oriented.

Tribal cultures tend to be "irrational," that is non-linear
or non-sequential in their reactions, intuitive, immediate
and total,—in part because the ear involves the whole body
more than does the eye. Speech is a cool medium because
the spoken word is participational, low in definition, and
leads to dialogue and intimate relations. Before the 8th
century B.C. the Greeks were tribal, and learned the poets
from memory. By the time of Plato, writing had changed
this. The tribal culture also is characterized by inter-
dependence, magical and mythical, harmony, sponta-
neity in reaction, humanism, and its sense of time and space
are non-visual, hence non-linear. McLuhan views the new
twentieth century tribal culture as possibly superior to any
tribal culture which has existed before.

McLuhan holds that, by giving man "an eye for an ear,"
the phonetic alphabet is the sole technology that has been
able to create civilized man with dogmas of individualism,
egalitarianism, and commitment to the open society.[3] Mc-
Luhan calls sight the most neutral and objective sense.
Written language, he states, stifles and slows down both
mental and emotional reacting, and divides human faculties. McLuhan uses such expressions as "detribalization
by literacy,"[4] and he writes of "literacy as a technology."[5]
He holds that Gutenberg's invention was the source of early
modern individualism and nationalism, and he believes that
since Gutenberg Occidental man has over-developed and
over-used his visual, and underused his aural-oral faculties.[6]

McLuhan writes of the "literacy victim." Modern man has been unaware of this schism in his faculties because men generally are unaware of how technological extensions of the body and senses affect them. McLuhan writes of "the typographical trance of the West," which has prevailed since Gutenberg. He believes that men are blind to the impact of media in part because they suffer from media narcosis, and in part because they focus on the impact of content rather than the medium itself. The content usually is of slight importance. "The medium is the message."[7] Hence, technologies usually have imperceptible, subliminal effects. The historian must know this, and must know that invention is aggression, for new technology always attacks the social and psychological equilibrium.

"All media," McLuhan writes, "are fragments of ourselves extended into the public domain."[8] He contends that new historical movements or styles occur when a new extension of our sense lives occurs, and each new extension eventually commands another one. Each media stereotypes, or dictates its own environment. McLuhan regrets man's dependence on material things, and declares that the only salvation from men being servomechanisms to the extensions of their bodies and senses is knowledge and awareness of the ways in which media enslave.[9] The only autonomous, free person, he believes, is the one whose awareness of the effects of material technology keeps him from being a victim of "media fallout." McLuhan holds that, as the men "of integral awareness," artists are the first to perceive and react to the impact of new technology. The Black historian, then, must reevaluate, in terms of media impact,—as this essay seeks in part to do—, the productions of such Black men as Frederick Douglass, William Wells Brown, Paul Laurence Dunbar, W. E. B. Du Bois, Carter G. Woodson, Louis Armstrong, Duke Ellington, Nat King Cole, Marcus Garvey, James Baldwin, Martin Luther King, Jr., Malcolm X, and Eldridge Cleaver.

Media and the Slave Era

"The trauma which affects Europe from Machiavelli to the present," McLuhan wrote in 1964, is "the print-made split between head and heart." In several of his books W. E. B. Du Bois expressed the belief that this trauma was the split between Occidental man's POCKETBOOK and heart,— or Christian dogma—, which was wrought by the early modern slave trade.

The controversy which has been waged among scholars on whether any elements of the African culture survived among blacks enslaved in the New World generally has failed to consider McLuhan's contention that hot, specialist, speed-up media such as print, industrial technology, and money fragment and erode non-literate tribal cultures. Also, considering McLuhan's view on the drastic changes which occur when man changes "an ear for an eye," it may be that the greater magnitude and intensity of slave revolts in Latin America, when compared with English or Protestant America, was due to a greater proportion of LITERACY among slaves in the Catholic countries. Indeed, the slave-owners in North America prohibited teaching bondsmen to read and write not just because of *what* the slaves might read, that is, the content. Here the planters knew that the medium is the message,—that literate slaves were more troublesome property regardless of what the reading fare might happen to be.

The greater militancy of Latin American slaves was also the voice of a more wholesome, more intact, healthier tribalism speaking. The Latin American slaves' greater freedom from oppression, which both Stanley Elkins and Eugene Genovese document, resulted in a healthier psyche that was more prone to assert itself by revolutionary action. This more wholesome psyche drew its strength not only from the facts that slaves in Catholic countries were baptized and had legal marriages and a higher level of literacy. This healthier psyche, character, and personality existed also because the beneficent aspects of tribalism—of which Marshall McLuhan writes—, existed in greater abundance in the Catholic countries. This is to say that slavery was less destructive of tribalism in the Catholic countries than was the case in Protestant areas.

Although the greater literacy of slaves in Catholic countries militated against the preservation of tribalism, because sugar cane culture left Blacks in larger units, because of the attitude manifest by church and state in the instances of marriage and baptism, and because there were so many more isolated pockets where the white man's presence and rule were absent, African culture, —which is to say African tribalism—, survived in Catholic countries to a greater extent. This more intact, more wholesome tribalism produced a healthier slave character and personality. The greater literacy which existed among Latin American slaves was not of sufficient scope or strength to negate the beneficent aspects of African tribalism.

African tribalism survived more in Catholic countries also because, when compared with Protestantism, the Catholic Church always has tended to be nearer, hence more sympathetic to manifestations of tribalism. Eye-oriented Martin Luther and John Calvin revolted against tribalism. Indeed, this may explain not only Marshall McLuhan's attachment to the Catholic church while he extols the virtues of tribalism, but also his conviction that something serious went wrong at the beginning of modern history when man substituted an eye for an ear. This also probably means that, except for Communism's atheistic and materialistic bias, the Catholic church might well find it attractive. The Protestant church's greater individualism and greater commitment to the literalism which Norman O. Brown attacks in his book, *Love's Body*, causes Protestantism to be more hostile to tribalism than Catholicism. In this sense, Catholicism never became as "modern" as Protestantism, hence

was never able to support the very modern institution of
slavery as completely. Catholicism, then, was less destructive of African tribalism because it had more of an uncon-
scious bias in favor of tribalism. However, contrary to the
position long-held by E. Franklin Frazier, tribalism among
North American Blacks was not completely destroyed. This
is a truth which Marshall McLuhan recognizes, which earlier such a scholar as Miles Mark Fisher in his book *Negro
Slave Songs* recognized, and, indeed, which Frazier himself
inadvertently recognized when he often complained about
the "peasant mentality" held by many twentieth century
Afro-Americans. Out of the beneficent aspects of Black
North American tribalism came such gifts to the United
States of America, and the world, as the Negro's Spirituals,
secular songs, dance, laughter, optimism, and commitment
to humanism and democracy.

The image of the slave constantly praying for deliver-
ance, and then singing the soul-stirring spirituals has caused
men to label the culture of the bondsman "Sacred," while
that of his profit-seeking owner is sometimes called "Profane." This accords with McLuhan's view that a Sacred culture is ear and spoken-word oriented while a Profane
culture is visual oriented.[10] "The visual," McLuhan declares, not only detribalizes, it "desacralizes." In his book
The Negro's God, Benjamin Mays has shown that increasing
literacy among twentieth century Afro-Americans was a
factor in a rising agnosticism. Yet, in his book *The Negro
Church*, E. Franklin Frazier declared in 1963 that the religious heritage of Negroes was still viable,—even among
most black college students—, thereby revealing that many
blacks were still strongly ear-oriented.

Because they were aural-oral oriented, many more slaves
believed that God would bring their emancipation than
could have been possible for eye-oriented bondsmen. Tribal
man is more "fascinated by hidden forms that produce
magical results."[11] For the same reason many more slaves

believed in such things as ghosts and forms of black magic than would be the case with the eye-oriented Negroes of the post-1865 generations.

Since most slaves and free blacks have been deliberately evasive and enigmatic vis-a-vis whites, in this relationship most Afro-Americans have been "cool." Among themselves blacks always have been "hot." The Uncle Tom Negro is one who has been "hot" vis-a-vis whites. Also, the food of the poorest people everywhere has tended to be "cool" food, that is, an inadequate core which had to be filled in with left-overs or bits of this and that, and a lot of imagination.

Slaves were relatively more patient about oppression and degradation than has been the case with twentieth century Afro-Americans. To visually-oriented man time is linear and divided into uniform segments. This, says McLuhan, creates impatience. "Work" and "time" result from fragmentization. The time and work senses of the literate visually-oriented Afro-American of the twentieth century are different from those held by most of the ear-oriented field-hand slaves. The same difference existed between the field hand slaves and their clock-oriented overseers and owners. This, of course, is not to say that the field hand slaves never exhibited impatience. Blacks long have been accused of not appreciating the value of time,—of wasting too much of it—, thus proving that many of them have never been obsessed with Gutenberg time. In the Electric age the field hands' orientation to time and work is back in vogue.

Numerous persons have observed that the slaves were "playful," fun-loving human beings. Since Blacks never have abandoned so completely the aural-oral orientation, they have not lost the "depth participation" in games to the same extent as the white Occidental.[12] McLuhan writes: "Men without art, and men without games, tend toward automation."[13] "In fun and play," he concludes, "we recover the integral person."[14] McLuhan holds that games are "models of a culture," and are extensions of man which have counter-irritant or counter-stress functions.[15] He points out the need which oppressed minorities have for art and games when he writes that "the game, like any art form, is a mere tangible model of another situation that is less accessible."[16] Due to the arbitrariness of fate or the human oppressor, victims of great poverty and oppression constantly live in a world where uncertainty is king. For the oppressed mere survival is the only constant goal, hence the oppressed are more concerned with processes than with goals. The life of the oppressed is hard, but it is often more exciting than that of the goal-oriented oppressor. The oppressor is forced by his many goals to be more serious. The life of the oppressed has much in common with the world of play, which McLuhan holds, "is necessarily one of uncertainty and discovery at every moment."[17] He who plays is an artist, "a maker rather than a mere consumer."[18] Many Black Americans often have said that white Americans would love to be "niggers on Saturday night."

McLuhan refers to the myth of Cadmus, who, by introducing into Greece the phonetic alphabet, sowed dragon's teeth which sprang up armed men. It is no accident that Nat Turner, Denmark Vesey, and most of the prominent black abolitionists were literate men, or that the first Black college graduate was also the first black newspaper editor, and a militant. It is no accident that the abolitionist William Wells Brown was also the first successful historian and novelist, or that Frederick Douglass was an outstanding newspaper editor as well as a great abolitionist. More than being baptized by a church, or anything else, literacy made some slaves and free Blacks *equal* to the owning class. During the eighteenth century this was partially recognized by whites in the treatment which they accorded such persons as Phyllis Wheatley, Jupiter Hammon, John Chavis, Moses Horton, and Benjamin Banneker.

The industrial revolution, which began in England during the last quarter of the eighteenth century grew out of Gutenberg's invention, and, it, too, worked to produce such revolutionaries as Gabriel Prosser, Nat Turner, and Denmark Vesey. Each equilibrium-upsetting new technology is bitterly opposed because, "each innovation is not only commercially disrupting, but [also] socially and psychologically corroding."[19] Yet, beginning in 1831 most of the annual Negro conventions championed industrial education of Blacks. Frederick Douglass was a very active leader in most of these conventions.

Before the slave era disappeared, a number of characteristics and beliefs about Blacks had become fixed into a hardened mould. Some of these characteristics and beliefs follow.

According to McLuhan the speedup engendered by electric technology retribalizes culture. The already-tribalized are better able to understand and confront an Electric age.[20] The process whereby a Gutenberg culture converts to an Electric culture is less painful for those who never abandoned so completely the aural-oral orientation.[21] Backward people are "cool"; such electric media as television is cool.[22] The telephone is a cool medium.[23] Blacks long have been thought of as peculiarly able to react from the depths of their nervous systems. Now that electricity has "outered" everyone's central nervous system, this uniqueness has been lost.

The Black man long has been defined as "irrational" or "non-rational." The Occidental concept of rational, McLuhan states, is based on the visual, linear, uniform bias. The non-visual, immediate, patterning of the Electric age has ended concern with this concept of the "rational."[24]

Because of their status as an oppressed minority, many Afro-Americans have not cared much for rugged individualists; "All for one and one for all" has been the preferred motto. Thus, during slavery, and since, Blacks have been in step with the mosaic participational group-minded culture and out of step with the Gutenberg mechanical, individualism, visual culture.

Just as the great contribution to music and dance made by Central Europeans is due to their long retention of a greater aural-oral orientation, the same is true of the Afro-American's great contribution in these fields. McLuhan believes that in the Electric age the world's "backward" or "deprived" peoples hold some advantages over the more literate and advanced because the latter are locked into the attitudes and postures fostered by eye-orientation. Since the more aural-oral oriented Central Europeans are better equipped to comprehend nuclear physics than eye-oriented Caucasian Englishmen and Americans, one wonders why by 1969 more Afro-Americans were not numbered among top-level nuclear physicists.[25]

Oral propaganda and persuasion, or ideological warfare, is another area in which the aural-oral oriented are supposed to excel in the Electric age.[26] Also, "Tribal man," McLuhan states, "can spot the gaps in the literate mentality very easily."[27]

From the slave era to the end of the 1960s, the Black American has presented the nation with a version of spoken English whose humor, "slang and dramatic vigor" have been cherished by many persons. McLuhan appreciates the black man's spoken English in part because the regular "educated speech" of Occidentals has been so flattened out with "literate uniform qualities" that it is a "facsimile of the uniform and continuous visual effects of typography."[28] Also, the Black American long has been viewed as a uniquely superstitious being. Now McLuhan writes of "the scientific return to magic."[29]

McLuhan writes of each technology as a form of self-amputation,—for social uses—, which leads to alienation and pain. By the late 1960s Afro-Americans were among the less amputated citizens of the Occidental world. The Black man has been viewed as an eternal provincial or agrarian.

McLuhan writes that the electric and agrarian societies are highly campatible.[30]

Slavery disappeared throughout the Western world during the nineteenth century because electric technology was eroding the whole Gutenberg culture. In 1844 Samuel Morse's first telegraph line was opened. By 1858 the first transatlantic telegraph cable had been laid. On this McLuhan writes: Telegraph brought the "integral insistence and wholeness of Dickens, and of Florence Nightingale, and of Harriet Beecher Stowe. The electric gives powerful voices to the weak and suffering."[31] In the 1870s, the telephone was invented.

The Gutenberg era was an age of fragmentation, specialization, and high definition. Caste and slavery are aspects or elements of fragmentization and specialization, which the Electric age doomed, hence destroyed caste and slavery. Fragmentization and specialization constitute the hallmark of modern capitalistic and industrial development. Even the earliest manifestations of the industrial revolution foreshadowed the doom of slavery because of the need for homogenization of the affected populace.

Like all of the black abolitionists, Frederick Douglass was aware of the impact of the technological revolution which began in England during the last quarter of the 18th century. In an 1858 address in Boston, Dr. John S. Rock, Negro physician, lawyer and abolitionist declared that in the United States "money is the sympathetic nerve which ramifies society, and has ganglia in every man's pocket." He continued:

> When the avenues to wealth are opened to us, we will then become educated and wealthy, and then the roughest looking colored man that you ever saw, or ever will see, will be pleasanter than the harmonies of Orpheus, and black will be a very pretty color. . . . Then, and not till then, will the lip of prejudice be sealed.

If it was the railroad that aided greatly in keeping the South in the Union in 1861, a decision made in the air and electric age might well be to let the Confederacy secede in peace. Electricity decentralizes.

Black Americans who considered Abraham Lincoln during the 1960s and made his racist expressions and acts the preeminent consideration needed to remember that (1) no person who believed in granting immediate freedom and equality to the slaves could have been elected President in 1860, and (2) from mid-1861 to at least 1870 Abolitionism was institutionalized, hence not only different from but much more effective than the pre-1861 brand. While Blacks tend to choose their main Abolitionist heroes from the pre-1861 period, they must be mindful that the institutionalization of any movement is necessary for its greatest success, and that when this occurs movements often find pragmatism enthroned where formerly there was pure idealism. Regardless of each Union soldier's beliefs about race, in terms of his *achievements* every Union soldier was a John Brown and Nat Turner. Despite his slowness and personal beliefs and desires, the same is true of the Commander-in-Chief of these Union soldiers. Lincoln had a many-sided personality and character. Still, he led the nation's military and governmental machinery and men in a war which he, at Gettysburg, admitted was to achieve the destruction of chattel slavery. This racist reluctant-Abolitionist might have resigned from the Presidency rather than go so far to help Black people and the nation. All giants have areas in which they are pygmies.

Media and The Freedmen To 1930

In his volume *The Negro in American Life and Thought* Rayford W. Logan constantly refers to the impact of industrialism and the laissez-faire—Social Darwinism philosophy in pushing Negro rights and opportunities to their nadir between 1877-1900. Archibald Grimke also wrote of the Bargain of 1877 and the end of Radical Reconstruction. Grimke stated:

> The clamor of all (the) million-wheeled industry and prosperity was for peace. 'Let us have peace,' said Grant, and 'let us have peace' blew forthwith and in deafening union, all the big and little whistles of all the big and little factories and locomotives, and steamships from Maine to California. Every pen of merchant and editor scratched paper to the same mad tune. The pulpit and the platform of the land (joined in). The loud noise of chinking coin . . . drowned the agonizing cry of the forgotten and long-suffering Negro.

If immediately after the Civil War the freedmen had known one-half of the negative effects of changing an ear for an eye, they would not have been so intensely interested in learning their A B C's. With Afro-Americans, as all Occidentals, the impact of the Gutenberg technology was not due so much to learning A B C's as having the opportunity to adopt the principles of uniformity, repeatability, and continuity. The 13th Amendment to the federal constitution increased the opportunities for Blacks to acquire not just their A B C's, but all elements of the Gutenberg culture.[32] For example, literacy created individualism, McLuhan holds. Among the second generation of post-1865 Blacks, and commonly since, an often-heard complaint was: "Negroes just won't stick together."

McLuhan defines clothing and housing as extensions of the skin. Until the electric age people wanted their clothing to be visually impressive. In slavery, and since, poverty marked the Negro in this regards. Yet before and after 1865 many Blacks were very clothes-conscious and played the dandy at the slightest opportunity. Even the field hand bare-footed slave sang . . .

I got shoes, you got shoes,
All God's children got shoes,
When I get to Heaven go'in to put on my shoes,
An shout all over God's Heaven.

I got a robe, you got a robe, etc.

In the visual age rags made men feel unworthy. The freed-man dressed "to-kill," in spats, top-hat, and vested suit, was declaring his status. Doubtless the posture of post-bellum black dandies is explained in part by McLuhan's reminder that "clothing itself is a systematic form of aggression."

Although Frederic Douglass opposed the post-Civil War exodus of Blacks from the South, he said: "In no case must the Negro be 'bottled up' or 'caged up.' He must be left free like every other American citizen, to choose his own local habitation and to go where he shall like."

McLuhan refers to Arnold Toynbee's findings in support of his view that slave persons in a warrior-society react by deliberately specializing so that they can become "indis-pensable to their masters."[33] Reminiscent here is Booker T. Washington's advice to his race to stay in the South either in agriculture or in crafts which would make them indis-pensable to the white South. McLuhan's criticisms of spe-cialism as leading to a fatal rigidity may be used to support W. E. B. Du Bois' contention that Blacks should pursue a more flexible liberal education. When Booker T. Washing-ton wrote the book, *Working with the Hands*, and urged his race to learn trades, Washington was not properly aware that the inroads made by electric technology made much of his advice out-of-date. The same is true of his advice that most Blacks should remain on Southern farms. Washington may have been aware of the ultimate impact of the electric age. "God for two hundred and fifty years, in my opinion," he wrote, "prepared the way for the redemption of the Ne-gro through industrial development." Again Washington said:

I plead for industrial education and development for the Negro not because I want to cramp him, but because I want to free him. I want to see him enter the all-powerful business and commercial world.

The dominant social philosophy of the period 1500-1900 A.D.,—the Protestant Ethic—, gave an exalted place to the Gospels of Work, Success, and Asceticism or Frugality. Asceticism, or masochism, in the life and thought of Blacks in North America is a subject which deserves special study. Much of Booker T. Washington's philosophy and program was based on a plea to his race: "Deny thyself!" Because the impact on Afro-American thought of the Protestant Ethic was still felt when Washington made his famed Atlanta speech in 1895, more Afro-Americans could agree with him then than is possible for the post-mid-Twentieth century Blacks who live in the Age of the Freudian Ethic. The creed of the new ethic is: "Indulge thyself!"

During the 1890s an intensified tribalism was revealed in the lives of whites and blacks throughout Occidental civilization. This is the period of the New Imperialism, when boxing, football, and body culture first became popular, of the racism of Thomas Dixon, of the minstrel tradition, the Jingoism of James G. Blaine and others, the immigration restriction movement, and intensification of lynchings and race riots. Tribalism also was manifest in the life and thought of Afro-Americans in such ways as Zionist agitation and movements to the West or to Africa, the popularity of the dialect poetry of Paul Laurence Dunbar, the militant novels of Sutton E. Griggs and the novels and poetry of Dunbar, Charles Chesnutt, Frances Ellen Watkins Harper, J. McHenry Jones, Yorke Jones, Claude McKay, Thomas H. B. Walker, Henry F. Downing, William Stanley Braithwaite, Anne Spencer, Leslie Pinckney Hill, Charles B. Johnson, Fenton Johnson, Joseph Cotter, Everett Hawkins, Lucien Watkins, Roscoe Jameson, and others, the make-the-most-

out-of-segregation philosophy of Booker T. Washington, formation in 1896 of the National Association of Colored Men,
founding of the American Negro Academy in 1897, formation in 1900 of the National Negro Business League, growing interest in Afro-American history evident in novels, autobiographies, and the studies of W. E. B. Du Bois, Carter
G. Woodson, and others, and the formation before 1915 of
the National Urban League and National Association for
the Advancement of Colored People. Strengthened tribalism also can be seen in the search of Benjamin Brawley,
Carter G. Woodson, and others for the "Negro genius."
Also, between 1870-80 the number of Negro periodicals in
the nation doubled from ten to twenty. Before the eighties
were over the number had increased to approximately
thirty. In 1892 the Baltimore *Afro-American* was launched,
the Norfolk *Journal and Guide* in 1900, the *Chicago De-
fender* in 1905, the Amsterdam *News* in 1909, and the Pittsburgh *Courier* in 1910.

In contrast to the generally oral character of the American press, the Black press,—like that of Russia—, long has
had a literary or book-like character. Also, except for the
editorial page, the modern newspaper is a cool mosaic medium. This is one reason why the hot editorials in Afro-
American newspapers have been subjects of unique interest.

Photography shifted Occidental man from the Age of
Typographic Man to the Age of Graphic Man.[34] McLuhan
holds that the photograph, a hot medium, makes people
more critical of the negative aspects of their personal and
social existence.[35] Also, photography acts as a social leveller.
Before this invention only the privileged classes could have
a likeness of themselves, in such forms as oil painting or
sculpture. Also, McLuhan implies that the popularity of
the snap-shot, by increasing the visual orientation of the
ear-oriented, may have increased their self-esteem and ambition as well.[36] Similarly, a drastic increase in the numbers of mirrors in the slave quarters of the Old South might

have led to many more slave plots and revolts. Also, because money has an effect on a culture similar to that of writing, the field-hand slaves would have been much more troublesome-property if they could have handled more money.[37]

Despite the generally racist portrayal of Afro-Americans which prevailed in the movie industry, since the medium, and not the content, is the message, as an implosive force the movies worked to help give birth to the egalitarian global village. Yet, as an echo of the racist structure and practices of the general American society, the early movies may be a rebuttal to the contention that the content of a medium is of slight importance only. To McLuhan the movies constitute the dividing line between the Gutenberg and the Electric cultures.[38] But artists saw the change coming long before it was clearly manifest to others. McLuhan states that the movies brought an end to the nineteenth century in the following manner. The Victorian Age was specialized and ugly, hence led to a lot of private dreaming which the movies could better satisfy.[39]

As hot media, the radio and movies "pepped up everybody" and produced the Roaring Twenties.[40] Movies have been called "a harem of beautiful visions and adolescent dreams."[41] But the movies were largely based on the lives of affluent white people, while the majority of Black Americans were poor and either excluded or demeaned. McLuhan agrees with James Joyce that movies turned much of society to a world of fantasy. Still, poverty, oppression, and their lower level of literacy doubtless kept a higher percentage of Negroes more realistic than "reelistic."[42]

Was their vision of the liberating power of electricity the main source of the optimism and militancy shown by Monroe Trotter, George Forbes, W. E. B. Du Bois, and other Blacks near the opening of the twentieth century? Was this vision the primary source of the call for Black manhood as the object of Afro-American education which W. E. B. Du Bois made in 1903 in his volume *Souls of Black Folk?*

More than the earlier horse-drawn street-car, or railroad, or later airplane, the automobile gave the Black American an unrivalled feeling of freedom and power. McLuhan writes of the automobile as human clothing, and of clothes as a weapon,[43] and he reminds us that the automobile,—"an extension of man" that, by its power "turns the rider into a superman"—, was a "great leveller of physical space and social distance."[44] White Americans saw that the automobile made Blacks more "uppity," and their reactions during the 1930s and 40s caused some Blacks to fear to drive a very expensive car in small southern towns. The automobile, says McLuhan, levelled upward rather than downward.[45]

McLuhan declares that new technologies alter the balance between our senses; use one more, or less, and the others are affected. Also, new technologies cause "cultural blues," and recently extinct technologies cause "phantom pain."[46] Radio affected men by reawakening their tribal memories,[47] and changed individual man into collective man.[48]

The radio strengthened Black tribalism. It is, in part, the tribalism, or aural-oral bent, of such movements as Father Divine, the holiness churches, and the "Black Muslims" which account, among other things, for their puritanical postures on such matters as sex, alcohol, drugs, and cigarettes. The hot medium of radio "provided the first massive experience of electronic implosion," and had its greatest impact on those groups and nations which had lost less of the aural-oral orientation.[49] Afro-Americans, Germans, Russians, and other East Europeans were among these groups, while the English and white Americans were not. McLuhan declares that radio thus made it possible for the "tribal songs and dances" of Afro-Americans to dominate "the Roaring Twenties."[50] While radio aroused the tribal energies of Europeans and Afro-Americans, television first achieved this result where white Americans are concerned.[51]

McLuhan holds that the radio produced Oswald Spengler and Adolph Hitler as prophets of doom for the old visual culture. "The medium for frenzy," the white-controlled radio strengthened black tribalism by strengthening blues, jazz, and dialect in such forms as the Amos 'n Andy, and Eddie "Rochester" Anderson presentations.[52] Hot media, like the radio and movies, exclude or leave very little to be filled in or completed by the listener, viewer, or user. Such media is low in participation. Cool media, on the other hand, includes, is participational, which is to say that the observer or user must fill in a lot.[53]

McLuhan sees the impact of the electric age as the chief impulse behind the rise of jazz during the World War I era.[54] Without the phonograph, also a hot medium, "the twentieth century as the era of tango, ragtime, and jazz would have had a different rhythm."[55] Like the telegraph and telephone, the phonograph aided greatly in bringing Occidental mankind back to the aural-oral orientation from which he had been alienated by Gutenberg.[56] These electric media "inspired the strange new rhythms of 'the jazz age,' the various forms of syncopation and symbolist discontinuity that, like relativity and quantum physics, heralded the end" of the Gutenberg era's insistence on uniform patterns.[57] Jazz stresses not only the discontinuous and the deep, but also the spontaneous, the unique, and participation. Because it is a "free verse" medium, jazz has special appeal to proscribed, oppressed minorities. This "performance as composition" is not far removed from the tribal minstrel or bard.[58] When the impact of the movies and radio was at their height during the thirties and forties, jazz was "hot." "Cool jazz" became popular when the cool medium of television came into vogue.

In his book, *The Heart of Man*, Erich Fromm reminds us that everyday language is based on conscious experiences only. Very deep feelings must be based on extraordinary language or symbolism. Among passionate black writers W. E. B. Du Bois and others have used lavishly the symbolism of the Bible and Greek literature, while Eldridge Cleaver used profanity. The Spirituals, blues, and jazz are other examples of the depth involvement which long has been characteristic of black Americans.

"As a reviver of archaism and ancient memories," and as a "decentralizing pluralistic force," radio turned the thoughts of many Blacks to "Mother Africa" and earlier arts, languages, and religious forms.[59] Under the aegis of radio, not only did Garveyism appear, and flourish for a while, but Carter Woodson produced such works as *The African Background Outlined, African Heroes and Heroines,* and *African Myths and Proverbs*; W. E. B. Du Bois wrote *The World and Africa* and *Gifts of Black Folk*; and Langston Hughes wrote, "I've Known Rivers." This list could be lengthened.

Many Afro-Americans felt during the 1920s, 30s, 40s, and since, that the Number One place to go and the Number One hero were the night club or bar and the Jazz musician. Previously the church and the clergymen had held these positions in their lives. By 1969 the mentality and culture of the Jazz musician had become the dominant outlook and culture of many Afro-Americans. This included the musician's posture of being different in dress and behavior, "cool," contemptuous, and the conviction that his gift or genius made him naturally a superior being. James Baldwin, for example, removed the church and pulpit from the exalted place they once held in his life, and raised to a higher place the culture of the Jazz musician. Baldwin, Eldridge Cleaver, and Leroi Jones were among the sizeable number of Black writers whose values and beliefs had much in common with the culture of the Jazz musician. The moral fervor of these writers indicated that, perhaps unconsciously, they did not reject the church and pulpit as completely as they might claim, but rather merged the religious with the secular.

If electricity was the central force behind the "Negro Renaissance," it is altogether fitting that this movement should have been centered in the uniquely electric city of New York, in Harlem. Electrically illuminated night clubs, in what Carl Van Vechten called "Nigger Heaven," were a center of this movement.

McLuhan writes: "Of all the great hybrid unions that breed furious release of energy and change," none surpasses "the meeting of literate and oral cultures."[60] Out of such meeting of cultures "new form is born" and new insights are acquired as men are temporarily released from the "ordinary trance and numbness" which result from contact with media.[61] The slave had essentially an aural-oral tradition and culture. By the 1920s there was a strong Afro-American element of the Gutenberg visual linear mechanical culture.

Like the fifteenth century Renaissance, the one in Harlem during the 1920s drew inspiration from the fact of publishing. Because their words, thanks to Gutenberg, could reach audiences numbering in the hundreds of thousands, and stretching over the decades, the leading figures of both of these renaissance movements had a heightened sense of personal power and importance. Also, just as the Gutenberg literacy,—based on linear vision and repeatable use of type,—served at the beginning of modern time as a catalyst for the scientific orientation, perspective-oriented art, point of view literature, and the historical perspective, these outlooks and emphases were repeated with literate twentieth century Black Americans. This had much to do with the fact that in 1915 Carter G. Woodson launched the Scientific Afro-American History Movement and that it quickly became a success. Woodson's efforts were soon supported by W. E. B. Du Bois, A. A. Schomburg, and others. Indeed, these same factors and influences make it no accident that Du Bois, the first Afro-American to receive a Ph.D. degree in any of the social sciences, won this degree in History in 1896. The historical collections of materials on Black people at such places as Fisk, Howard, and Atlanta Universities came into being because of the work of these same factors and influences.

But even the literate "New Negro" usually was not as eye-oriented as his white counterpart. N. P. Tillman stated in *Phylon* in 1950 that obsession with race has made the Black writer "so thoroughly a part of his subject that he has been usually unable to view it objectively." Hugh Gloster points out, in the same journal, that because of his deep concern with race the Black writer's "philosophical perspective" has been diminished so much that "he has made only meager contributions to national and world ideologies." That the Afro-American's art has been participational is seen in the observation of Alain Locke. Until very recently, Locke wrote,—also in *Phylon* in 1950—, Black literary expression "ran a one-dimensional gamut from self-pity through sentimental appeal to hortatory moralizing and rhetorical threat—a child's gamut of tears, sobs, sulks, and passionate protest." In this same journal L. D. Reddick wrote: "Even Negro intellectuals tend to read and talk, rather than read and write."

The movement led by Marcus Garvey was in part counter-resurgence of the old Black oral culture. The same is true of the Black nationalism of the 1960s which had Elijah Muhammed, Malcolm X, and the so-called Black Muslims at its center. Afro-American nationalism always has tended to be a resurgence of the old against the new,—efforts to preserve a primal innocence and purity. The first nationalism in modern history, "an intense new visual image of group destiny and status," was created by literacy.[62]

Not until the Black race developed a fairly large eye-oriented class was there a notable reaction against any non-violent Black leader on the grounds that he was "too emotionally oriented." Much of the opposition to Marcus

Garvey which came from Black intellectuals was due to the traditional hostility of the eye-oriented, fragmented man and his refusal to accept persons who are totally integrated into a role.[63]

Garvey, a hot personality, would never have risen to great prominence if the cool medium of television had been the dominant medium of the twenties instead of radio. Garvey's colorful parades, uniforms, grandiose dreams, acts, and speeches, and his naïvete fitted into "the era of the hot mommas, jazz babies, of sheiks and shebas, of vamps and gold-diggers and the fast buck."[64] The 1920s was still the Gutenberg era, "a world still innocently engaged in expanding and exploding, in separating and teasing and tearing."[65]

By 1900 some Black college students were reacting against dialect poetry and the dialect-wording of the spirituals and slave songs. During the 1920s the Black intelligentsia was at times estranged from the masses because one group was visually-oriented and the other aural-oral oriented, one was literate and the other semi-literate or illiterate. The same is true with the so-called Black Militants of the late 1960s. The appeal of such persons as Stokely Carmichael and Rap Brown was tribal, while the legal-action orientation of Roy Wilkins and the National Association for the Advancement of Colored People appealed to the eye-oriented, individualistic, detached, objective, Gutenberg culture Blacks. Because they were of this latter orientation, James Baldwin in *The Fire Next Time* rejects much of the "Black Muslim" philosophy and approach, just as Richard Wright had done with Communism in a book entitled, *The God That Failed.*[66]

McLuhan believes that new technologies inflict pain, and pain inflicted by the new medium of radio during the 1920s was reflected in the blues.[67] The greater impact of electricity during the 1960s, he believes, caused pain of so vast a scope that the blues of the 1920s and 30s would be only a minuscule effort at expressing it.[68] Yet, when it comes to expressing pain, for black Americans only the Watts, Newark, and other riots of the 1960s were comparable to the Negro blues of the 1920s, 30s, and 40s. Also, if "the confusion and pain" felt by Caucasians during the 1930s was "created by radio" and "lavishly expressed in the blues," as McLuhan contends, it is clear that the confusion and pain which Afro-Americans expressed in the blues had further, and perhaps more important roots, in economic deprivation and the oppressions of white racism.[69]

The return to isolationism, lynchings, and race riots of the immediate post-World War I period reveal an intensification of tribalism in the United States of the 1919-1929 period. Again intensified White tribalism was matched by intensified Black tribalism, and vice versa. Strengthened Black tribalism manifested itself in a number of ways, and was to be further intensified by the fears and destitution wrought by the Great Depression. Although World War II ushered both black and white Americans into larger concerns, fears which this war engendered also brought a return of Intensified White and Black Tribalism, especially after the integration push that was led by Martin Luther King, Jr. During the 1920s, James Weldon Johnson's song, "Lift Every Voice and Sing" became a "national Negro anthem."

In the urban centers of the North and South fundamentalism in religion asserted itself in such forms as the new holiness denominations and, during the thirties in the movement led by "Father Divine." Showing a keen interest in folklore, the anthropologist Zora Neale Hurston published *Jonah's Gourd Vine* in 1934, and in 1937 *Their Eyes Were Watching God.*

Still, there were larger currents as international concern was to be seen in such novels as *Dark Princess* (1928) by W. E. B. Du Bois and George Schuyler's, *Slaves Today: A Story of Liberia* (1931), Eric Walrond's *Tropic Death*, and

Claude McKay's *Banjo* and *Banana Bottom.* A high-water mark of the black tribalism of the thirties was reached after the end of the decade when, in 1940, Richard Wright's great novel *Native Son* appeared. Wright had published his first volume in 1938.

McLuhan writes that the radio, by shifting American values away from the Gutenberg culture emphasis, caused the depression of 1929-39, and that the impact of television during the 1950s and 60s worked to create a similar depression.[70]

CHAPTER VI

BLACK AND WHITE TRIBALISM

It took ten years of television to "Europeanize" white Americans, but because of their greater illiteracy, poverty, and cultural isolation Afro-Americans were already "Europeanized" when television appeared.[1] Like the radio, television is re-tribalizing Gutenberg man.

Television's mosaic pattern of presenting pictures with dots requires use of all the senses in filling in the empty spaces. The sense of touch is the most involving of all the senses. Television, an extension of this sense, and of the human nervous system, is a cool medium, but it has made eye-oriented Americans more susceptible to radio, a hot medium.[2]

The fact that race relations seemed during the 1960s to be at one of the worst levels of crisis ever was misleading. By promoting the cool depth reaction, television brought greater maturity to the views on race of both black and white Americans, and this,—together with the rapidity of social change—, is what accounted for the deep concern about the problem. Solution of the problem was nearest just when it seemed to be farthest away. Yet, McLuhan wrote in the March, 1969 issue of *Playboy* magazine, the possibility of a race war also was nearer than ever.

Since television has intensified everyone's "drive to participation," to this medium must go a large part of the concern during the late 1960s for "Black Power." Electric media in general, and television in particular, had created by 1969 a "now"-oriented impatient generation. Small wonder that Martin Luther King, Jr. entitled one of his books, *Why We Can't Wait*, and the so-called Black Militants chanted, "Freedom, NOW!" and seemed to want too much too rapidly.

The prevalence of the mosaic effect engendered by electricity ought to lead to greater acceptance by society of the different ethnic and cultural groups. The Gutenberg era image of man was based on fragmentation, uniformity, detachment, objectivity, and singularity of point of view, hence this image was more congenial to strong ethnic and cultural bias. The old images of man tended to be hot, or high in definition and low in participation, hence were easily frightening. The opposite is the case with the Electric era images of man.

McLuhan believes that the speed of events in the twentieth century, and the extension of man's central nervous system as electricity, means that mankind now lives "integrally" and "mythically," but the thoughts of men are still rooted too much in the past mechanical age. The new concern is for wholeness and involvement in depth.[3] The mechanical age of 1500-1900 A.D. was one of expansion or explosion, while the instant speed of electricity has created a "global village," in which all of the nations and races, classes and ages are deeply involved in each other's lives. All men are now committed, concerned, and want to participate or be involved. McLuhan sees this effect of electricity as the primary source of such revolts of the 1960s as the move for "Black Power" and "Student Power."[4] More than ever, he writes, society in the Electric age is one organism, a global village in which every "thee" is a "me." Other evidences which McLuhan sees of the return of Europe to tribal culture are the fascism of Adolph Hitler, Benito Mussolini, and Francisco Franco, Communism, the European Common Market, and Cubism and Surrealism in art. McLuhan urges contemporary man to be eclectic and choose what it is desirable to keep from the Gutenberg culture, and not to be totally, blindly tribalized.

By the 1950s Americans of both races were keenly aware

that three-fourths of the population of the Global Village was colored,—yellow, brown, and black.

The new electric age culture emphasizes the visceral rather than the visual. McLuhan writes of the "orientalization" of the Occident.[5] Thus it is, that to arrive at their profound insights into the Occidental culture of their day, such Black spokesmen as James Baldwin, Malcolm X, Stokely Carmichael, and Eldridge Cleaver would not have to read such men as Soren Kierkegaard, Frederick Nietzsche, Oswald Spengler, Arnold J. Toynbee, Pitirim A. Sorokin, T. J. Altizer, Jean Paul Sartre, Herbert Marcuse, or Norman O. Brown. For the sensitive man, the air was saturated with these ideas because the implosive effect of electricity was reversing the old postures and attitudes.

As Thomas Edison's sensibility was not weighted in favor of any one of the senses, so it has been with many Afro-Americans. The message of the Black man never has depended heavily on eye-orientation, but has been expressed in such ways as laughter, inarticulate prayer, cursing, dance, song, or moan of the voice or jazz instrument. From Giambattista Vico to James Joyce to Norman O. Brown to Eldridge Cleaver there is a call to recapture the symbolic or dialectical vision,—to give up literalism or focusing on parts only; to see WHOLE—, unite VISION and FEELING. Like Jean Jacque Rousseau and others, the Black revolution of the 1960s championed a return to nature in the highest sense. It viewed Occidental man as slave to man-made things, hence an alienated, artificial, heartless, automaton. The new culture is organic in that actions and reactions are instant and total. Cubism in painting, surrealism, and nuclear physics all are evidences of the new concern with wholeness rather than with parts.

Western mechanism has not penetrated the Afro-American psyche any more than it has the Russian or Japanese psyches. By the 1960s such men as James Baldwin, Malcolm X, and Eldridge Cleaver knew this, and they knew that the Afro-American was better off for not having been penetrated. What McLuhan calls Occidental man's mechanical, blind, fragmented, "robot condition," Malcolm X called the condition of a soul-less "devil," and he viewed the black man's condition as that of a god. It was not so much that the black man was primitive, but rather that Occidental culture was primitive once more.[6] McLuhan writes of people, such as those of twentieth century Africa, China, and India, being "tribal in the noblest sense of the term," because they "never had a nineteenth century."[7] These people still have intact their interpersonal relations systems and depth reactions and involvements. Like Marcus Garvey and Elijah Muhammed before him, Malcolm X saw that Negroes had been deliberately brain-washed by whites. Malcolm did not understand as well that, more often than they realized, the "white devils" were conditioned "non-perceptive somnambulists."[8]

During the 1950s and 60s the identity of Afro-Americans was profoundly disturbed by the earlier winning of independence by the people of such states as India, Israel, and the African states, as well as by racial integration within the United States. Declaring that the overheated medium, or the overextended culture, reverses itself, McLuhan points to Arnold J. Toynbee's reminder that during the fourth century A.D. Germans who were working for the Romans showed a new pride in their own German culture.[9]

In their quest for a more relevant religious posture, during the 1960s some Afro-Americans proselytized for Islam and others for Judaism, a black Christ, or some other basic change in the traditional posture. Much of this coincided with the "God is Dead" movement which wracked the white Christian world, and it was all related to the cataclysmic shift from the Gutenberg to the Electric age.[10]

Names, or other words, as symbols, have origins related to faith in magic. Adam in the Garden of Eden, it is said, gained power over other living things by giving them names.

Was belief in magic one factor,—among numerous others—, in the desire which numerous Black Americans felt during the 1960s to find new names for such things as their race, jazz, blues, and many other things; to magically rid everything of the white man's domination?[11]

There can be little doubt that a significant factor (but by no means the only one) behind the negative stereotyping of Whites by Black writers, and vice versa, during the 1950s and '60s was aggression or hatred engendered by unenlightened tribalism. By 1969 Blacks had made very few direct scientific studies of the mind, character, and personality of Caucasians, hence could base their generalizations in these areas largely only on the studies made by others in these areas, on studies of White political, economical, and other institutions, and on an analysis of the historical record. Although the latter two were most-often used, Blacks could boast of having produced few—if any—, scholarly analyses of White culture of the scope and depth of Thorsten Veblen's *Theory of the Leisure Class.* The historical record led as the basis for the generalizations which Blacks made. This was true of the thought of Marcus Garvey, Elijah Muhammed, Malcolm X, and others. Although the historical record might be considered adequate to document the indictment brought against White racism, it could not be used for such a charge as the one which declared that White adult males were sexually inferior to Black adult males. For some of the elements in their negative image of Caucasians, Blacks could cite only their personal experiences or the conclusions of White critics of Occidental culture. This, Black critics needed to keep in mind, together with the fact that their status as an oppressed people led them to *need to accept the negative images of Whites.* The same observations apply to the negative stereotypes of Blacks which Whites have held, that is, they have been based on abuse of the historical record; too-few personal experiences; few,—often-faulty—, scientific studies; and,—because of their role as oppressor—, Whites have needed to accept these stereotypes to justify their maltreatment of Blacks.

In an interview published in the March, 1969 issue of *Playboy* magazine, McLuhan deplored the recent national tendency to try to educate Black Americans for the dying Gutenberg culture,—to detribalize them—, while white youth were rejecting this culture and becoming tribalized. By indirection McLuhan appeared here to support the efforts of Dr. Vincent Harding and others to transform predominantly Negro colleges into uniquely black colleges and universities. In this interview McLuhan held that the white Occidental world's "cultural aggression" against Blacks and Indians was due primarily to the white man's recognition that he was the *inferior* of these tribal groups rather than their superior as he claimed. When in this interview McLuhan indicated a belief that Afro-Americans did not properly appreciate the worth of their traditional culture, he revealed his inadequate acquaintance with the writings of such persons as Carter G. Woodson, W. E. B. Du Bois, Marcus Garvey, J. A. Rogers, Elijah Muhammed, Malcolm X, and Eldridge Cleaver.

Just as backward nations of the post-mid twentieth century,—because they do not have shells created by modern technology or media to paralyze and blind them—, have great advantages in the Age of the Global Village, so does the Afro-American have similar advantages for the same reason. During the eighteenth century America, as a very backward nation, had similar advantages vis-a-vis Europe.[12] A similar advantage is held by teen-agers and young adults of each generation. Thus it is, too, that young Blacks with no college or university training to paralyze and blind them, such as Richard Wright, James Baldwin, Marcus Garvey, Malcolm X, and Eldridge Cleaver are often more perceptive and relevant than blacks who possess college and university degrees.

In part, it was the impact of electricity in the form

of television which ended the passion of Afro-Americans for racial integration. Until television began to make a strong impact on American life, Afro-Americans had demanded integration as a reaction against the fragmenting, separating tendencies of Gutenberg technology. Although, since the popularity of Malcolm X, many Blacks have not found the idea of a chosen racial segregation distasteful, this does not mean that they either hate whites more or are more indifferent to whites. For both races, television compels a *greater* depth interest in and involvement with each other.

The Gutenberg era was unable to achieve racial integration because "literate man naturally dreams of visual solutions to the problems of human differences."[13] Literate man wants to obliterate racial differences, while Electric-age man ultimately accepts these differences. Electric technology tends to promote equality of individuals.[14] Also, advertising is a social leveller because, instead of presenting a private point of view it presents a message "that is for everybody or nobody."[15] In the Electric age "we wear all mankind as our skin."[16] Also, the black man of the Electric age is aware that he is part of a delicate social organism, and that all-out war against him would be genocide for white men as well as black men.[17]

In the Age of Automation electricity decentralizes, hence is a decided factor in the assertion by Blacks, heard repeatedly during the 1960s, that they happily will accept separation with Black control of the institutions in the predominantly-Black communities. While some persons saw the riots in Watts, Newark, and other cities during the 1960s as, in part, a quest of young blacks for manhood, McLuhan writes of "violence in its many forms, as an involuntary quest for identity."[18] Later, in a day when some people were predicting a "race war," McLuhan wrote of "war as a quest for the recovery of identity and respect."[19] He made it clear that violence is the angry, irrational response given when a world is slipping away. Writing in his book *Identity: Youth and Crisis*, of a proper "species-hood" and a pseudo-species for man, Erik Erikson also affirms that man in the state of "identity panic" becomes a killer more vicious than anything else that lives. During the late 1960s black students on predominantly-white campuses were more fearful of becoming Caucasianized,—of losing their identity—, than most of them would have admitted. The demand to bring into these schools Black teachers, coaches, and administrators, black dormitories, more black students, and a Black Studies Program were prompted not only by the desire to extend democracy by ending racism and paternalism, but also by the desire to transplant Soul culture to these campuses so that the black students would be less alone and in less danger of becoming Caucasianized. One subconscious trigger of explosive Black anger was: "You all are trying to paint me white!", just as some whites complained that Negroes desired to paint the nation brown or black.

Whether he was telling stories, singing, dancing, playing an instrument in a jazz ensemble, or engaging in athletics, the black man long has been thought of as an artist. The true artist always has been *avant garde* in sensing and interpreting the impact of media. Here the black man has performed a distinct service for white America. In the Age of the Global Village all men must and will be artists.

Historical Experience and the Changing Sensory Ratio

Marshall McLuhan mentions often the manner in which media—such as print, photography, radio, or television—create "new men" by changing the sensory-ratio of populations. Where Afro-Americans are concerned, *perhaps equal to media in changing the sensory-ratio has been that historical experience which is the more traditional concern of historians.* As witnessing "a thing of beauty is a joy forever," every experience which a man has in depth alters his sensory ratio forever.

Regardless of where he was or what he did from 1861-65, every Black American "fought" in the Civil War, and although this experience did practically nothing to alter their ability to read or write, they all were different Blacks when the war ended from what they had been when it began. Certainly they were not the Black Militants of the 1960s, but they were more "on their way" in 1865 than they had been in 1861.

Similarly with the Reconstruction experience of 1867-77. The taste of freedom and power experienced during these years altered the sensory ratio of black Americans forever, and during the 1950s and 60s they often spoke of the "movement" of these decades as "The Second Reconstruction" which would complete the work of the Emancipation Proclamation and the Thirteenth, Fourteenth, and Fifteenth Amendments to the Federal Constitution.

Most Black Americans never accepted the ugly charges brought by the enemies of the Reconstruction effort, and were elated in 1935 when W. E. B. Du Bois, in his thick volume *Black Reconstruction*, successfully demolished many of these charges. The graft and corruption, Du Bois pointed out, were national in scope and these Reconstruction governments did such commendable things as provide for a Southern public school system, universal manhood suffrage, and more liberal constitutions than the South ever had; ended imprisonment for debt and such inhumane punishment as branding, cropping, and flogging; and established numerous eleemosynary institutions. Although these Reconstruction governments were overthrown, no Afro-American would ever forget that, for a brief moment in American history, Black men were in both houses of state and federal legislatures, held such offices as Lieutenant Governor, Secretary of State, Secretary of the Treasury, State Superintendent of Education, and sat on Southern state supreme courts.

With these experiences the Black man's sensory ratio was changed forever.

The same is true of experiences which Black Americans had such as participation in the Southern Fusionist Movement of the 1880s and 90s, fighting in the Spanish-American War, the boxing exploits of Jack Johnson, the scholarly achievements of W. E. B. Du Bois, Carter G. Woodson, Alain Locke, Charles Drew, and others; and the literary and artistic accomplishments of Charles W. Chesnutt, Paul Laurence Dunbar, James Welson Johnson, and others. Since the days of Phyllis Wheatley every high achievement of any Black individual or group has altered the sensory ratio of all Afro-Americans. The same is true of every act of protest against racial degradation,—from the days of Crispus attacks, David Walker, Gabriel Prosser, Nat Turner and Denmark Vesey to the present—, all have become part of the developing Black ego and Black psyche.

Perhaps no experience since 1861-65 so drastically altered the Black Americans' sensory ratio as his participation as soldier and civilian in World War I. This, plus the accompanying dramatic shift of the black population to cities of the North and South, and a rising level of literacy, joined with such influences from recent decades as those mentioned above, to create the much-more-self-confident "New Negro" of the 1920s and 30s. Participation by Afro-Americans in World War II was a force of comparable scope and intensity in altering the Black Americans' sensory ratio. Since 1945 there have been added to this such powerful influences as participation in the Korean and Vietnam wars; racial integration of sports, the military, and other segments of national life; and the successful independence movements in Africa, India, China, and other places. Still, there is not even a slight jump from the spirit of such persons as Harriett Tubman, Sojourner Truth, Henry Highland Garnet, Frederick Douglass, William Monroe Trotter, W. E. B. Du Bois, Carter G. Woodson, and Marcus Garvey to that of such persons as James Baldwin, Martin Luther King, Jr., Medgar and Charles Evers, Malcolm X, Stokely Carmichael, Cassius Clay and Eldridge Cleaver. Black achievement and Black militancy, new only in intensity and scope, both have lengthy histories. The larger scope and intensity of each during the 1960s owed their existence to a new sensory ratio which had been created as much by *experiences* as by *media*.

Black and White Tribalism

As used herein, the word tribalism might include not only ethnic groupings, but groupings based on such things as religion, class, nationality, or sex. The chief concern here, of course, is tribalism based on notions of race.

The polarization of attitudes evident in the alternating postures of White tribalism toward Black America are informative about the heights of idealism and the depths of "realism" which are components of the White psyche. Throughout the course of American history "the Negro question" has been a chief mirror in which White America has viewed itself. Many White men have seen the salvation of their souls resting on their posture and stand on the question of the Black man's status and rights. This is just as true of a John Brown as it is of the head of the Ku Klux Klan.

White tribalism—synonymous in some ways with nationalism—, was not well-enough articulated to develop a serious open schism when the status and future of slavery were debated by the Continental Congress and Philadelphia Constitutional Convention. However, intermittently, and always imperfectly, from the Missouri Compromise question in 1819 until 1877, White tribalism was divided—sometimes almost irreconcilably—, over the "Negro question" or the rights, privileges, and status of Black tribalism. The inevitable reaction set in around the time of the Bargain of 1877 and lasted until the United States Supreme Court school desegregation decision of May 17, 1954. Once again a schism existed in the ranks of White tribalism over the status and rights of Blacks. This division lasted until 1964-65, at which time another reaction set in and White tribalism again closed ranks against the Black man.

In their impact on each other, black and white tribalism not only at times have evoked alternating general postures of greater aggression or greater neglect of each other. The periods of greater black-white aggression also have created or aggravated divisions and aggressions on each side of the racial divide. Thus have white versus white and black versus black aggressions been effected, and from this environment-versus-counter-environment posture, both good and bad benefits have flowed.

In the United States, on both sides, juxtaposed black and white tribalism has joined the frontier and Open Society as a source of chronic identity conflict for all Americans. In one sense the Black man has not allowed whites to have much peace or rest, while at the same time the Black man has pointed the way to a more humane and humanistic world in which there would be more peace and rest for all. Since conservative mankind at times abhors growth, small wonder that both races have wanted so often to end the tension between them, either through a "return" of Blacks to Africa, emigration elsewhere, or the imposition in America of a rigorous and complete separation of the races. Some Americans, perhaps unaware that some tensions are creative,—hence desirable—, may even have desired the creation of a police state to end these tensions.

Integrationist efforts of Black Americans have had to surmount the great odds of assuming or winning the good-will and support of white Americans, the repression by Blacks of the deep hostility and suspicion which the majority long have held toward whites, and the need for reformation of the "mainstream" culture. Integration has thus had widest appeal to the most economically and culturally advantaged Blacks,—those few to whom "thinking white" seemed to have the greatest immediate grounding in common sense because they had benefitted the most from white paternalism. Thus it is that the Black organizations and movements which have had widest and deepest appeal to Afro-Americans have been those that were based on Intensified Tribalism such as the Garvey and "Black Muslim" movements. With these movements the Afro-American has been able to give full vent to his hostilities, fears, and suspicions rather than being compelled to repress them as integration movements necessitated.

The dying of the Gutenberg culture creates pain and crises of identity for men everywhere, and, as they seek desperately to recapture their old damaged identities, various forms of violence and war are omnipresent. McLuhan writes in the March, 1969 issue of *Playboy* magazine that just as the old tribalism of the European Jew was seen as a threat by the new tribalism of the Nazis, the old tribalism of the Afro-American is viewed as a threat by the new tribalism of the Caucasian American. McLuhan fails to see that, somewhat like the Blacks, most white Americans never ceased being tribal.

McLuhan writes of pain "as the natural accompaniment of innovation," and goes on to indicate why Black Americans experienced during the 1960s a vigorous reaction against integration.[20] Like the white South vis-a-vis the North during the 1800-1865 period, Blacks of the 1960s began to experience deeper than ever the fear of being swallowed up,—of losing all of their identity. Thus the Martin Luther King, Jr.-led integration efforts of the 1950s served as the basis for the popularity of Malcolm X during the 1960s. The mistaken notion that the King-led integration efforts would be successful, and radically change the relationship between the races, caused many American whites, of all regions, also to experience the fear of loss of identity. The "white backlash" resulted from this and other factors. McLuhan writes that people who find their "entire identity endangered by physical or psychic change," feel certain that they have "a mandate for war," and lash "back in a fury of self-defense."[21] "The old image," he writes, "must be recovered at any cost."

But there was more here than fear of the danger of being swallowed up, devoured. That the "main-stream" culture actually needed many reforms there could be little doubt. Also, after a certain point, mankind recoils from any added burden of stimulation, in much the same way that persons long-blind whose sight is restored by an operation often long to return to the world of more limited stimulation.[22] Such persons also require a long time to "make sense of" this new, chaotic, frightening, world. Doubtless some black and white Americans were not patient enough with the "unique sensory environment" of the world of racial integration. Lack of patience, however, was by no means the only problem that was involved.

During the 1950s and 60s some efforts were made to prepare Black students *academically* for integration, but no one prepared them psychologically. No one warned them not to panic when they began to fear loss of their identity. No one told them that as certain as the sun rises, as a Black minority in an ocean of whiteness, they would come to feel that they were being devoured and swallowed by some giant monster. No one warned them of the many serious short-comings of the nation's major colleges and universities. Most Blacks,—like most whites—, had become conditioned to racial separation, hence integration would be a traumatic experience even if the institutions were modernized and many whites were not saturated with racist attitudes and beliefs. During the days of slavery Blacks usually preferred to be around one another instead of association with whites. Yet, the two races must eventually learn to live in a world of considerable integration. Each race must achieve a larger identity. Neither race can afford to retreat into an even narrower identity—a more-blind, more-cruel tribalism. Nor is such retrogression possible in the coming age of the

Global Village. A better job of education must accompany the needed reforms. Each side must be told *beforehand* how to deal with inevitable personal subjective reactions without over or under-reaction. Each side must be warned beforehand of the crisis of identity which progress and integration inevitably bring, and each side must be cautioned that this crisis must not be viewed as a mandate for the traditional reactions based on blind fear. Proper adjustments of men and institutions must be made.

In an age in which television is making cool values dominant, it is well to remember that the Black American long has been the "coolest" of all Americans, and that perhaps he can teach his white brethren much about life in the Electric age. In the sense that living things need anti-environmental elements, black and white Americans have heightened and intensified each others awareness. Some of this has been good and some bad. Through greater use of courage, and *rational* rather than merely *visceral* reactions, the good can be multiplied and the bad eliminated.

Intensified Tribalism appears among Afro-Americans when they feel that, not only are they farther from achieving equality of status and opportunity in the American mainstream, but that their physical or cultural extinction has become a much greater possibility. Regardless of appearances, whether of the 1890s or 1960s, or some other period, Afro-American Intensified Tribalism is always a movement toward conservatism, and is both twin and child of Intensified White Tribalism and Conservatism.

Also, as Erik Erikson points out in his volume *Identity: Youth and Crisis*, all strong manifestations of tribalism evidence the conservatism of "incestuous fixation." The tribe often is a mother substitute and incestuous fixation is a sign that one's birth process has never been completed. Thus, to cling to the tribe is to cling to mother. Intensified Tribalism puts all non-tribal persons beyond the pale of love and respect, and views them as the "threatening enemy" who ought to be killed. Ralph Ellison said that the minority tribe is invisible to the majority tribe, while W. E. B. Du Bois said that his group was not only not seen but not heard.

White tribalism is white narcissism, a god to which not only the black ethnic minority, but even God Himself, often has been made subservient. To end white or black racism, then, is to end idolatry; to accept the teaching that love should not stop at the boundary of class, nation, or race.

Tribalism among the slaves was intensified by the hopes aroused when the American Colonization Society was most active, and by the fears aroused through the reaction against slave revolts and plots to revolt. In his volume *Negro Slave Songs*, Miles Mark Fisher has shown that slaves produced "Caution songs" during such times of repression and fear as followed the Nat Turner uprising or the Gabriel Prosser or Denmark Vesey plots. The words of one of these songs ran—

> You better mind how you talk,
> You better mind what you talking about,
> You got to give an account at the Judgement,
> You better mind.

During slavery Intensified Tribalism was characterized not only by greater caution, and greater concern with mere survival of the race, but also, as a part of this posture, greater reliance on patience, fortitude, and on God. Cultural survival was not much of an issue during the slave era. During the slave era, and since, the swing away from tribalism by Blacks has been characterized by greater optimism and faith in American whites and in the American Dream of equality and material affluence, and greater individualism in thought and action. With Intensified Tribalism individualism wanes and group-mindedness is called for. Since 1865 the intensified Afro-American tribal emphasis also has championed separatism, self-help, and economic development of the Black community. Doubtless, even during the slave era Intensified Tribalism called for less conversing with and being around whites, unless carelessness violate the spirit of intensified caution. In the post-bellum period Booker T. Washington was the first major spokesman for Intensified Tribalism, just as Frederick Douglass lived in and spoke for an era in which many American whites seemed intent on being sincere and effective allies in making the American Dream a reality for American Blacks.

In a paper entitled, "The Tyranny of Racism over Southern Politics," which was published in the First Quarter, 1969 issue of the North Carolina Mutual Life Insurance Company journal, *The Whetstone*, Samuel Du Bois Cook writes as if there have been almost no moments or hours when the mind of the white Southerner was not filled with thoughts of the Black people in his midst. It is not true that the white man has been as obsessed with fear or thoughts of Blacks as Dr. Cook states. White Southerners always have gone many long periods, and have indulged in many various activities, without any thought at all being given to Blacks. White tribalism has focused on Blacks largely when Black activity seemed to threaten the status quo. White tribalism has been intensified largely as a reaction to the actual or seeming intensification of Black tribalism, and vice versa. This chain reaction may be set off, in divers ways, from either side. For example, the agitation of northern abolitionism between 1831-1860 triggered the intensification of white southern tribalism. During the 1895-1917 period Black tribalism was intensified by the disfranchisement movement of the 1895-1905 period, and by the slight attention paid to the problems of Blacks by Presidents of the United States after 1876.

Tribalism may be healthy or unhealthy, desirable or undesirable. There is nothing wrong with a white tribalism (and vice versa) which consciously transcends mythology, recognizes its actual and potential strengths and weaknesses, and respects and seeks to help Black tribalism develop its critical awareness and beneficent potentialities. In fact, tribalism which recognizes proper limits,—which does not deny the humanity, dignity, and rights of any other individual or group—, has much to commend it. In the past black and white tribalism often have lacked this critical awareness and unselfishness. Societies need diversity, communication, rationality, and cohesion. There is no need, however, for the closed society of arbitrarily defined absolutes.

From the days of slavery until past the middle of the twentieth century, there is an alternating rhythm of weak to strong tribalism in the history of Afro-Americans. In this often-times ugly symphony, the majority group usually determines the moods and shifts of the music. Black tribalism weakens whenever white tribalism weakens, that is, when the behavior and pronouncements of white Americans appear to be aimed at the weakening or destruction of racism. On the other hand, when Black Americans become convinced that white Americans are intent on strengthening and maintaining racism, Black tribalism is strengthened. This alternating rhythm, now several centuries old, creates a symphony of the rising and crashing hopes of both white and black Americans. There are those who would contend that, for each race, the low point of each valley of despair is higher than the last one, hence there is ultimate progress in this repetitious climbing and falling. If this is true, such an important matter should not be left so much to accident or chance.

Almost four centuries of eye-oriented American whites having in their midst aural-oriented Afro-Americans has tended to save white Americans from some of the negative effects of changing an ear for an eye. Each intensification of Afro-American tribalism has been matched by an intensification of white American tribalism, or vice versa. McLuhan errors in not seeing the persistence of white tribalism,—in both the United States and Europe—, throughout the period from 1500-1900 A.D. He sees tribalism among white Occidentals before 1500 A.D. and after 1900 A.D. But, as he indicates in the case of Germany and Russia, tribalism never yielded absolutely to the onslaughts of Gutenberg's invention. In the United States of America Black tribalism prodded White tribalism into continued existence and vitality, more in the South than in other regions. In both the Old and New Souths numerous whites took pride in being more tribal than white Northerners. Although white Americans were at times isolated from Europe, they were practically never isolated from Black Americans.

When two tribes occupy the same soil, the minority tribe seeks to ape the majority in just about every detail. But to justify and maintain its superiority, the majority tribe proscribes and denies this right to the minority. The latter are blocked,—often viciously—, in their efforts to assume the attitudes, postures, and roles of the majority. Only among equals could these ambitions of the minority tribal members be realized. The minority is slow to learn that when spokesmen for the majority proclaim their faith in equality, justice, brotherhood, and similar values they have in mind only the members of the majority group.

Throughout much of the earth, wrote Erik Erikson in 1968, the struggle of many men was again propelled by the motor force of many older historical revolutions,— the quest for a larger or more inclusive identity.[23] Practically always, Erikson stated, this more inclusive identity was a process which went from a condition where two groups "had come to depend on each other's negative identities (by living in a traditional situation of mutual enmity or in a symbiotic accommodation to one-sided exploitation)" to a condition where each group borrowed from the other to the mutual benefit of each.[24]

The chief sin committed by civilizations, as pointed out by Arnold J. Toynbee, is that of clinging fatally to an *identity*, such as the city-state or nation-state. Men must learn

to die,—to give up identities—, in order that they may end
rigidities and have the flexibility of life. Excessive rigidity
is the hand of death; change and growth constitute the essence of life. Yet, since for every identity given up a new
one must be acquired, more men, in both races, must become artists skilled in renewing identities and institutional
machinery. Often, new identities cannot be based on old
institutional machinery.

In his volume *Identity: Youth and Crisis,* Erik Erikson
states that women,—once they are fully accepted and integrated into areas of vocational and artistic endeavor—, may
make a unique contribution to culture and civilization. This
contribution will be based in part on their unique physical
attributes and the unique experiences which have been
based, in part, on these biological endowments.

In a predominantly-white world the skin color of Afro-
Americans,—along with other mythical physical qualities—,
has been used in part as a basis for forcing Blacks to have
unique experiences. The Black man and the White woman
both have been victims of many of the same stereotypes.
Both have been grossly exploited and thought of and treated
as immature dangerous beings. Because of their unique experiences, once the era of tokenism ends,— and Afro-Americans are fully accepted into all areas of vocational and artistic endeavor, and the institutions are humanistically-
oriented—, the Black historian and other Afro-Americans
also may add immensely to their already-significant unique
contributions to this nation and mankind.

In his volume *Negro Slave Songs,* Miles Mark Fisher
contends that white Americans adopted from blacks such
things as shouting in church and philandering after marriage. Although Fisher doubtless exaggerates in this matter of cultural borrowing, there can be little doubt that by
the late 1960s such things as the white Americans' sense
of rhythm, speech, humor, and attitude toward "morals,"
the human body, and life itself had been vitally affected

by his lengthy proximity to Blacks. This means that by the late 1960s white and Black Americans were not as different from each other as both often imagined, and that, if the sun of one race was setting forever because fatal cultural elements had been irrevocably embraced, the chances were good that the sun of the other race also was setting forever. It means, too, that if Blacks, because they had preserved certain positive cultural elements, possessed unique possibilities for making a fairly smooth transition from the Gutenberg to the Electric age,—and not only helping to save Occidental civilization, but being good denizens of the Global Village—, white Americans also possessed some of these same unique potentialities.

As the Black historian watches the abortive efforts of numerous national crusades against such things as crime and "loose sexual morals," and ponders the record of his race barely "inching along" in the struggle for freedom, equality, and manhood, he is less likely to succumb to despair than to wonder whether Occidental nations hope only to reasonably control rather than eradicate problems of crime, sex, and racism. All three problems have persisted, in part, because practically everyone is tainted with some degree of guilt of thought or deed.

If White America was prepared forever to live with the problems of racism, as with those of crime and sex, by 1969 Black Americans had a different determination. They were thoroughly tired of the oppressive crushing weight of racism, and many were convinced that they could force White America to view this problem more seriously. They knew that the crime and sex problems produced no Gabriel Prossers, Denmark Veseys, or Nat Turners, and, by 1969 numerous Blacks had been quoted in the public press as stating that if, in order to end racism, they had to commit arson, murder, and wage unremitting guerilla warfare against White America, they would not hesitate to do so. By 1969 it was clear that a really enlightened White tribalism could eliminate the basis for all such thoughts and deeds.

By the time he wrote *The Wretched of the Earth*, Frantz Fanon had seen that where they constituted the overwhelming majority of the population, the goal of the colonized should be to take the place of the colonialists. In the United States of America, this course was closed by the fact that exploited Blacks comprised only ten percent of the population. It seemed clear by 1969 that no possibility existed of effecting and safeguarding the rise of African-Americans except that of finding some means of civilizing White Americans. Blacks had to find some way of persuading White men to rise, thus making possible security for the rise of Black men in their midst. Contrary to the teachings of Mr. Elijah Muhammed, the ultimate fate of Black Americans was inexicably tied to the ultimate fate of White Americans. They had to rise almost in concert or they would enter oblivion almost in concert. White Americans might choose to wage a war of extinction against Blacks,—which might be "successful"—, but no America worthy or capable of existence could survive this "solution." Some persons long had hoped that miscegenation would lead to the disappearance of the Negro, but in 1969 the New Black Man was in no mood to choose this or any other road which obviously led either to extinction or continuing the traditional roles and relationships.

It long had been said that White men could not rise unless they allowed the Black man to rise. Now it was clear that Blacks could not rise and have any security therein unless White men rose. Blacks might choose the alternative of creating a Black "nation" in or near the one from which they emerged. Initially this might well be the quickest way for Black men to rise, but what real long-term security could they have? Unless White racism abated, what would keep its atomic and hydrogen bombs ultimately from exterminating the Black "nation?"

Doubtless no one in the Thirteen British colonies could have guessed that the easy decision to cultivate enslavement of Africans would result in this eternally permanent tying-together of the ultimate destinies of the Black and White populations. It seemed clear by 1969, that for both races, there always would have to be a "Me and Thee,"—or Nothing!

A central meaning of the mid-1969 landing on the moon of astronauts Neil Armstrong and Edwin Aldrin is its testimony to the power of human intellect. Now we must know that intellect can solve not only problems not yet conceived, but many old ones with which men have wrestled for centuries. Sigmund Freud urged men to be strong enough to take Id off the throne, in many areas of their lives, and let Ego rule. Intellect can end exploitation and oppression, and thus end blind fear and blind hatred. Intellect which produces enlightened tribalism can solve the so-called race problem.

When he received the nation's highest award for achievement in his field, Thornton Wilder, author of *The Bridge of San Luis Rey*, stated that the bridge between the world of the living and the world of the dead is love. If in this nation there are the often-times separate Black and White worlds, the moon-landing ought to say to us that when love is blocked, intellect can be a sufficient bridge.

That there is an awful reality named "racism" was bountifully clear by 1969. Also, perhaps the word needed sharper definition. Not every anti-Negro act of every white person was racist. At least a few of these acts grew out of ignorance, and some, doubtless, out of good intentions. Doubtless, too, a great quantity of these acts derived largely from the tendency toward tyranny which is shown by most or all majorities. In the latter instance, it was the White South which, before 1865, had shown the greatest concern with finding a way to protect minorities against the tyranny

of majorities. But the Old South,—seeking herself to preserve slavery—, really was not victimized by the tyranny of
a majority. In this instance the South was in the wrong.
Only when the majority uses its power to impose wrong on
a minority is there tyranny, for minorities ought always to
desire to support that which is right. All unnecessary actions or alterable conditions which militate against the liberation and elevation of any human being are evil.

A more enlightened black tribalism must handle in a
more mature fashion not only its relationship with the white
tribe, but also its own internal ordering. The disharmony
of institutions and culture created by decades of oppression,
paternalism, and self-hate must be replaced by a reordering
of the total life of the black tribe so as to effect the maximum amount of pride, independence, and creativity. By
1969 this task had barely begun.

Writing in the August, 1969 issue of *Ebony*, Lerone Bennett, Jr., said that while a Black Rebellion existed, a Black
Revolution had not yet developed in the United States of
America. Yet, by 1969 the only proper Black Revolution
was well-launched in the nation. Those Blacks were revolutionist who had decided to accept the goals of affirming
blackness, ending racism, paternalism, poverty, and war,
and struggling to make the total culture freer, healthier,
happier, and more decent and humane. As a person is good
by virtue of his sincere commitment to goodness,—and not
by the victories over evil to which this commitment leads—,
so a black person was a revolutionist by virtue of his sincere commitment to these goals. By 1969 so many persons,
—white and black—, were committed that they had won numerous victories and others were almost certain. No one
could predict the form or quantity of these future victories.

In his essay mentioned above Lerone Bennett, Jr. pondered such questions as where the Black Revolution was
headed, and when it would end? It was clear that, unlike
those colonial situations where an oppressed majority aimed

at the specific goal of displacing an oppressing minority, the Black Revolution in the United States never could end. The tendency toward tyranny of majorities is an eternal reality. To become a Black revolutionist in this context is to take on a role which one must endure for a life-time, and then bequeath to all future Blacks. Here "eternal vigilance is the price of liberty" never had better application.

By 1969 the ten percent of the nation's populace that was black sometimes thought too-much of their situation vis-a-vis the ninety percent that was white, and vice versa. Many Blacks could not think of their plight without feeling that rage,—a mixture of impotence, fear, envy, despair, hope—, which, perhaps, all dwarfs feel when giants confront them. Only some type of separatism could remove that awesome reminder,—the physical presence of Whites. But such separatism would be, in large part, victory achieved by embracing an illusion. This is so because the ten per- cent of the populace,—however separated—, could only be a proud island of blackness in or near an ocean of white- ness. In this sense, whether integrated or separated, the black American was fated to remain a dwarf.

But the Afro-American also could remember always that he was part of the earth's population majority that was over two-thirds black, brown, and yellow. He could remember also that, *on that individual basis of personal commitment, growth, and service,* many white Americans are dwarfs and many black Americans are giants. The black American could remember always that Uncertainty, Time, Aging, Pain, and Death are giants before which all men are dwarfs. He could remember always that often whether one is a giant or dwarf is purely a matter of perspective.

For many years white people could "accept" Blacks only if the latter were in the role of the semi-illiterate maid, cook, chauffeur, or something similar. Always Blacks had to be the presumed-inferior in the relationship. Such Negroes as the White-created stereotype,—natural-born eternal-children

—, could pose no real threat to any white person with a weak ego. At the same time Whites reserved a special hatred for Blacks who held college degrees or whose speech, manner, or affluence indicated that they might pose a threat to the status quo. By 1969 this tragedy had reversed its form, and many Blacks could "accept" white people only if the latter were stereotyped as fragmented, alienated, doomed, cold, calculating, sexless, devils. Such Whites as this Black-perpetuated stereotype depicted could pose no threat to any black person with a weak ego.

Doubtless one of the greatest and most common of all human errors or sins is that of "separating off" or the tendency of men to accept only the portion of reality which they find pleasurable. In their weakness, egoism, greed, ignorance, and utopianism men constantly deny dialectical wholeness, thus,—in their efforts to achieve the impossible they destroy their chance of achieving the highest that is possible. Opposites are not two things but one thing. White or black racism is only one of the multitudinous forms of "separating off." "Separating off" was Job's great sin. He believed that only good should come to a good man. The psychological mechanisms of repression, projection, and sublimation are all forms of "separating off," as is also the literalism which Norman O. Brown brings under assault in his book *Love's Body*.

A Black Scholar and Black and White Tribalism

A book similar in some ways to the indictments of the black bourgeoisie by E. Franklin Frazier and Nathan Hare is Harold Cruse's *The Crisis of the Negro Intellectual* (1967). This is, in a number of ways, a brilliant much-needed book,—an excellent commentary on what herein is called "Black and White Tribalism." Cruse also brings the ideology and practice of the cult of individualism under constant and powerful siege. He shows the unreality and essential conservatism of many tenets of this ideology and practice, and points out that most black and white "revolutionists" in the United States of America have been reformist only, and that they had scant idea of what the elements of a revolution would be. The clear need for those who talk of revolution to define it, and the emphasis which he places on group or nationalistic rights, responsibilities, privileges, and power are among the most valuable insights presented. Cruse pleads for a Black tough-mindedness, courage, and wisdom that can cut themselves free from any and all manifestations and expressions of white paternalism. The latter, he declares, always waters down and diverts Black programs and efforts to the point where the interests of the black masses are always betrayed.

As Cruse knows, but does not adequately emphasize, democracy's failure where Blacks are concerned did not begin in the 1920s but when the slave ships landed in Africa. The chief responsibility and blame for the persistence of the racist blight does not rest with any of the sons and daughters of the former black slaves, but with the white majority that has persisted in the thought and action patterns of the slaveholding class. Because he places too much of the blame for the Black American's problems of the 1960s on Negro intellectuals, Cruse is forced into the error of over-valuing the errors of the period from 1920 to 1960.

One shortcoming of the Cruse study is his failure to have a more broadly psychological orientation. Although Karl Marx and C. Wright Mills are paid homage, there is no evidence in Cruse's book that he has used anything written by Sigmund Freud or such persons as Erich Fromm or Norman O. Brown. Yet, behind all institutions and movements,—whether cultural, political, economical, or otherwise—, stands men who are either mainly of the phallic (egoistic power-hungry show-offs) or non-phallic orientation. If they are of the former type, regardless of whether they are integrationists or nationalists, socialists or capitalists—, they can be true friends or allies to no one,—not even to themselves.

The arrogance of power, in both its individual and collective manifestations, is at the root of the problems of mankind. Although the collective form of this arrogance,—as in white racism—, is readily understandable, the individual manifestation,—derived from the infant's fantasies of omnipotence and intensified by a "spoiled" upbringing—, is less understood. When caught in the grip of the arrogance of power, both the individual and the group are excessively egoistic, convinced of their omnipotence and invincibility, overly-convinced that their actions are logical and right, contemptuous of altruistic thought and behavior and of the common masses of men, insatiably greedy, and believes that might makes right. Many years ago, the Book of Habakkuk in the Old Testament gave an adequate characterization of this "Chaldean" type of individual or group. This problem, plus that of hereditary aristocracy, are very high on the list of the chief woes of every capitalistic society.

Cruse writes as if the "race problem" would be solved if Negro intellectuals and the black bourgeoisie only had embraced black nationalism at the time that Martin Delany proposed it during the 1850s. Cruse fails to mention that this course might well have intensified white tribalism's aggressions to the point where a "final solution" to the Negro problem such as Adolph Hitler attempted against Europe's Jews would have resulted. Cruse depicts American Jews of the twentieth century as being hypocritically nationalistic for themselves while condemning nationalism for Blacks. Yet he does not consider all of the possible implications of the practice of ardent Black nationalism during the 1865-1914 apogee of white racism. Instinct for survival, rather than stupidity, may have been a part of the Negro intellectual's guide here. The "race problem" of the period since 1920 may have been worse, instead of improved, had a staunch pre-1920 Black nationalism existed. Still, if this is so, it also should be true that by 1969 white tribalism's potential for enlightenment has been so developed that a more nationalistic course for Blacks was not only safer, but also wiser.

Cruse often treats racial integration versus black nationalism as an either—or matter. Yet the best course for black Americans is probably a mixture of these two positions. Both integration and separatism exist and doubtless both will and should continue to exist. These two are not diametrically opposed, although integration based on any disrespect whatever for Black people, or on the desire to see the black group become extinct, is wrong and ought to be opposed.

Cruse points out that the Black-White relationship is over-simplified unless the fact is considered that among whites there are competing religious and ethnic groups (mainly Anglo-Saxon-Protestant, Catholic, and Jewish),— white tribalisms. Cruse admits, however, that when it comes to their thoughts and acts where black people are concerned, there is scant difference among these white groups. Thus, the problem still is essentially one of "White over Black,"—a problem of the power, arrogance, and cruelty of a numerical majority. Cruse pleads for Blacks to match Whites in group pride and solidarity. This, of course, is sorely needed, but the solution of the Black-White problem can come only if there is a concomitant achievement, by enough members of the majority, which involves an expansion of their attitudes and values where Blacks are concerned. For Blacks to learn to play the power game,—and nothing more—, only "solves" the problem within the old context of "realism." On both the international and domestic scenes, unless power and economic affluence cease to be the highest elements in the "realistic" outlook, the entire human race is doomed. Men in high places too often are unaware that in an age of atomic and hydrogen bombs, they cannot conduct business-as-usual.

By 1969 black nationalism certainly had its beauty, power, and wisdom. That its champions were capable of exaggeration was also clear. Cruse wrote in 1967 that "in the rundown ghettoes are the accumulated results of years of black middle-class social irresponsibility." Certainly this is an exaggeration of the potential of the black bourgeoisie. White America has allowed only a few Blacks to "make it." These few, the black bourgeoisie, could not at the same time also have rescued the black masses. The root cause of this problem has been white racism, and absolutely no one has provided the answer to the question of how to get a sufficient number of the white majority to change their attitude and behavior toward Blacks. Regardless of the wisdom and courage of its actions, no physically-conspicuous minority of only ten per cent of the populace, afloat as an island in an ocean of white racism, can have more than a small amount of control over its fate. Black power can move only *some* mountains. Contrary to the implication made by Cruse, Jews, Irish, Poles, and other ethnic groups in the United States "made it" not because of their nationalism but because first, they are white, and second, because they never had to overcome the effects (on themselves and on their oppressors) of more than two centuries of enslavement as chattel property. Cruse refuses to accept the fact that the masses of white Americans have been the authors and finishers of the plight of the black masses. To blame excessively the black bourgeoisie, Jews, Marxists, or "white liberals" here is to indulge in scape-goating. All of these groups share some of the blame, but not the major portion of it.

Since Cruse misplaces the major blame for the plight of Blacks, he also is led to minimize too-much the role that Whites must play in the salvation of the black masses. Over-rating the self-help potential of Blacks often leads the would-be rescuers of Black people to propose programs which are very masochistically-oriented. The weak and sick, except in rare instances, cannot save themselves. If all whites and the black bourgeoisie are too sick to help the black masses, as some persons contend, then there is little hope for either race. The exaggerated element in black nationalism may well be what accounted for what Cruse calls "the only real flaw" in the thought of W. E. B. Du Bois,—his inconsistency about black nationalism.

When Cruse implies that Frederick Douglass does not belong in the tradition of "Black Power" and Black Nationalism, Cruse does this great man a gross injustice. To cite just one example, *The North Star* is in the tradition of Black Power. Also, long before Booker T. Washington's 1895 Atlanta Speech, at numerous of the National Negro Conventions Douglass promoted industrial education for Blacks. Finally, Josef Stalin,—perhaps the greatest of all Russian nationalists—, opposed Leon Trotsky's efforts to have the Soviet Union promote revolution abroad as well as at home. Is Douglass to be denied the label "nationalist" because he,—like Stalin—, felt that recently "freed" Afro-Americans were too weak to fight on two fronts (the U.S.A. and Africa)?

When considering their own interests, to think and act in a manner diametrically opposed to the dominant white thought on the matter always has been the greatest difficulty encountered by Afro-Americans. This has been a prime source of the acceptance by Blacks of white paternalism. The other prime source has been the attractiveness of the money which this paternalism has dangled before the eyes of Blacks.

There is a great deal of egotism in each of the three types of human relationship delineated by Erich Fromm. However, the mature strong ego is manifest only in the democratic relationship, and in neither the sadistic (where you are *over* someone) nor the masochistic relationship (where someone is over you). Hence the weak egos possessed by most white and black Americans have been evident not only in the war between the sexes, generations, classes, and regions,—and in the extreme ambivalence of the attitude toward Europeans, Asians, and Africans as foreigners—, but in the relationship between the races as fellow-countrymen or fellow-citizens.

White and black Americans always have feared racial integration for the same basic reason that they have been isolationists in foreign relations—the realization that intimate contact with even slightly-different peoples and cultures would lead to death in the form of destruction of their weak egos. The racial separatism which existed during the era of classical slavery, and from 1865 to 1950,—like isolationism in foreign relations from 1789 to 1945—, probably was a blessing in disguise which saved the weak identities of black and white Americans from extinction.

By 1945 the wealth, technology, and other achievements of American education and energy dictated an end to isolationism in foreign affairs and in domestic race relations. Persistence of the weak ego in foreign affairs was evident during the 1950s and 60s in the super-nationalism in such phenomena as McCarthyism, and the political stance of the Ku Klux Klan, many Goldwaterites, Birchites, and Wallace-ites. As might be expected, persistence of the weak ego in race relations found its greatest manifestation in the thoughts and actions of these same groups, now joined by some of the Black nationalists. Often the groups which seem the strongest, are the weakest.

By 1969 it was clear that weak egoism was a cancer which in both foreign affairs and domestic race relations needed to be excised. The period when isolationism and racial separatism were necessary to save the weak identities of black and white Americans had lasted too long. By 1969 the ego of each group should have been strong enough not to need such defenses. A weak ego is understandable when national resources are weak, or when men are slaves. But men usually have greater resources than they realize, and slavery has multitudinous forms. The rise of the city, modern technology, and the Global Village dictated the need for black and white Americans to know that the ego that is strong enough is in no danger. This is probably one of the deepest truths in the statement by Socrates that no evil can come to a good man.

CHAPTER VII

THE NEGRO AND THE CENTRAL THEME
OF SOUTHERN HISTORY

Although practically everyone agrees that the people called "Southerners" are somehow different from Americans designated as "Northerners" or "Westerners," there is a very considerable variety of opinion as to just how and why Southerners are different. The effort to find answers to these questions has been designated the quest for a central theme of Southern history.

During the 1920's Southerners became acutely conscious that industrialization, urbanization, and other factors were creating a New South. The pace of change in the region produced, for many persons, a crisis-of-identity. In the eyes of these, the region was becoming so much like the North that it was difficult to determine (1) remaining areas of dissimilarity, and (2) whether the South as a distinctive culture was disappearing altogether. Some Southerners were unhappy about this development, and many were led to ask such questions as "Who or What am I?" "Do I represent a disappearing breed?" "What, if anything, makes the Southerner unique among Americans?"

"The threat of becoming 'indistinguishable,' of being submerged under a national steamroller," one scholar wrote in 1960, "has haunted the mind of the South for a long time."[1] As if to reassure themselves, in 1957 fourteen Southerners took a "look at their home" and published a volume entitled *The Lasting South*.[2] Here the editors declared:

The fourteen writers who contribute their thought on the matter [The thesis that the South's identity is worth preserving] share one underlying assumption about the South, and that is that in an increasingly modern and cosmopolitan world, there is more than ever need for the persistent individuality of the South.

The tension generated by this juncture in history, and such questions as these, served as a great catalyst to Southern thought and literature, and probably had much to do with the occurrence of that happy phenomenon that is often called the Southern Literary Renaissance. During the 1920's and since the South produced its first really great group of writers in such persons as Eudora Welty, Ellen Glasgow, Thomas Wolfe, William Faulkner, Erskine Caldwell, Robert Penn Warren, Allen Tate, Tennessee Williams, Bell I. Wiley, C. Vann Woodward, Francis Butler Simkins, and others.

Since the 1920's the pace of change in the region has continued to be rapid and dramatic, and these same questions have been (and are still being) asked with rising interest and intensity of demand for an answer. Over the years many answers have been attempted.

Among others, in the 1960's C. Vann Woodward, in a volume entitled *The Burden of Southern History*,[3] wrote at length on this theme; Rice University had as a feature of its semicentennial celebration a symposium which used as its theme, "The Idea of the South,"[4] and an article which appeared in *The Yale Review*, in 1961, entitled "Enigma of the South,"[5] pondered these questions.

Most scholars have agreed that a major characteristic of the mind of the Old South was its sense of having a way of life that was unique. There has been little agreement, however, as to what the elements of that uniqueness were or when it first appeared.

Carl Bridenbaugh has held that there was no unique mind of the South during the colonial period.[6] Yet Allen Nevins states that "We might trace far back into Colonial times the Southern conviction of superiority to Northern and British shilling-grabbers."[7] Merrill Jensen has found the "roots of antagonism that led to war between the North and the South in the era of the American Revolution."[8]

In 1957 John R. Alden held that sectional strife began to manifest itself at the beginning of the War for Independence, and "The South had emerged as a section and the Southerners as a people different from Northerners" by "the end of the Revolutionary era."[9] Differing with this judgment, another scholar states that, "When the two sections allied in common cause against England, their alliance by no means embraced a common culture. Their cultures were becoming increasingly divergent."[10]

Some scholars have seen the mind of the South first manifesting itself at the Philadelphia Constitutional Convention.[11] The South became a "conscious minority," according to Jesse T. Carpenter, at this time.[12] Francis B. Simkins dates the origin of a unique mind of the South from the Missouri Compromise controversy,[13] and in 1936, R. S. Cotterill also held that there was no unique mind of the South before 1819-1820.[14] Apparently William B. Hesseltine also once dated the origin of a unique mind of the South from the 1819-20 controversy over slavery.[15]

Just as scholars differ on when the South emerged as a unique region, they differ on what causes and constitutes the differentness. The South's distinctiveness has at various times been based on the region's "faults or weaknesses," such as laziness, lynching, the poll-tax, hedonism, sharecropping, secession, states-rightism, paternalism, moral parochialism, clanism, and one-party demagogic politics, or on the region's strengths or "brighter side" such as hospitality, sunshine, pretty virtuous girls, fast horses, fried chicken, waterwelons, or ham and hominy.

Nineteenth century Occidental scholarship placed special emphasis on climate and race as explanations and justifications for such things as institutions, cultures, patterns of immigration, the prevailing imperialism or colonialism, and expected levels of national achievement and destiny.

In 1928 Ulrich Bonnell Phillips utilized the race theme and wrote a now-famous essay entitled, "The Central Theme of Southern History," in which he held that what makes the South unique is the everlasting desire and effort to preserve white supremacy.[16] Involved here is the racial-purity argument and the white South's claim to so-called Anglo-Saxon purity.

Borrowing in part from the ideas of Frederick Jackson Turner, Wilbur J. Cash, in his oft-quoted book, *The Mind of the South*, held that the South's uniqueness resulted from agrarianism and the persistence of behavior and attitudes adopted during the region's frontier days.[17] This uniqueness, Cash held, manifests itself as a pronounced proclivity for exaggerated self reliance alongside deplorable paternalism, violence, romanticism, and hedonism. The historians William Hesseltine and Francis Butler Simkins also have made much of agrarianism as the central source of the Southerner's uniqueness. In 1930, however, several Southerners, often called the Vanderbilt, Nashville, or Southern Agrarians, issued a volume entitled, *I'll Take My Stand*,[18] which is the most noted argument that the uniqueness and glory of the Southerner and his histoiy derive from long-standing cultivation of the soil and preference for the rural values and pattern of life. Of this effort, one scholar stated: "The twelve Southerners who joined in this profession of faith categorically rejected the industrial way of life, which they regarded as the prevailing or American way, and with equal conviction they subscribed to an agrarian way, which they identified as a Southern way. They hoped to carry this Southern way to the nation through 'a national agrarian movement.'"[19]

"As of old," wrote Clarence Cason in 1935, "the climate and the presence of the Negro are the main conditioning elements in southern culture."[20] "During the three cen-

turies of his residence in the Southern States," Cason continued, "The Negro has had almost as much as the sunshine
to do with conditioning the lives of the white people of the
region."[21] Thus with Cason, as with U. B. Phillips and some
others, the Black man is considered to be a major factor in
the central theme of Southern history.

David Potter's explanation of Southern uniqueness is
that folk-level or folk-type culture persisted in this region
"long after it succumbed to the onslaught of urban-indus-
trial culture elsewhere."[22] Howard W. Odum also places
the Old South under the heading of a folk culture, and
states that such a culture derives its "social character from
societies that are small, isolated, reflecting love of liberty,
loyalties, homogenities of structure. The folk culture is
closely knit, cohesive, nonorganizational, with behavior primarily spontaneous, personal, traditional. . . ."[23]

Thomas P. Govan, in an article entitled, "Was the Old
South Different?,"[24] has pointed out that in the Old South
as in pre-1865 North, there were divisions between farmers
and city folk, "the educated and the uneducated," "the rich
and the poor," and "the powerful and the weak."[25] Govan
deemphasizes the differences that have existed between the
South and the North.

One leading Southerner asked in 1957: "Could it be that
there is no essence of Southernism—that it is a myth used to
justify whatever status quo was then being attacked?"[26]
This scholar then goes on to point out that there has indeed
been such a myth thus used. Yet focus on differences between the regions has persisted, and several volumes have
been written to advance or attack various of the explanations and arguments for the uniqueness of the Southerner
and his culture.

Preservation of democracy and freedom was the chief
goal that Thomas Jefferson believed would be realized by
forever keeping America a society of small farmers.[27] The
idea that independence and freedom in a state are best pre-

served when the small family farm is predominant has been widespread and is not peculiar to either Americans or the modern period of history.

Numerous histories of the Old Southwest and biographies of Eighteenth and Nineteenth century Americans have shown that there was an affinity between agrarian democracy and plantation aristocracy. The two were not opposites, as is often thought, but rather both were products of frontier-type democracy and freedom. "There is no universal law," stated one scholar in 1948, "that equates agrarianism and democracy or family farming and democracy."[28] "On the contrary," he concluded, "historical evidence to date seems to indicate that democracy has flourished most in the countries, with the notable exception of Germany, that have attained a high degree of industrialization and urbanization." This same scholar continues:

> Democracy did not spring full-flowered from the soil. It has grown from men's minds and spirits in the commercial and industrial atmosphere of cities as much as . . . in the agrarian atmosphere of the country.
>
> If there were democratic magic in agriculture, why is it that men have been farmers for thousands of years, yet democracy as we know it is not two hundred years old and claims a minority of the earth's peoples as its disciples? . . . Farmers have been called the backbone of every form of government in the world, including fascism. . . . Whatever truth the proposition may have held in the United States of Jefferson's age, it has lost a little of it with each succeeding generation.[29]

David Potter denounces the theory that the South's uniqueness rests on agrarianism because of his belief that the paternalism, hierarchy, monoculture, and commercialism which practically always existed in the region negate the theory.[30] Of the Nashville Agrarians, Potter has written:

Whether they advocated populism or elitism no one could make out.

They were accused of medievalism and of quixotically renouncing all the benefits of modern science and technology.

The historical significance of agrarian thought has still never been adequately analyzed.[31]

And:

. . . it is clearly evident that agrarianism appealed to many liberals, both before and after the Nashville group, partly because they were looking for an alternative to the prevailing American way of Life. . . . Here . . . was a way in which a man could renounce industrial capitalism and all its works without becoming a Marxist . . . without going outside the American tradition.[32]

Again Potter stated in 1961:

Again a whole generation of writers have made this tempting equation between Southernism and agrarianism, it requires only a limited analysis to see that in many respects, the Southern economy and the Southern society have not been agrarian at all—in fact; have embodied almost the antithesis of agrarianism.[33]

Potter states that in F. L. Owsley's *Plain Folk of the Old South,* "and many other writings, a number of time-honored propositions continued to find acceptance: That American democracy has been nourished primarily from agrarian roots; that agrarian attitudes are inherently democratic; and that the South peculiarly embodies the agrarian tradition."[34] But, says Potter, Arthur Schlesinger, Jr.'s book, *The Age of Jackson,* published in 1945, held that "Jacksonian democracy owed more to the East and to class conscious urban workingmen than to the frontier and its coon skin equality,"[35] while Richard Hofstadter's volume, *The Age of Reform* (1955) "has gone even further by arguing that Populism had little affinity with liberal democracy, and was in fact a seed-bed for such-illiberal manifestations as prohibition, nativism, immigration restriction, red-baiting, and the like. Thus according to Schlesinger, democracy was not agrarian, and according to Hofstadter, agrarianism was not democratic."[36]

The effort to see all or most Southern traits as derivatives of agrarianism—rather than the larger context which includes such elements as American isolation, relative weakness of the central government, and the impact of the world frontier—has led to a debunking of even the genuine derivatives of national and Southern ruralness. There was democracy and freedom in early America not because of supposed virtues inherent in farming, but because of the widespread ownership of, and easy access to land. Also, the low state of development of industrial, commercial, and governmental powers left most individuals with a high level of independence.

Although theories of the magical powers of farming have been discredited, there can be no denying that, when compared with Northerners, Southerners kept in closer contact with the natural environment simply because more of them remained on farms. Throughout history the belief that there are significant differences between the outlook and style of life of farmers and city folk is too common among writers, scholars, politicians, and the laity to be without some basis in fact.

In the late 1950's one scholar examined the U. B. Phillips thesis that the uniqueness of the South rests on the effort to preserve racial segregation. "What is the relation, if any, between farming and the Southern way of life?",[37] he asked. He continued:

> The Southern way of making a living has been largely, and still is predominantly, farming. We may

expect, then, that the Southern way of life will have much to do with farming. It will also have much to do with the association of Negroes and whites, because it is through this association that we have farmed. But to include this total productive association of whites and Negroes and land in the bare term segregation, and then to say that this segregation is our way of life, is to fail to see that segregation is rather a principle of dissociation than of association, and as such is a source, not of spiritual value, but of spiritual disvalue. The earlier institution of slavery, largely though of course never entirely accepted by those involved, and existing for the purpose of economic production, did tend to moralize itself; it created obligations, duties, loyalties; it became a way of life. The institution of segregation, never really accepted by the Negroes though necessarily acquiesced in and existing in part merely to satisfy the desire of the whites for superiority, has developed few moral implications, and is therefore but slightly a way of life. It might more properly be called a way of not-life.[38]

Among Southern historians who were active in the 1960's, Francis Butler Simkins found it possible to agree with the U. B. Phillips thesis. On this, Simkins wrote:

[Liberal modern white historians of the South] should know that the color line was created to sustain the most important fact in southern history. Two biologically aggressive races have dwelt together in large numbers for 335 years without the ruling race losing its integrity of blood. Without this fact there would be no South in the social or psychological sense; the region between the Potomac and the Rio Grande would be just a geographical expression.[39]

In 1937 Charles W. Ramsdell also agreed with Phillips,[40] and, writing in 1965, Dwight Dumond accepted the Phillips' thesis unqualifiedly.[41] In 1961 David Potter chided liberal historians for rejecting the Phillips conclusion that the "core of distinctive Southernism" was the "fixed purpose on the part of the southern whites to preserve biracialism, or . . . to assure that the South shall be and remain a white man's country."[42] "It is in some ways ironical for liberals, concerned as they are with the sick South," Potter declared, "to reject a formula which explains so cogently the chronic nature of the illness."[43]

In a 1960 essay entitled, "The Central Theme Revisited," George B. Tindall stressed the fact that the South's virtues and vices usually have been the same as the nation's and that everyone should be more mindful of the Southerner-As-American rather than the Southerner-As-Unique. Later, in 1964, Tindall stated that perhaps the true central theme of Southern history is not going to be found in the realm of facts at all, but "at last on the new frontier of mythology."[44] This frontier of mythology, he thinks, is new in the sense of being a new area for scholarly study by historians.

During the 1960's several scholars felt that the best thinking on the problem of the central theme tends to get away from the old single-factor explanation.

Tindall agreed with C. Vann Woodward and others that pluralistic explanations of the South's uniqueness are probably superior to monistic ones. Potter also was sympathetic with this view, and endorsed the items—as offered by Tindall and Woodward—that should go into such a pluralistic explanation. Each of these writers, however, indicated his uncertainty, and fascination with the single-factor explanation, by presenting his own "monistic" theory. Woodward wrote:

> The better studies of group or national character in late years have tended to go beyond circumstances and purpose, beyond natural environment and public policy, and to stress experience as the influence of first importance.[45]

He then proceeded to list experiences which the South has had that Americans of other regions have not had, such as being defeated in a major war and placed under an army of occupation; having had much greater economic deprivation; and, having had to carry a larger burden of guilt because of the greater acuteness of the region's race problem.[46] Woodward has attacked many of the explanations of the South's uniqueness on the grounds that they are based on conditions that were temporary,[47] and he makes the quest for a central theme a search for a permanent theme in Southern history. This tendency may well be due in part, to mankind's persistent desire, ever more pronounced in times of rapid change, to find security by clinging to something absolute or eternal. This scholar failed to indicate clearly that a region's history, like a nation's foreign policy, may, over a period of time, have different central themes, each valid for only a few decades or generations.

Because they, too, are Southerners, relevant here is the argument that sometimes rages as to how or whether Afro-Americans are different from other Americans, and if so, "What is the central theme of Afro-American history?"

Like the planters of the Old South, in the 1960's the Ku Klux Klan still held that Afro-Americans are different in that they are inferior to other Americans, but by then the "Black Muslims" had achieved considerable notoriety with their claim that Blacks are different in that they are "superior" to white Americans. On the "positive" side Blacks have been held to be more athletic, musical, humorous, playful, innocent, and religious than white Americans, while on the "negative" side they have been held to be more stupid, lazy, dirty, larcenous, childish, and emotional. In the twentieth century the Black man generally has been acutely aware of his difference in terms of skin color, hair texture, lower level of poverty and culture, and of being an outsider or parish group, and many Blacks, in many ways, have worked long and hard to change all of these differences.

Utilizing the idea that a fundamental difference between regions, nations, classes, ethnic groups, or individuals is caused by the fact that they have had different experiences, it can be seen that while Afro-Americans are
neither better nor worse than Caucasian-Americans, in some
very significant ways—other than just pigmentation of
skin and texture of hair—Blacks are different.

Of course black and white Americans are alike in many
ways, and this not only because they share a common biological and cultural heritage, but because they have shared
much by way of common national and regional history. But
the Afro-American's experiences often have been different,
and they have evoked both hatred and love (each in considerable abundance) for white Americans. Not all of the
elements of the Afro-American's past are like all of those in
the past of white Americans. The enslavement of the black
race is unique in American history.

As a slave, and often since, the black man was unfree
in a country that worshipped freedom, poor where wealth
was worshipped, denied ownership of his body when a man
was measured by what he owned, black where whiteness
was worshipped; denied achievement where success was the
goal; denied religion, education, and learning where they
were uniquely cultivated; denied home and family although
a man's home was generally held to be his castle; and, in a
land that boasted of its past, the Black race was held to
possess no history that a self-respecting person would own.
No other group in the American populace has been treated,
with such conscious deliberate persistence, as a parish
group, and the black man is the only American who had the
question of his freedom made a central issue in a long and
bloody fratricidal war. The 13th, 14th, and 15th Amendments to the federal constitution, as well as more recent
federal civil rights legislation and judicial rulings, came
into being because of the uniqueness of the Afro-American's history, condition, and problems.

Once when a Black professor was engaged in a conversation with a white member of their predominantly-Black college faculty, it was suggested that the latter's department might interest itself more in subject matter and courses of a Black idiom or genre. The reply of the white faculty member was—"I thought Negroes wanted to get away from being Negroes." The Black teacher was too stunned to answer, for he was convinced that Afro-Americans can never get away from being "Negroes," and that only those persons who are ashamed of the identification either want to make this dissociation or believe that it is possible.

Some Blacks don't like the celebration of "Negro History Week" and would like to forget that their race ever had dramatically unique and often-times ugly experiences and treatment. It is very human to deny, to repress, to refuse to accept facts that are unpleasant. This, of course, is why people deny the insanity, murders, suicides or other dramatic failures in their immediate families, or why Occidental culture notoriously represses the fact of death. Yet, for a region, nation, class, race, or individual, there can be no maturity until the ability or honesty or strength is acquired which makes it possible to deal objectively with the past. This is so because acceptance of one's past is nothing less than acceptance of self. There can be no maturity that is not based on objective self-acceptance.

No Black man of today, or tomorrow, can escape this past that so many find to be a painful thing to contemplate. He is associated with it forever. He may allow the past to overwhelm him or he may transcend it; he may use it in many ways and for many purposes, but he cannot escape it. As long as any Americans are associated with the word "Negro," they will be associated with the unique past experiences of blacks, and in this sense they will always be different or unique. And for the same reason, so long as any Americans are called "Southerners," they will be associated with not only Yorktown but Ft. Sumter and Bull Run and

Gettysburg and Appomattox, and this stamp of past experience upon them will always make them unique, however similar they may be in all other ways. Because the past can not be altered or erased, and because the past is always a part of the present, neither the Southerner-as-Caucasian nor the Southerner-as-Black can ever disappear.

The U. B. Phillips thesis stresses the coercive or hatred side of Black-White relations. Still, by placing the black race at the center of the equation, Phillips came closer to the central theme of Southern history than those scholars who see a central theme which either omits the black man or makes him peripheral.

In *Edmund Ruffin, Southerner,* Avery Craven stated that the presence of the black race and the Cavalier ideal were the main sources of the uniqueness of the South.[48] In his volume, *The Militant South,* John Hope Franklin has shown that the Old South's militaristic and Cavalier proclivities were intensified by the presence of the slaves.[49] The subtitle of a recent volume on Alabama history also is among the many studies which reveal the central position of the black man in the central theme of Southern history. The volume, by M. C. McMillan, is entitled *Constitutional Development in Alabama, 1789-1901: A Study in Politics, The Negro, and Sectionalism.*[50] In his *Myths and Realities: Societies of the Colonial South,* Carl Bridenbaugh gives primacy to the presence of the black race in determining the uniqueness of the South.[51] The same is true of a recent treatise by D. F. Dowd.[52] Echoing many other scholars, Thomas P. Govan indicates this when he writes of the causes of the Civil War.[53] He states:

> The South did not secede because of differences in culture, nor even because of the tariff or the Bank of the United States, but rather because of its 'peculiar' sectional interest. The one important sectional conflict in the nation's history arose from the fact that Negroes were held as slaves in the southern

states until 1865. The defense of slavery . . . led
[Southerners] to seek independence outside the American Union.[54]

In his *magnum opus* James Ford Rhodes viewed slavery as
the central cause of the Civil War. "If the negro [sic] had
never been brought to America," he wrote, "our Civil War
would not have occurred." In their volume, *Growth of the
American Republic*, Samuel Eliot Morison and Henry S.
Commager also contend that slavery was the central cause
of the Civil War.[55] Although J. G. Randall and Avery Craven contended that slavery and the black man were unreal
issues of the 1830-1860 period, Arthur Schlesinger, Jr. and
others have directly attacked their arguments.

Those scholars who place the black race near the bottom of the list in a multiple-factor explanation of Southern
uniqueness sometimes forget the intimate relationship which
exists between the black man and most or all of their other
factors. On this, one scholar wrote in 1964:

A frontier civilization which grew in waves of westward settlement, the South developed a rustic cast
reinforced by abundant, thinly settled land. Rustics
are normally fiercely independent, industrious folk,
jealous of rights and chattels. Southerners had all
these traits, but they were conditioned by one constant peculiar to the South: slavery. The slave system in its economic, political, and social implications
added an intangible something to the violent strain
running strong in Southerners.[56]

As this scholar, Frank Vandiver—and Phillips, Potter,
Cason, Cash, and others—imply, slight the black race in
studies or theories on Southern history and culture and the
truth is always missed. Even Cash probably fails somewhat in this regard. In his discussion of the uniqueness of
Southern character the frontiers made by geography and by
the Yankee sometimes seem to practically push the black

man out of the picture. The same criticism is valid for the effort of Howard Odum and others to explain the South by stressing the fact that it has been a region with an acute economic problem.[57] Odum and his associates wrote in 1936 of the plight of "southern farmers" without direct discussion of the distinct plight of Southern blacks. Thus, concluded one critic, "their survey of Southern problems left out the greatest problem of all."[58]

The major objection to the Phillips thesis is not, as C. Vann Woodward would have it, that it dealt with a passing phenomenon—the effort to preserve white supremacy—; or, as George B. Tindall would have it, the thesis was focused too exclusively on the political aspect of Southern history and life. Like the rest of America, freedom is the central theme of Southern history. The central theme of Southern history is the effort of the white man to preserve a superabundance of freedom, and the concomitant desire of the black man to acquire the freedoms denied to him. The central theme of Afro-American history is the quest of Black Americans for freedom, equality, and manhood. The chief objection to the Phillips thesis, therefore, is that it encompasses only one-half of the freedom-concern which has been the real central theme of Southern history.

CHAPTER VIII

THE WHITE TEACHER OF BLACK HISTORY

Most White Americans who desire either to teach special courses on Afro-American history, or who desire to integrate this history into traditional American history courses need emancipation from elements of the world of traditional White thought and feeling. One example of this need is furnished by a pamphlet which a noted White American historian has written. This scholar, Louis R. Harlan, wrote a pamphlet which was published in 1965 by the American Historical Association's Service Center for Teachers of History, under the title, *The Negro in American History*.

Some of the observations which follow are not criticisms of the pamphlet, but concern information which might have been included. For example, when he discusses "The Era of Slavery," Harlan says nothing about the much-debated question of African survivals, the question of how much, if any, of the original culture of the slaves survived in the New World. Also, to his brief information about the *Journal of Negro History*, he might have said something about the great value and usefulness of the many scholarly articles and book reviews which have been carried in this journal. An examination of the titles of these articles will readily reveal that, though many may be a decade or more old, in numerous instances nothing further has been written on the subject. Also, while he points out that the *Negro History Bulletin* was originally "aimed at high school readers," he neglects to mention that, for various reasons, some issues of the *Bulletin* have carried articles that also were aimed at the graduate student and scholar.

Since the Service Center for Teachers of History pamphlets were not designed for much discussion of primary materials, one cannot accuse Mr. Harlan of sinning in any way because he fails to mention the collections of materials for Afro-American history which are to be found in several states. However, anyone who is giving close attention to the materials of Black history ought to mention these special collections, the most famous of which is the Schomburg Collection at the 135th Street Branch of the New York Public Library. Among others are the Booker T. Washington and Monroe Work Collections at Tuskegee Institute, Atlanta University's Slaughter Collection, Howard University's Spingarn and Moorland Collections, and the Fisk University and Hampton Institute Collections.

The Harlan pamphlet ignores too much, and is otherwise too disrespectful of the contributions of the black historians who pioneered in this field and whose labors and achievements made Afro-American History a respected and accepted area for historical specialization.

Whether the area is American economic or diplomatic history, or the Renaissance, Reformation, or French Revolution, as time passes most of the earlier works of scholarship are superseded by later studies. Each generation of scholars knows that this is the ultimate fate of their labors. Harlan is aware of this. Still, one must disagree with what seems to be the tone and conclusion of his judgment about the black makers of Afro-American history and their work. On this subject, Harlan refers to "the segregated, somewhat sectarian Negro history of an earlier generation." On this, he continues:

> One of the assumptions [of this pamphlet] is that historical writing of the past two decades answers more of the different questions we are asking of the past than most books written a generation or more ago. Though the latest insights should not be equated with eternal truth, every generation of scholars has

built its own intellectual city on the rubble of the previous generation's interpretations. It is ironic that the Negro history movement begun fifty years ago is part of that rubble.[1]

Only part of the problem here is caused by the fact that practically all of the scholars consigned by Harlan to the rubble-heap are black. More is involved.

In the paragraph following the quote just given, Harlan discusses the contributions of George Washington Williams and Carter G. Woodson. Because of the magnitude of his contribution, W. E. B. Du Bois should have been included here.

Regardless of whether the field is art, music, philosophy, the novel, or historical scholarship, the living tend to be overly-conceited, and overly-disrespectful toward the achievements of previous generations. Perhaps in no area of historical specialization should one be as convinced as Harlan is that "historical writing of the past two decades answers more of the different questions we are asking of the past than most books written a generation ago." To consider just one subject T. J. Pressly's, *Americans Interpret their Civil War* does not confirm Harlan's position. Probably for no field of historical specialization should one speak of the previous generation's achievements as "rubble." Persons who attempt to teach and write Negro history today will err seriously if they accept Harlan's view "that the Negro history movement begun fifty years ago is "[now] rubble."[2]

Everyone should commend the generally high quality of writings on Afro-American history produced during the last two decades. But, we also must be aware that this historiography has produced few, if any, new interpretations of significance, and its quantity is so slight that on many subjects we have only the older works which Harlan assigns to rubble.

The Negro college has made an outstanding contribution to the development of this nation. Where histories of these institutions exist, there is generally only one per institution, often one or two decades old. This always has been a neglected field. These are still-valuable histories. Assign them to rubble and we are left with nothing. The same is true of that important institution of black people, the church. In 1958, Earl E. Thorpe's book, *Negro Historians in the United States* appeared with a section on "Negro Writers of Church History." Although a number of the books mentioned there were already a decade or more old, not so much has been done in this area during the past two decades as to allow us to classify these earlier works as "rubble." The religious history of the Black American always has been a neglected field. These are still-valuable histories. Assign them to rubble and we are left with practically nothing.

The same picture holds if we turn to such areas as Black business, lay fraternal orders, college sororities and fraternities, some biographies of Negro personalities, and to the organizational efforts and activities of Black women. Here again there is a pattern where often only a single work exists, often at least one or two decades old. Because the primary materials used may have been lost, the author leaned rather heavily on interviews and personal memory, or similar reasons, if we assign these histories to the rubble heap, we have little or nothing left.

Of Booker T. Washington and Frederick Douglass, Harlan writes:

> Anyone now interested in Washington should begin with [August] Meier's volume. Though Washington succeeded Frederick Douglass as the Negro father-figure, Negro scholars have avoided this obviously important biographical subject, possibly because of alienation from his social philosophy and the lack of a tradition of critical biography.[3]

Harlan goes on to call Spencer's life of Booker T. Washington "an ultrafavorable treatment of limited usefulness."[4]

The extent to which Washington was a "Negro father-figure" is questionable. Also questionable is whether Blacks lack "a tradition of critical biography." The list of Blacks who have written good biographies includes Charles W. Chestnutt, Benjamin Brawley, Shirley Graham, W. E. B. Du Bois, Miles Fisher, Roi Ottley, Charles Wesley, Benjamin Quarles, and Lawrence D. Reddick. In addition, many good critical biographical sketches written by Black Americans have been published in the *Journal of Negro History* and *Negro History Bulletin.*

The truth which Harlan can state here is that the quantity of biography written by Afro-Americans is relatively small. But this is true of almost any field which might be mentioned. Although the quantity, quality, and value of Black literary and scholarly production are much higher than has been generally appreciated or known, it is still true that Negroes have not written "enough" plays, poems, or novels. They have not written many scholarly studies of the colonial period, the Civil War, or Reconstruction eras, the Progressive Movement, American diplomatic history, and so on. Considering that over 80% of the black population were chattel slaves a little over a century ago, and the handicaps imposed since 1865, one must make his own judgment as to what the quantity and quality of achievement in these areas should now be.

Also, while the Spencer biography is "favorable," it is not an "ultrafavorable treatment" of Washington's life.

One must dissent from Harlan's statement that the "personal foibles" of W. E. B. Du Bois "indicated inner insecurity"[5] and that the Broderick biography, in Harlan's words, "pricks the bubble of Du Bois' reputation as a scholar and literary artist."[6] It is doubtful that Harlan, in any capacity, will have such impact on his time as to be the subject of the number of full-length biographies that will be written on W. E. B. Du Bois. Whether a man's greatness rests on his personal psychic illness, or on the sickness of the culture in which he lives, is a debate that has centered around John Calvin, Martin Luther, Samuel Adams, John Brown, and others. We should not now have to suffer the charge that Du Bois was any sicker than the rest of us.

One can argue just as easily that Du Bois was a great American because he had more,—not less,—inner security than most men of his day. His doctoral dissertation, which was published as the first volume in the Harvard Historical Studies series, his book, *The Philadelphia Negro*, and his volume entitled, *Black Reconstruction*, are landmarks in the history of scholarship in this nation. Scholars ought to be big enough not to need to attack this giant of an American.

Harlan appreciates too little the contributions to the literature of Afro-American history made by Black Americans. Where the names of authors are used in his bibliography or "References," at least thirty-seven are white and only fourteen are black, and of these fourteen one-half are not historians. Without violating in any way the purposes to be served by the Service Center for Teachers of History pamphlets, one can readily add significant recent works by Black historians to this list of references. Not enough is listed from the works of A. A. Taylor, Charles Wesley, Du Bois, Rayford Logan, Carter G. Woodson, Benjamin Quarles, or John Hope Franklin, and such completely omitted authors as Lorenzo Greene, L. D. Reddick, Merze Tate, Helen Edmonds, and George Woolfolk might well have been listed.

Some Afro-Americans believe that it is impossible for a Caucasian to do justice to the teaching and writing of Black history, or to participate genuinely in the cause of the uplift of the black masses. Any white American can do all of these things who is willing to be critical of his repressions and projections, and to stay on guard against the ethnic and class biases and stereotypes which abound throughout modern Occidental civilization. In the vernacular of today, he must be able to think black. Thinking black is thinking sympathetically about the history, culture, and plight of black people. The Caucasian who can do this has had the transcendant experience of being "born again." Unfortunately this is rare, because it is difficult and painful. An identity based on white racism must die in order that a larger identity can be born.

In his article which appeared in the June, 1969 issue of *The Atlantic Monthly*, Eugene Genovese stated that, because every Southern historian "worth his salt" must carefully study Black history, they qualify as teachers of Black history. Yet, by 1969 most "able" White Southern historians either had shown too-little concern or too-little respect for Black people to qualify as teachers of Black history. For example, members of the so-called Dunning School were "able" Southern historians, but their racism disqualifies them as teachers of Black history. The same is true of an Ulrich Bonnell Phillips or most other leading White southern historians.

Anyone who can read Harriet Beecher Stowe's book, *Uncle Tom's Cabin*, and find his sympathies more with Simon Legree and his bloodhounds than with Liza and her infant; who can read of the thousands of lynchings of Black Americans and sympathize more with the lynchers than the lynched; whose sympathies are more with the assassinators of persons like Medgar Evers and Martin Luther King, Jr. than with the assassinated; whose sympathies are more with Police Chief "Bull" Connor than with the demonstrators, or more with the men in Birmingham, Alabama who threw a bomb into a church and killed Black girls attending Sunday School than with the dead girls; who believes that there are superior and inferior races; who believes that White people can never learn to treat Black people decently; who believes that during riots twelve year old Black "looters" should be shot; who joined the Ku Klux Klan or White Cit-

izens' Council,—and still has the same racial views as when
he joined—, no one of these should attempt to teach Black
history.

Such books as E. Franklin Frazier's *Black Bourgeoisie*,
and Nathan Hare's, *The Black Anglo-Saxons*, show that many
Afro-Americans think white instead of black. By this is
meant that they over-value Europe and whiteness and den-
igrate Africa and blackness. Thus it is that many Afro-
Americans, especially the semi-privileged, also must be born
again.

All of this is saying that we cannot properly help, teach,
or write about human beings when we believe that they can
never be our equals.

Integrating Afro-American History

The methods of integrating black history into traditional
American history courses are mainly such traditional ones as
including it in lectures, having students present oral and
written reports and term papers on aspects of Afro-American history, and examining them on their reading from
source materials on this history. Also, regular major ex-
aminations may be used to emphasize Afro-American history. Although little, if any, "problems in history" materials
which featured Afro-American history existed by 1969, these
too, if soon available, ought to be used.

To integrate black history and the traditionally-taught
American history one must first learn some Afro-American
history. When it comes to the history of this nation, the
teacher is largely limited to what he knows,—what he is
ignorant of is omitted. Where a despised minority is concerned, he can easily justify the omission on grounds other
than ignorance. He can say, for example, that black people
never did anything of any importance.

When one knows something about the contributions of
black people, he finds that there are few, if any, areas or
movements in American or world history where the black

man has not made an impact. His story begins before and with the first civilizations and had attained epic proportions before the modern period begins.

The Portuguese who, following the work of Prince Henry the Navigator, preceded Columbus in the quest for a water route to the East, early encountered Africa and her people. It has been held that there was at least one Black man in the crew of Columbus. Blacks were members of the expeditions of Balboa, Cortez, DeSoto, and many of the *conquistadores*. The brawn, brains, and blood of these Blacks were widespread and important in the establishment of New Spain and all of the great colonial empires.

Only twelve years after the first successful English settlement was begun, the black man began to play a very considerable role in the history of colonial English America.

The story of Black slavery in the New England and Middle Atlantic colonies has not yet been properly told. In the South the black slave made a contribution to American history which is seldom properly appreciated. There were skilled slave artisans and millions of common laborers. They worked not only in the fields but in the cities and mines and factories, and on the ships and other places.

A great amount of literacy and literary art are required to tell properly the story of the black slaves' contribution in shaping American economic, political, religious, and social life, music, dance, folklore, and practically every other aspect of the national culture. There is an impressive bibliography on this, and he who wishes to integrate Afro-American history must be familiar with this bibliography if he is going to do justice to the task.

Just as the story of the contribution of the slave is broader and deeper than most American historians realize, the story of the free Negro is also important. There is a significant literature on this subject also.

The War for Independence probably would have been lost if George Washington had stuck to his early decision not to use Black troops. The black historian William Cooper Nell preceded Benjamin Quarles in telling the story of the Negro's role in the War for Independence. Yet, following the general pattern of excluding or denigrating the story of the Black man, such media as history books and the movies often have given the impression that only white people fought in the Revolutionary War and the War of 1812, and the Civil and Spanish-American Wars. Here the contribution of Black men ought to be included.

Traditionally the story of Westward expansion has been taught as if Blacks were not an integral and important part of this movement. From most presentations one could not guess that there were black cowboys or that many Blacks participated in the California Gold Rush and in the life of the many mining towns throughout the West.

Although the nation has been willing to extend limited recognition to the black athlete and entertainer, judging by history books, and by the public pronouncements of politicians, and the movies, newspapers, and other media until very recently, one could not guess that since the beginning of American history there have been distinguished Black inventors, lawyers, physicians, scientists, businessmen, clergymen, scholars, teachers, and writers. This situation must be changed. Until the story of these black men and women is added, American history is incomplete and distorted.

Traditionally in history Blacks have been lumped together as groups, such as slaves, free Negroes, freedmen, and so forth. This must be corrected by the inclusion of more names of individual Blacks.

So far as it has been included in American history, the story of the Black man is presented largely as "The White Man's Problem." Either directly or indirectly, the Black man's character, personality, and contribution are presented as something negative, bad, ugly. American historiography, like so much else in the culture, has been permeated by the disease of racism.

In every area of American life, historiography *not* excepted, there has been too much *disrespect* for black people. In the history books, movies, newspapers, political arenas, and other places Afro-Americans have been depicted as eternally irresponsible children, wild animals, savages or clowns. Even the so-called "Auntie," and "Good Nigger" male black, were never regarded as the equals of white people. Anyone who hopes to integrate successfully Afro-American history must rid himself of all attitudes, ideas, and convictions of Black inferiority. Also, the white teacher of black history must get rid of the notion that this history is propaganda. As Dr. Nathan Hare points out in the April, 1969 issue of the journal *Social Education*:

> There are the ultra 'objective' who, though they think nothing of teaching a 'regular' history course without ever mentioning 'the Negro' except as a slave and a spark for the Civil War, are quick to wail self-righteously that to teach from a black perspective is political rather than academic.

Also, white Americans who would teach some Afro-American history need to gain acquaintance with the inner life of Black Americans. This can be achieved through such means as reading poems, plays, novels, and social criticism written by Blacks; looking at Black painting, sculpture, and dance; and listening to the spirituals, work songs, blues, jazz, and other music composed and performed by Blacks. If Blacks can learn to "appreciate" Shakespeare, George Bernard Shaw, Bach, Chopin, DeBussy, and Beethoven, perhaps whites can learn to "appreciate" such persons as Richard Wright, Ralph Ellison, Saunders Redding, Le Roi Jones, Eldridge Cleaver, James Brown, Ray Charles, Mahalia Jackson, and Aretha Franklin. White Americans who want to do justice to the business of integrating Afro-American history, probably will find it helpful to take out a subscription to the *Journal of Negro History, Phylon,* and *The Jour-*

nal of Negro Education, and to a popular organ such as *Negro Digest, Jet,* or *Ebony,* and to read at least occasionally a Black newspaper such as the *Pittsburgh Courier* or *Baltimore Afro-American.*

In the teaching or writing of Black history it is possible to give great stress to either the Black Americans' failures or successes, sorrows or joys, oppressions or freedom from oppression; to the White man's villainies or humanitarian acts;—or, it is possible to attempt to achieve a balance between each of these opposites. Doubtless the proper approach ought to be a natural one, which is to say that the historical record ought to dictate the emphasis. When the sorrows and oppressions were predominant, the account should reflect this. If the opposites were balanced, the account should reflect this,—but, in an abuse of "objectivity," *the balance should not be forced.*

As just one gauge of success it should be remembered that any healthy personality who has been properly taught black history will be more sympathetic to the struggles which blacks have made,—and are making—, to end their exclusion and degradation.

Another White Scholar

One of the books on Black history, to appear during the 1960s, by a white author, which was in no way offensive to the sensibilities of Black critics, was Richard Wade's *Slavery in the Cities.* Of course this book was not the sole one in this category. A book which appeared in the last year of the 1960s, which had very pronounced strong and weak points was S. P. Fullinwider's, *The Mind and Mood of Black America: Twentieth Century Thought,* which was published by the Dorsey Press.

Fullinwider writes well. He has acquired depth and breadth of learning and insight about Black history and culture. But his sins of omission and commission are serious. His chief sins of omission are:

1. The failure to appreciate or give any attention at all to the thought and achievements of the Negro History Movement which Carter G. Woodson led from 1915 to 1950. Woodson's name and those of such persons as Charles H. Wesley, A. A. Taylor, Luther P. Jackson, William Savage, A. A. Schomburg, Benjamin Quarles, John Hope Franklin, L. D. Reddick, Lorenzo Greene, Merl Eppse, and J. A. Rogers appear no where in the volume. Nor do any of their books appear in his "Selected Bibliography." At times Fullinwider over-simplifies; at times he exaggerates. When he makes W. E. B. Du Bois and Benjamin Brawley just about his only Black historians, he not only sets up a straw man. He misrepresents the work of these two scholars.

2. Although Mahatma Gandhi and nonviolence are discussed in connection with Martin Luther King, Jr., Fullinwider says absolutely nothing about the world independence movements of black, brown, and yellow peoples as an influence on the thought of Afro-Americans during the 1940s, 50s, and 60s. During this period he sees mainly the urban ghetto and bitterness about the "White backlash" as new influences on Afro-American thought.

3. Fullinwider's discussion of "Soul" is all of the secular variety. A few months earlier *Esquire* magazine brought out an issue featuring "Soul" which also discussed almost exclusively the secular variety. A discussion which stresses the religious side of "Soul" is the article in the May, 1964 issue of *Negro Digest* entitled, "The Essence of 'Soul.' "

4. Although Fullinwider discusses "Daddy" Grace and "Father Divine," Elijah Muhammed and Malcolm X are not mentioned a single time.

All of these are serious omissions.

The chief sins of commission are: (1) his arbitrarily-imposed pattern or method, and (2) what appears to be a hypersensitivity about Blacks who are very critical of whites.

Fullinwider's method is to depict the thought of the earliest twentieth century Black thinkers,—from 1880-1920—, as strongly mythical; that of the middle group or "Harlem Renaissance" thinkers of the 1920s and 30s as less-mythical; and the thought of Afro-Americans since Richard Wright's book, *Native Son* appeared in 1940 as a return to the strongly mythical. Is this method valid?

The central concern of all of twentieth century Black thinkers was—"How can the 'race problem' be solved?— which is to say, how can the freedom, equality, and manhood of Black Americans be achieved?" Only when the "race problem" is finally solved can anyone know the real pattern of sound thinking on the subject. Certainly the answer,—if found by 1969—, had not been implemented. This being so, it is clear that 1969 was too early to give any of the approaches or answers labels such as "strongly mythical" and "less mythical." The Fullinwider method is clearly arbitrary and imposed. Here he claims a wisdom that no one possesses.

The real or non-mythical influences on the mind of Blacks which Fullinwider mentions are largely Christianity, sociology, racial oppression, the artist-as-ideal, Marxism, and the urban ghetto.

The mind of Fullinwider can be gauged by consideration of the persons whom he never accuses of myth-making. Persons who, as he sees it, are not very angry and who refuse to moralize about the behavior of whites, such as the "Harlem Renaissance" writers who were committed to the art-for-arts-sake perspective, as well as "sociologically-oriented" persons such as Booker T. Washington, Charles W. Chesnutt, E. Franklin Frazier, Charles S. Johnson, Zora Neale Hurston, Alain Locke, James M. Lawson, and Bayard Rustin are in this category. Fullinwider obviously does not like Blacks who are angry, who hate, and who throw stones at white people. It is also obvious that Fullinwider's sympathies are mainly with those Blacks who are integrationists and assimilationists. Yet, when in the last line of the book, he writes of white society's long "unyielding resistance to reason," he makes it clear that the position with which he has greatest sympathy also may be mythical.

Fullinwider attacks the idea of Black cultural superiority on the ground that the idea of a racial soul is mythical. So it is. It is not mythical, however, that such things as greed, hopes, fears, abilities, and opportunities of men determine their experiences, and that the *experiences* of people numb and blind them about some things, while sensitizing them to, and bringing more clearly before their eyes some other things. Because they have been largely kept out of the mainstream of Occidental culture, Blacks have been less contaminated by the negative elements of that culture. It is primarily the *experiences* that men have which make them different,—not race, Intelligence Quotient, nationality, or class.

Behind experiences are commitments or interests.

To a very considerable extent, the character of men is determined by their commitments or interests. Slaveholders are committed men. They must think and act in such a manner as to justify and protect their interests. The tragedy of many men is not their character, but the commitments or interests which mould and dictate this character. Since they have had no wealth or power, and have not been allowed to be the oppressor, Black Americans have seldom been committed to the thought and action patterns which possession of wealth, power, and the oppressor role dictate. While this does not mean that the oppressed man is necessarily better than his oppressor, the oppressed man *wants to change* his role and behavior. Because of his interests, the oppressor *wants to preserve and continue* his role and behavior. The oppressor is more encumbered by evil, and he is its greater victim. *The probability of goodness is on the side of the oppressed.* This is the crux of the matter.

All Historians, white and black, tend to idealize their own group. By 1969 Blacks were still far from perfect. They always had been. There is the negative outside the mainstream. Still, an ounce of difference may be used to move mountains. The black American of the 1960s knew that he was a *product of history*. This is mainly why he was so strongly drawn to the study of Black history. When he asked himself, "Who am I?" he could not trust the answers to this question which traditionally had been given by most white historians. W. E. B. Du Bois knew all of this. As Fullinwider acknowledges on the last two pages of his book, in his basic attitude and position Du Bois was never far from the so-called Black Militants of the 1960s. Dr. Du Bois spent his life trying to change Occidental culture so that the arrogant men who compel the masses to have so many dehumanizing experiences would be deprived of their power.

Fullinwider states over and over again that Afro-Americans,—as an ego-defense mechanism—, have been strongly influenced by the notion that they are Christ-like. Not once does he indicate or point out that,—at least until 1945—, many white Americans were victims of the myth that *they* are more Christ-like than all Europeans,—who are decadent—, and all Red, Yellow, or Black men,—who are savages. White America also long has been obsessed with its *own* mission myth. Christ was not just meek, humble, and forgiving. He was also pure and innocent,—and Savior—, and it is chiefly this portion of the Christ-like myth to which white America has fallen victim. Are the ego-defense needs of the oppressor identical with those of the oppressed? Those Afro-Americans who have been victimized by the Christ-like and mission myths did not need to derive them from their own plight. They needed no literacy at all to *borrow* these myths from white America.

The idea that Blacks are better morally than whites,— what Fullinwider calls the "Christ-like mythology"—, did not emerge simply from the psychological needs of Blacks, as he contends. There is much more to the black man's case than the "ego-defense" hypothesis which Fullinwider presents on page 27 of his book. One searches this book in vain for any admission by its author that Caucasion-Americans have been morally wrong in their treatment of Blacks. According to him, all Black spokesmen who felt that moral right was on the side of their race were merely influenced by John Calvin, the Abolitionists, or Transcendentalists, but these Black thinkers were never *right* in their conclusion. They were myth-makers.

Despite Fullinwider's steadfast refusal to admit the long-standing rightness of the black man's case *vis-a-vis* white America, the black man's case is much more than simply "myth," "an irrational thing . . . an extension of the emotions" which took "from reality only those facts which [reinforced] it." (Preface). Rather, the idea of the superiority of the black man's moral position arose out of the omnipresent necessity to judge human behavior,—one's own as well as that of others. Is it myth or truth that, in their relationship, during the antebellum period the slaveowner was a greater sinner than the slave? Were the Blacks who, after 1865, were being deliberately denied their citizenship and human rights, in this relationship no better than the men who were oppressing and exploiting them? Were the Jews who were being fed to the gas chambers and ovens during that period no better than the Nazis who were dispatching them? One of the powerful and beautiful things about Kenneth Stampp's book, *The Peculiar Institution* is that Stampp admits and writes from the position that slavery was morally wrong. In contrast, Fullinwider,—obviously enamored by "the nonmoralistic sociological imagination"—, writes from a position of almost absolute moral relativism. While he displays no hostility toward such persons as the "Harlem Renaissance" writers who lived and wrote from the Neitzschean position that God is dead, he applies the label of myth-makers to Blacks who uncompromisingly called the slave-owner and compulsory-segregationist sinners. In his view, such moralists are old-fashioned and excessively influenced by the values of the pre-World War I Victorian era.

Although Alexander Crummell saw his people as "imbruted" by their experiences, although during the 1880-1900 period systematic "oppression rained hammerblows" on the Negro, and although Negro thought of the period shifted "From Hope to Hatred" (the title of Chapter I), still, on p. 31, Fullinwider accuses the Black clergy of a "peculiar blindness to oppression." These men were not blind to oppression. They knew that,—one way or another—, their church members might well be lynched if they militantly spoke and acted against oppression. Especially in the South, the black man of this period had little choice except to be "patient" and "forgiving." He knew that the nation's presidents, governors, legislators, judges, business tycoons, and white clergy were mainly either indifferent or hostile to the black man's plight. It is the white leaders (not the black ones) who during this period had a "peculiar blindness to oppression." In his book, *The Negro in American Life and Thought, 1877-1900*, Rayford W. Logan pointed out that it was white America which was blind to oppression.

In Chapter II, entitled "Racial Christianity," Fullinwider sought to show how Black clergymen of the 1880-1920 period interpreted and applied Christianity for Black liberation. He neglects to indicate or point out that the use by whites of theology and the pulpit to keep Blacks subordinate and degraded *also was racial Christianity*. If the blacks who preached racial Christianity viewed the white man as the devil, most white Christians of this era also viewed Blacks as wild, evil, barbarians.

W. E. B. Du Bois is handled roughly by Fullinwider not only because Du Bois was a moralist. He is also accused of being a racist. Reverdy C. Ransom, the young R. R. Wright (around 1915), and other militant Blacks are also called racists. Obviously here a semantical problem exists. If John C. Calhoun,—who believed in slavery—, was a racist, should not some other word be used for Du Bois who op-

posed slavery? Fullinwider calls the gentle, honest Marcus
Garvey a racist. Does Garvey deserve the same label as the
home-and-church-dynamiting Ku Klux Klan? Does Du Bois
deserve to wear the same label as George Fitzhugh, Josiah
Nott, Thomas Dixon, and Adolph Hitler?

At the beginning of his book, Fullinwider asserts that
Black spokesmen of the 1880s and 90s believed that Western civilization then was an embodiment of the principles
of Christianity; that Blacks did not then doubt the white
man's Christianity. This is not true. Before 1861 Frederick
Douglass,—who lived through most of these two decades—,
along with most of the other Black abolitionists, made long,
often repeated, and bitter attacks on the white man's Christianity. Fullinwider writes as if the first time that Black
Americans went from hope to hatred was between 1880-
1914. This had happened before,—between the era of the
War for Independence and the 1831 revolt led by Nat
Turner.

Fullinwider also errs when he assumes that Blacks of
the 1880s and 90s,—without serious qualification—, viewed
either their own or the white race in the "Christ-like image"
(kindly, forgiving, meek, humble, patient) for Blacks and
its opposite for whites. Indeed, much of the stereotype
which the freedmen actually held of their race,—that it was
notably musical, humorous, optimistic, and bouyant of spirit—, is so worldly in orientation as to be incompatible with
the popular image of Christ. The Christ-like image is more
complex than the narrow simplistic use which Fullinwider
makes of it. Also, when Black thinkers of this period spoke
to members of their own race about the "Christ-like" qualities, it was often to criticize them as the Black Abolitionists
earlier often had done. When they spoke of these "Christ-
like" attributes to whites (and they hoped whites would
read their books) the Black thinkers *often were constructing
propaganda.* They were asking whites to support Black causes
because they *knew that these were qualities which whites*

wanted Blacks to possess. Although it is true that many Black spokesmen conceived of their race as superior morally, this was only because their race had been the enslaved, and whites the slave-owners. But to be superior is not necessarily to be Christ-like. Certainly Booker T. Washington never thought that slavery left his race Christ-like. He often criticized his races "character," and he criticized its *impatience!* Washington asked the race to *adopt* the "Christlike" posture as the best way to win the hearts and cooperation of whites. Also, Frederick Douglass never thought that slavery left his race Christ-like. The Black spokesmen of the 1880s, 90s, and later, were not nearly so naive about either race as Fullinwider would have us believe. He throws the label "myth-makers" around loosely and freely, apparently unaware that he is creating some myths of his own. To call the more-conservative Negroes the "realists" and the militant Blacks "myth-makers" comes close to coining a new word for "nigger."

As late as 1969 much of liberal white America still seemed unable to accept the Black historian's contribution to scholarship. As Sociologist Fullinwider could omit discussion of the Black historian's thought and work, Louis Harlan and other white historians commonly slighted this contribution.

White "Masochism" and Mature Vision

One argument advanced during the late 1960s stated that White liberals who were strongly sympathetic to the cause of Black uplift were motivated largely by masochism. Especially was this argument used in 1969 against White teachers and students who supported the reformist-efforts of Black students who were enrolled in predominantly-White colleges and universities. Yet, if there is even a kernel of truth in many statements about the Black character and personality which were made by many persons during this decade, these maligned White liberals may well have been motivated far more by mature vision than by masochism. They may correctly have seen in Black Americans, and their fight, a model for the larger identity which White Occidentals needed to achieve. In this case the chief motivation would be the desire for growth rather than the psychic illness of masochism.

In his 1969 interview in *Playboy* magazine, Marshall McLuhan is quoted as saying that consciousness of the psychic and social superiority of Blacks and Indians long has been a source of White envy and maltreatment of these two groups. McLuhan, of course, bases this conclusion in large part on his belief that aural-oral oriented groups are happier, healthier, and less-alienated than eye-oriented groups.

Malcolm X and other so-called Black Muslims long have contended that the Black man has a superior destiny because he has a "healthier" history and psyche. These persons have had an intense awareness of History and the role of the-past-in-the-present. They have believed that "you reap what you sow"; that character is destiny; that—

> The past follows us from afar;
> What you have been determines
> What you are.

James Baldwin in numerous essays, and Eldridge Cleaver in *Soul on Ice* wrote of the Black man's superior acceptance of his body. In *Life against Death: The Psychoanalytical Meaning of History*, Norman O. Brown depicted alienation from the body as the chief sickness of Occidental civilization. In many of his books, W. E. B. Du Bois declared that, since the beginnings of the modern slave trade, wide-spread anti-humanistic thought and action-patterns constitute the chief evidence of the sickness of Occidentals. In *Civilization and Its Discontents*, Sigmund Freud depicted a Western civilization that was dying from the cumulative onslaughts of a death instinct. In biting terminology, Pitirim A. Sorokin often attacked "dying" modern Sensate culture. The list could be expanded with the names and contributions of such thinkers as Karl Marx, Frederick Nietzsche, Oswald Spengler, Thomas J. Altizer, and others. All have condemned the Western world's excessive concern with such things as power and money, and the Kerner Commission report condemned the excessive concern with skin-color.

In his book, *The Doctor and the Soul*, Victor Frankl states that all human values may be listed under one of three headings. Values, he writes, are either creative, experiential, or attitudinal. Creative values are those that are activated in vocations or avocations,—where there is freedom to act and express talent and abilities. Experiential values are activated in such ways as the contemplation and enjoyment of art, music, drama, or natural beauty. Attitudinal values are largely realized in mature acceptance of fate when life is severely proscribed by sickness or some other misfortune.

The opportunities and demands of the 1500-1900 A.D. Age of the Frontier produced the Protestant Ethic, the Gospel of Work, and the philosophy of Pragmatism, all of which pushed action and creative values to the forefront. By the system of chattel slavery, and proscriptions since 1865, Black Americans always have been denied many opportunities to actualize creative values. Throughout their sojourn in the Western world, Blacks largely have had open to them the opportunity to actualize only experiential and attitudinal values. Through unique emphasis in these two areas, they have had to compensate for the lack of opportunity to actualize creative values.

By 1969 creative values no longer held their old high position of eminence. Due to either the passing of the Age of the Frontier, or the psychic and cultural effects of the use of electricity, the dominant values of the new Age of the Global Village are experiential and attitudinal. Thus it is that the Black man's exclusion from the opportunity to participate fully in the mainstream of Occidental culture may have been the silver lining of a dark cloud. If, because of their exclusion and suffering Blacks are more naturally fitted for participation in the New Culture, they are proper models for White liberals and other reformers. To assist Blacks in their efforts to rise, then, is not masochism but mature vision. For Caucasian-Americans not to realize and accept this might well be the most tragic and final tragedy in the history of the relations between the races.

A Caucasian-American historian, C. Vann Woodward, provided a good answer to the question of why Black history became a popular mass movement during the late 1960s. In his Presidential Address before the April, 1969 annual session of the Organization of American Historians he called Black history "Clio with Soul." Wide use of such expressions as "Soul music" and "Soul food" indicated during the late 1960s that Afro-Americans were baring their souls as never before since the efforts and activities of the Black Abolitionists of the 1830-60 period and the Harlem Renaissance of the 1920s. 1969 was indeed a peak year of the Third Negro Renaissance, which had begun around 1950. Each of these three renaissance movements drew its strength primarily from the "identity problem," which is to say that impending or actual social change triggered in Blacks an intense need to answer that omnipresent question for humans,—Who am I? Black history, as the fullest spelling-out of the experiences congealed in such media as the Blues and Gospel music, was a central and vital element and vehicle in each of these three renaissance movements. A renaissance is not re-birth; it is *birth*, or the fullest baring of the human soul,—a showing-off in the interest of re-assurance. A renaissance is a people's non-violent way of healing a damaged identity.

In 1969 the teacher of Black history often played a role highly similar to that of the Black Abolitionist, preacher, or

Blues or Jazz artist. Each was "telling it like it is," and, like his audience, was "committed," hence,—as Charles Keil reminds us in his book *Urban Blues*—, was participating in a ritual. All four,—Abolitionist, preacher, Bluesman, and Black history teacher—, brought about catharsis by bringing to consciousness the repressed feelings and beliefs of the audience. Thus it was that,—as was the case during the earlier Black renaissance movements—, White Americans of the late 1960s who found the Blues, Jazz, and Black history appealing indirectly revealed (often-times the only way that society would permit them to do so) their own endorsement of the "Black Revolution."

White Americans are to be commended for their desire to join in the effort to end the neglect and insulting of that ten percent of the nation's population which happens to be black. They must never forget that what is at stake here is not just the present interests of thirty million Black Americans.

This civilization's dehumanization of black people is part of a larger tragedy. That Occidentals have never made up their minds whether man is to be respected as a person or despised as a thing is also reflected in the many wars which they have fought against each other, in the debunking of the body which Norman O. Brown has described, in the wars against the Open Society so ably depicted by Karl Popper, in the over-populating of hell in such theologies as Calvinism, in Thomas Hobbes' justification for the leviathan state, in Adolph Hitler's attempted extermination of the Jews, and in similar hideous ideology and phenomena too numerous to mention.

The study of the dehumanization of black people ought to teach both the black and white races that they must end these ambiguities in thought and deed. The culture which will not dehumanize Black people also will not dehumanize white people. If life is to continue to exist on this planet, both races must develop soon something which has never existed in the Western world,—a truly humanistic culture. Such a culture will include an American historiography which gives proper recognition to the contributions of the Black man.

CHAPTER IX

W. E. B. DU BOIS

For fifty years, with a pen dipped in gall, he has written in trenchant, classic English what he has deeply felt and deeply studied . . . his personal manner is purely scholarly. A little vanity perhaps appears in his neat, well-tailored clothes, in his nicely groomed hands and his carefully tended van dyke beard. But chiefly he is the dignified, restrained, almost shy, gentleman from New England. While he has hundreds of devoted admirers he has not attracted warm friends.[1]

Thus reads one reasonably accurate estimate of the personality and character of William Edward Burghardt Du Bois. The manner in which a scholar may attain such a large measure of notoriety and fame makes an interesting tale, and reveals at the outset, perhaps, that such a person did not confine his activities solely, or even largely, to scholarship.

Du Bois was born in Great Barrington, Massachusetts, February 23, 1868, of mixed Black and French ancestry. There were few Blacks in his home town and Du Bois was always proud of his ancestry.[2] Orphaned while still in grade school, he was able to enter Fisk University, Nashville, Tennessee, because a minister secured the necessary funds from his church members. Du Bois had dreamed of attending Harvard University, and went to Fisk only because this was the desire of the group financing his education.[3]

In his early years in Massachusetts, Du Bois had experienced little of the prejudice to which members of his race were subjected in most parts of the United States.

"Whatever of racial feeling gradually crept into my life," he later wrote, "its effect upon me in these earlier days was rather one of exaltation and high disdain. They were the losers who did not ardently court me and not I, which seemed to be proven by the fact that I had no difficulty in outdoing them in nearly all competition, especially intellectual."[4]

His experiences at Fisk University made Du Bois self-consciously a black man as his home town had never done. While there he even learned to "accept" segregation, and this, he states, helped him to accept the segregation which he later experienced at Harvard University.[5] At Fisk he also developed an interest in writing and public speaking, edited the school paper, became "an impassioned orator," and acquired an attitude of belligerence toward the color bar. This belligerence was to grow until it became the motor force of his entire life. "In my life," he writes in his autobiography, "the chief fact has been race—not so much scientific race, as that deep conviction of myriads of men that congenital differences among the masses of human beings absolutely condition the individual destiny of every member of a group. Into the spiritual provincialism of this belief I have been born and this fact has guided, embittered, illuminated and enshrouded my life."[6] Here lies the key to an understanding of the career of this genius.

The life of W. E. B. Du Bois is an outburst of literary genius, which is highly reminiscent of Voltaire, and of organizational genius, against the "race issue." In some ways this narrow interest of such a born-scholar represents a great tragedy in the history of American letters.

Du Bois graduated from Fisk University in 1888. He wrote on Otto von Bismarck for his graduation paper. Bismarck was then his ideal because this leader had used force to make a nation out of a bickering people.[7] Upon graduating, he applied for and received a scholarship to Harvard University. As a student there, he met such famous personages as William James, George Santayana, Albert Bushnell Hart, and Justin Winsor. Majoring in History and the social sciences, Du Bois was one of Professor Hart's "favorite pupils."[8] By this time the young scholar had become keenly conscious of race. He steered clear of members of the majority group. "In general," he writes, "I asked nothing of Harvard but the tutelage of teachers and the freedom of the library. I was quite voluntarily and willingly outside its social life. . . . For the most part, I do not doubt that I was voted a somewhat selfish and self-centered 'grind' with a chip on my shoulder and a sharp tongue."[9]

In 1890 he took the bachelor's degree from Harvard. One of six commencement speakers, he used the topic "Jefferson Davis," although this historic personage represented no hero to Du Bois.[10] A fellowship made it possible for him to remain at Harvard, and the following year he received the M.A. degree. His thesis was "The Suppression of the African Slave Trade from Africa to the United States."[11] At this time Du Bois received a Slater Fund Award to study abroad, and in 1892 he sailed for Germany. At the University of Berlin he studied under such scholars as Treitschke, Weber and Schmoller.[12] Thus Du Bois, at Harvard and later in Germany, had the opportunity to study under most-eminent scholars who were inaugurating the era of "the Scientific School" of history. One cannot doubt that the stimulation derived from studying with such scholars as these fired his ever-present ambition to great heights.

Du Bois had not yet become an economic determinist. Of the impact of his study abroad on his philosophy of history, he later wrote that it helped him begin "to see the race problem in America, the problem of the peoples of Africa and Asia, and the political development of Europe as one." "I began," he continues, "to unite my economics and politics; but I still assumed that in these groups of activities and forces, the political realm was dominant."[13]

After two years of study in Germany, and travel over

most of Europe, he returned to the United States to utilize his thorough training as a college teacher. Writing his dissertation on the same topic which he used for his master's degree, he was awarded the Ph.D. from Harvard in 1895. His first teaching position was at Wilberforce University, a Negro college in Ohio. Here he remained for only two years. He left because his duties were largely limited to teaching classical languages, while he wanted to teach the social sciences.[14] Then followed a year as a graduate assistant at the University of Pennsylvania, a position awarded him in order that he might make a sociological study of Philadelphia's Black population. This study appeared in 1899 as his epic, *The Philadelphia Negro*. Then followed thirteen years of teaching and scholarly activity at Atlanta University, Atlanta, Georgia.

At the beginning of his teaching career, Du Bois was gripped by the empirical method. "I was going to study the facts," he wrote, "any and all facts, concerning the American Negro and his plight, and by measurement and comparison and research, work up to any valid generalization which I could. I entered this primarily with the utilitarian object of reform and uplift; but nevertheless, I wanted to do the work with scientific accuracy."[15]

With an eighteenth century faith in the efficacy of education, Du Bois began his teaching career with the hope of improving race relations through education. "The world was thinking wrong about race," he opined, "because it did not know. The ultimate evil was stupidity. The cure for it was knowledge based on scientific investigation."[16] Also, democratic principles and practices were a part of his articles of faith. "My attention from the first," he wrote, "was focused on democracy and democratic development and upon the problem of the admission of my people into the freedom of democracy."[17]

While at Atlanta University Du Bois had his greatest success as a teacher and scholar. There he edited annually the "Studies of Negro Problems," the famed Atlanta University Studies, which appeared from 1896 to 1914. Reminiscent of the surveys of Negro life which Carter G. Woodson was conducting through the Association for the study of Negro Life and History, these researches covered reports on crime, health, business activities, landholding, professional groups, and similar topics.

Criticism of his growing radicalism on the race issue slowly caused Dr. Du Bois to give up classroom teaching. He took a lead in differing with the preachments of Booker T. Washington to the effect that the education of the Negro should be centered largely on manual training and that the race should concentrate on achieving economic security almost to the exclusion of interest and participation in any movement for political and social equality. His outspoken opposition to these ideas brought Du Bois into conflict with what he termed the "Tuskegee Machine." According to Du Bois, this one-man "machine" of Mr. Washington dominated all major grants and other aid to Negro colleges. His opposition to the famed founder of Tuskegee Institute was dangerous business. "It seemed to many who cared for this iconoclast," writes a Du Bois biographer, "that his opposition to Washington would be his undoing. On the contrary it was his making because it got him a following."[18]

From classroom teaching, in 1910 Dr. Du Bose became Director of Publicity and Research of the newly founded National Association for the Advancement of Colored People. He had aided greatly in the founding of this organization. "My career as a scientist," he wrote, "was to be swallowed up in my role as master of propaganda. This was not wholly to my liking. I was no natural leader of men. I could not slap people on the back and make friends of strangers. . . . Nevertheless, having put my hand to the plow, I had to go on."[19] He continued: "I did not hesitate because I could not. . . . My thoughts, the thoughts of Washington . . . and others, were the expression of social forces more than of our own minds."[20]

Du Bois slowly evolved in his thinking from a position of viewing the "race problem" as one peculiar to the Negro in the United States, to an internationalist outlook. On this point, he wrote: "At first . . . my criticism was confined to the relation of my people to the world movement. I was not questioning the world movement in itself. What the white world was doing, its goals and ideals, I had not doubted were quite right. What was wrong was that I and people like me and thousands of others who might have ability and inspiration, were refused permission to be a part of this world."[21] The success of the Russian Revolution of 1917, plus a visit to the Soviet Union by Du Bois shortly thereafter, caused him to change this thinking.

Just as his earlier radicalism caused him to give up classroom teaching, after becoming a convert to the Marxist viewpoint, his now-altered ideas on the race issue caused Du Bois to give up his work with the National Association for the Advancement of Colored People. He states that by 1930 he had become convinced "that the basic policies and ideals" of the Association were in need of change. "In a world where economic dislocation had become so great as in ours," he continued, "a mere appeal based on the old liberalism, a mere appeal to justice and further effort at legal decision, was missing the essential need; that . . . essential need was to guard and better the chances of Negroes, educated and ignorant, to earn a living, safeguard their income, and raise the level of their employment. I did not believe that a further prolongation of looking for salvation from the whites was feasible."[22] To some extent, Booker Washington, with whom Du Bois had disagreed so violently, had anticipated this economic determinism in his own program for racial uplift.

Du Bois started advocating a movement in which all Negroes in this country would organize their producing and purchasing activities in nationwide cooperatives. He was advocating socialism for the United States. The Negro was to socialize his activities in conformity with the coming pattern. The success of the Russian Revolution of 1917 had convinced Du Bois that socialism represented, as Marx had said, the next inevitable and desirable development throughout the Western world. And it appears that post-world war conservatism, lynchings and other manifestations of racial antagonism frightened Du Bois into thinking that the very existence of the colored race in the United States was threatened. He reversed his life-long struggle for integration of the Negro into the mainstream of American life and started advocating an acceptance and strengthening of the fact of segregation. "We are now segregated largely without reason," he wrote, "let us put reason and power beneath this segregation."[23] He had become an economic determinist and was now convinced that it was not ignorance which bred race prejudice, but rather that "economic exploitation of blacks was the greatest cause of continued discrimination."[24]

A Russian family in America, possibly Red agents Du Bois thinks, had sought him out in 1927 and financed his trip to Russia. "Since that trip," he wrote, "my mental outlook and the aspect of the world will never be the same." What significance may be attached to the fact that the revised type of economic organization which he was now championing for the Black American coincided with the Communist Party line in this country during the same period is debatable. This scholar began to tell his people of "things you must do for your own survival and self-preservation."[25]

Feeling that he had correctly gauged the future, Du Bois now wanted to launch the National Association for the Advancement of Colored People and the American Negro into the socialistic movement. He wanted to use *The Crisis*, the organ of this Association which he had founded and edited continuously, as an educational and propaganda device for his new ideas. Unable to get the Board of Directors to go along with him, Du Bois resigned. His resignation accepted, the organization gave unstinted praise to him. His work with *The Crisis* was termed "an unprecedented achievement in American journalism."[26] This commendation also stated that his efforts in general had been so effective "that the whole problem of the relation of the black and white races has ever since had a completely new orientation. He created, what never existed before, a Negro intelligentsia. . . . Without him the Association could never have been what it was and is."[27]

Upon leaving this organization, Du Bois went back to Atlanta University as a teacher, where his friend, John Hope, had in 1929 organized the Atlanta University System. In this period Du Bois wrote his Marxist study of Reconstruction,[28] and in 1936 he published a small study entitled, "The Negro and the New Deal." To this work he appended a statement and credo of the Negro which read, in part, "We believe in the ultimate triumph of some form of socialism the world over; that is common ownership and control of the means of production and equality of income."[29] This credo was rejected by the publishers.

In 1931 the Phelps-Stokes Fund called a committee to prepare and publish an encyclopedia of the Negro. Du Bois was made chairman of the editorial board. A scholarship award in 1936 made it possible for him to go back to Germany to study conditions there. From there he took a world tour. In 1938 he got permission from his publisher to rewrite his book entitled *The Negro* which had appeared in 1915 in the Home Library Series. The result was his *Black Folks Then and Now*, published in 1939.[30]

Although retired from classroom teaching, after 1939 the activities of Du Bois were many and varied. In 1940 appeared his autobiography, *Dusk of Dawn*, and in 1945 the preparatory volume of the Encyclopedia of the Negro. No subsequent volumes of this endeavor were published, although such a work was long on the agenda of the Association for the Study of Negro Life and History. Also appearing that year was his *Color and Democracy.*[31] After 1939 he also was engaged in writing other works of fiction, and one in history, and launching and editing the Atlanta University review of race and culture, *Phylon*. He also was a leader of the short-lived Progressive Party and ran unsuccessfully for the United States Senate on the New York Labor Party ticket in 1950. In 1951 he was tried and acquitted on a charge of serving as a representative of a foreign country without registering. This charge grew out of his prominent role in circulating the so-called Stockholm Peace Appeal in this country. Subsequently he moved to Ghana where that country's then-political leader, Kwame Nkrumah, assisted him in efforts to produce an encyclopedia of the Black man. He died in Ghana and was buried in Accra, the capital city.

In many ways the life of Du Bois was a mirror of his time. He received his training when the new "Scientific History" was just beginning to make its imprint on historical writing. Yet it is also true that the latter half of the nineteenth century saw passing as scientific sociology the racial views of such writers as Count Gobineau and Houston Chamberlain. This also is the period in which Radical Reconstruction made its brief appearance, only to be overthrown before the turn of the twentieth century. Ante-bellum teachings of the slave-holding South as to the nature, character and destined position of the Negro in society seemed to many to be vindicated. Caught up in the emotional heat engendered by these pseudo-scientific doctrines, Du Bois forged his excellent training and organization and literary genius into a weapon of propaganda. Rampant industrialism, colonial problems, and modern warfare also played their part in shaping the life and changing outlook of this scholar. Ultimately his mind came to rest on socialism as the solution to not only the race problem, but to most of the ills which beset the modern world. Highly opinionated, and a man of action as well as of ideas, it seems that, while he began his career as a fighter against historical and sociological doctrines which he termed propaganda, he shifted to a position where he felt it advisable consciously to forge propaganda himself out of historical and sociological facts. He expressed criticism of the non-utilitarian nature of history as a science, and against its teachers. "It is perhaps the greatest indictment that can be brought against history as a science and against its teachers," he wrote, "that we are usually indisposed to refer to history for the settlement of pressing problems. We realize that history is too often what we want it to be and what we are determined men shall believe rather than a grim record of what has taken place in the past."[32]

It seems not inappropriate to end this discussion of the forces which moulded Du Bois, and the forces which he moulded, with another quotation concerning his personality and influence. In 1927 another writer, this time a woman, characterized him thus:

> Among the distinguished Negroes in America, none is so hated by the whites as Burghardt Du Bois. And for an excellent reason. He insists upon making them either angry or miserable. So great, moreover, is his genius, that it is impossible to read him and not be moved. Anger or misery, according to the disposition of the reader, comes from his merciless portrayal of the white man's injustice to the black.[33]

"There is a cruel look," continues this writer, "in Du Bois's sensitive, poet's face. It lurks somewhere about the mouth —a half sneer, a scorn."[34] Yet she admits that "No man in this century has done more to secure the white man's reluctant gesture of respect for the Negro's attainments than Burghardt Du Bois."[35]

His Books

The dissertation of Du Bois was published in 1896 as Volume One in the Harvard Historical Studies.[36] In 1969 it was still considered an authoritative study of the suppression of the slave trade.[37] Vernon Loggins and other critics praise unstintedly the objectivity and thoroughness of research which characterize the volume. "The historical method employed is that of the strictest scholarship," states Loggins, "while the style is that of the scholar who is seeking the effect of accuracy and truth. . . . There is a certain charm in the sense of the logic with which the study is planned, in the discrimination with which the facts are grouped, and in the freedom from bias which we associate with all sound history."[38] On the significance of this volume in the history of Black Literature and scholarship, Loggins writes:

> *The Suppression of the African Slave Trade to the U.S.* was by far the greatest intellectual achievement which had by 1900 come from any American Negro. It taught the colored man that if he were to be considered a historian he had to produce work which could meet the requirement of high standards. It prepared the way for a number of specialized historical studies of excellence which have come from American Negroes during the past thirty years.[39]

Even upon its appearance, observers saw that this initial volume was destined for permanence.[40]

Throughout his life, Dr. Du Bois viewed the question of slavery in the United States as essentially a moral problem. This viewpoint is typical of Black historians in general, who have leaned heavily on the views of William Lloyd Garrison, Frederick Douglass, and other abolitionists. Thus, until recently, Black historians have not given equal consideration to political, economic, constitutional, and psychological aspects of the slavery controversy.

W. E. B. Du Bois 185

In presenting this initial volume to the public, Du Bois wrote, "I . . . trust that I have succeeded in rendering this monograph a small contribution to the scientific study of slavery and the American Negro."[41] Of the sources, scope, and limitations of the study, he explained:

> This monograph was begun during my residence as Rogers Memorial Fellow at Harvard University, and is based mainly upon a study of the sources, i.e., national, state, and colonial statutes, Congressional documents, reports of societies, personal narratives, etc. The collection of laws available for this research was, I think nearly complete; on the other hand, facts and statistics bearing on the economic side of the study have been difficult to find, and my conclusions are consequently liable to modification from this source.[42]

The first 197 pages of the volume are divided into twelve chapters. Appendices cover from pages 201 to 289. The bibliography and index bring the total to 327 pages. The chapter titles are: "Plan of the Monograph," "The Planting Colonies," "The Farming Colonies," "The Trading Colonies," "The Period of the Revolution, 1774-1787," "The Federal Convention, 1787," "Toussaint L' Ouverture and Anti-Slavery Effort 1787-1807," "The Period of Attempted Suppression, 1807-1825," "The International Status of the Slave Trade, 1783-1862," "The Rise of the Cotton Kingdom, 1820-1850," "The Final Crisis, 1850-1870," and "The Essentials."

The purpose of the monograph was "to set forth the major efforts made in the U.S.A., from early colonial times until the present, to limit and suppress the trade in slaves between Africa and these shores."[43] In Typical doctoral dissertation fashion, the volume is very thoroughly documented.[44] Apart from the inadequate economic data which the author mentions, perhaps the volume does not give enough consideration to moral reasons for anti-slavery sentiment in the colonies and the young republic. Du Bois sums up the anti-slavery movement to 1774 as follows:

In the individual efforts of the various colonies to suppress the African slave-trade there may be traced certain general movements. First, from 1638-1664, there was a tendency to take a high moral stand against the traffic. This is illustrated in the laws of New England, in the plans for the settlement of Delaware and later, that of Georgia, and in the protest of the German Friends. The second period, from about 1664 to 1720, has no general unity, but is marked by statutes laying duties varying in design from encouragement to absolute prohibition, by some cases of moral opposition, and by the slow but steady growth of a spirit unfavorable to the long continuance of the trade. The last colonial period, from about 1760 to 1787, is one of pronounced effort to regulate, limit, or totally prohibit the traffic. Beside these general movements, there are many waves of legislation, easily distinguishable, which rolled over several or all of the colonies at various times, such as the series of high duties following the Asiento, and the acts inspired by various Negro plots.[45]

After 1820, he stated, "The history of slavery and the slave-trade . . . must be read in the light of the industrial revolution."[46] In assigning a cause for the disappearance of the slave-trade and slavery in the United States, Du Bois wrote that the cause was "a peculiar and almost fortuitous commingling of moral, political, and economic motives."[47]

This volume is, almost in its entirety, thoroughly objective, scholarly, temperate, and follows a broad interpretation. The only clear evidence of Du Bois's proclivity for, and almost irresistible tendency towards proselytizing, is found in the last topic of this volume. This topic is entitled "Lessons for Americans."[48] "It may be doubted," he writes, "if ever before such political mistakes as the slavery compromises of the Constitutional Convention had such serious results, and yet, by a succession of unexpected accidents, still left a nation in position to work out its destiny."[49] Du Bois fails to answer, or consider, the question of whether adoption of the Constitution could have been secured without these "slavery compromises." "We must face the fact," he continues, "that this problem arose principally from the cupidity and carelessness of our ancestors. It was the plain duty of the colonies to crush the trade and the system in its infancy: they preferred to enrich themselves on its profits. It was the plain duty of a Revolution based upon 'Liberty' to take steps toward the abolition of slavery: it preferred promises to straightforward action."[50]

Du Bois continues his condemnation of the lack of moral integrity on the part of the early Americans thus:

> With the faith of the nation broken at the very outset, the system of slavery untouched, and twenty years respite given to the slave-trade to feed and foster it, there began, with 1787 that system of bargaining, truckling, and compromising with a moral, political, and economic monstrosity, which makes the history of our dealing with slavery in the first half of the nineteenth century so discreditable to a great people. Each generation sought to shift its load upon the next, and the burden rolled on, until a generation came which was both too weak and too strong to bear it longer.
>
> It behooves the United States, therefore, in the interest both of scientific truth and of future social reform, carefully to study such chapters of her history. The most obvious question which this study suggests is: How far in a State can a recognized moral wrong safely be compromised? And although this chapter of history can give us no definite answer suited to the ever-varying aspects of political life, yet it would seem to warn any nation from allowing, through carelessness and moral cowardice, any social

evil to grow. . . . From this we may conclude that it
behooves nations as well as men to do things at the
very moment when they ought to be done.[51]

"No persons," Du Bois states, "would have seen the Civil
War with more surprise and horror than the Revolutionists
of 1776."[52]

The Philadelphia Negro

In 1899 appeared *The Philadelphia Negro,* a sociological
study, which also carried a special report on domestic service by Isabel Eaton.[53] Two years previously, Du Bois had
submitted to the American Academy of Political and Social
Science a plan for the study of Negro problems. *The Philadelphia Negro* was "an essay along the lines there laid down,
and . . . thus part of a larger design of observation and research into the history and social condition of the trans-
planted African."[54] "Until [the scholar] has prepared the
ground by intelligent and discriminating research," Du Bois
wrote, "the labors of philanthropist and statesman must
continue to be, to a large extent, barren and unfruitful."[55]
Du Bois hoped that similar studies would be made of Negro
life in such cities as Boston in the East, Chicago and Kansas
City in the West, and Atlanta, New Orleans and Galveston
in the South. This would result, he felt, in "a trustworthy
picture of Negro city life."[56] Almost two years of continuous
research were spent in gathering data for *The Philadelphia
Negro.* Du Bois contacted over 10,000 Philadelphians. The
study had been made possible when Miss Susan P. Whar-
ton, a member of the Executive Committee of the Philadelphia College Settlement, asked the administration of the
University of Pennsylvania to sponsor it as a philanthropic
guide.

In this volume Du Bois censures the city of Philadelphia
for not planning conditions so that a superior Black citizenry
would be bred by the local environment. The work carries

statistics on crime, death rate, marriage status, occupation, and almost every conceivable aspect of life in the city. The last chapter is entitled "A Final Word," and is similar to the concluding portion of *Suppression of the African Slave Trade*. The first topic under "A Final Word" is "The Meaning of all This."[57] This section tells the nation what it must do for Blacks and tells the latter what they must do for themselves to improve their lot.

The *Philadelphia Negro* was one of the first scientific sociological treatises to come from the pen of an Afro-American. With this work, and the "Atlanta University Studies" which continued the pattern here outlined, Du Bois joined Carter G. Woodson in laying the foundation for subsequent scientific studies of the conditions of the race. Other university trained Afro-Americans were soon to appear and advance the work inaugurated by these two men. The rise of graduate schools in the United States had much to do with the increase in the quantity and quality of scholarly productions by Blacks after the first decade of the twentieth century. Still, "When Dr. Du Bois appeared he gave to his people a sense of pride. The race had had scholars before, but not one of such distinction and influence. To younger men accordingly he became an inspiration and a challenge."[58] The same can be said of his distinguished contemporary, Carter Godwin Woodson.

The Negro in the South

In 1907 appeared a volume which Du Bois co-authored with Booker T. Washington. It bore the title *The Negro in the South*,[59] and consisted of four essays, two by each of the authors. In this volume, Du Bois states that the industrial revolution both fastened slavery on the South by creating markets for cotton, and doomed slavery at the same time by creating a free laboring class.[60] "Such a system at such a time carried its own sentence of death," he wrote, "because it demanded extensive rather than intensive land culture, increased and made compulsory ignorance of the laboring class, and the rearing of a complete system of caste and aristocracy."[61] Yet, he states, freedom meant for the freedmen only another type of bondage—industrial slavery.[62]

Like many intellectuals in all ages, Du Bois could never see any intelligence in, or much need for war. He termed the American Civil War "that disgraceful episode of civil strife when, leaving the arguments of men, the nation appealed to the last resort of dogs, murdering and ravishing each other for four long shameful years."[63]

In this volume may be found the position on Afro-American participation in Radical Reconstruction which Du Bois was to amplify thirty years later in *Black Reconstruction*. "Although the new voters . . . introduced in the South were crude and ignorant, and in many ways ill-fitted to rule," he wrote, "nevertheless in the fundamental postulates of American freedom and democracy they were sane and sound. Some of them were silly, some were ignorant, and some were venal, but they were not as silly as those who had fostered slavery in the South, nor as ignorant as those who were determined to perpetuate it, and the black voters of South Carolina never stole half as much as the white voters of Pennsylvania are stealing today."[64] Du Bois then goes on to outline virtually all of the arguments which he later used in *Black Reconstruction*. Only the Marxist slant of the latter work, and its more thorough documentation, seem to be missing from *The Negro in the South*.[65]

In 1909 appeared a biography of John Brown which was written by Du Bois for the American Crisis Biographies series. This series was edited by E. P. Oberholtzer.[66] The author admitted that he had no new materials on Brown to bolster that already published in the biographies by Hinton, Connelly and Redpath, or the autobiography of Brown edited by Sanborn. Du Bois gave his excuse for writing the volume as being to "lay new emphasis upon the material which they have so carefully collected, and to treat these facts from a different point of view."[67] This scholar believes that John Brown, "of all Americans has perhaps come nearest to touching the real souls of black folk."[68]

The volume is well written and ably documented. The tone is one of moderation, and the volume deserves, perhaps, greater acclaim among the works produced by Du Bois than it has received. Indeed, he himself seldom mentioned in later years that he had written this work.

In summing up the miscarried effort of John Brown, Du Bois re-echoes the moral theme with which he concluded *Suppression of the African Slave Trade* and *The Philadelphia Negro*. "Only in time is truth revealed," he writes, "Today at last we know, John Brown was right."[69] The "right" thing which John Brown taught posterity is that "the cheapest price to pay for liberty is its cost today."[70] Though he states in this volume that "John Brown was right," later he deprecates and disavows the use of violence and advocates a greater exercise of Christian principles.[71]

The Negro

This volume was written for the "Home University Library of Modern Knowledge" for popular reading.[72] "In this book," he writes, "we are studying the history of the darker part of the human family, which is separated from the rest of mankind by no absolute physical line, but which nevertheless forms, as a distinct mass, a social group distinct in history, appearance, and to some extent in spiritual gift."[73]

Eight of the twelve chapters treat African history. The remaining four treat the slave trade, the Negro in the West Indies and Latin America, and in the United States. Du Bois here stated his belief that the American Negro was a part of the world-mass of colored peoples who were being exploited by capitalistic Europe. He expressed the belief that there was coming a unity of working classes all over the world and that everywhere the color line would disappear.

The Gift of Black Folk

This volume appeared in 1924, bearing the sub-title "The Negroes in the Making of America."[74] It was one of the "Knights of Columbus" racial series, and was for the author, "an attempt to set forth more clearly than has hitherto been done the effect which the Negro has had upon American life."[75] The thesis of the volume was that "despite slavery, war and caste, and despite our present Negro problem, the American Negro is and has been a distinct asset to this country, and has brought a contribution without which America could not have been; and that perhaps the essence of our so-called Negro problem is the failure to recognize this fact."[76] Here again is to be seen the persistent belief that mis-education or lack of education concerning the true nature of the achievements of the Negro constituted the primary basis of discrimination and prejudice against him.

The volume traces the aid given by Blacks in the discovery of America and indicates the significant contribution of anonymous black labor to the founding of the Nation. It also shows that members of the race served in all of the Nation's wars and influenced the growth of a broader democracy through the humanitarian interest which was fanned by the issue of slavery. It shows that Blacks contributed significantly to the body of American literature and art and states that the race brought a "peculiar spiritual quality into American life."[77] The volume, like most of the writings of Du Bois, was received with mixed criticism, mostly favorable.[78]

Black Reconstruction

This volume was published in 1935.[79] In 1910 its author had read before the American Historical Association a paper entitled "Reconstruction and its Benefits," "which greatly exorcised Ulrich Phillips, protagonist of the slave South, but brought praise from Dunning . . . Hart and others."[80] *Black Reconstruction* was, in part, an enlargement of this paper. Du Bois began the larger study through a Rosenwald grant received while he was with the National Association for the Advancement of Colored People. After leaving this organization and returning to the classroom at Atlanta University, he completed it.

By this time, as stated earlier, Du Bois had become a Marxist convert. *Black Reconstruction* was the first of his writings in which he clearly revealed himself as an economic determinist. Most of his subsequent volumes were to reveal this orientation. "It was not until I was long out of college," he wrote, "and had finished the first phase of my teaching career that I began to see clearly the connection of economics and politics; the fundamental influence of man's efforts to earn a living upon all his other efforts."[81] And again, "It was the Russian Revolution of 1917 I believe which first caused me to see clearly."[82]

The author admits that *Black Reconstruction* was based "very largely upon secondary material; upon state histories of the Reconstruction, written in the main by those who were convinced before they began to write that the Negro was incapable of government, or of becoming a constituent part of a civilized state."[83] He also admitted that he had neither the time nor money to consult many important sources in the Library of Congress and the Widener Library, such as the papers of Johnson, Wells, Chase, McCulloch, McPherson, Sherman, Stevens, Schurz, Greeley, Sumner, and others. Had Du Bois been able to use these sources, he believes that his case would have been "vastly strengthened."[84]

The thesis of *Black Reconstruction* is that the Negro "is an average and ordinary human being, who under given environment develops like other human beings."[85] Actually, this represents a poor statement of the thesis of the book because the above is the thesis of *all* of the writings of this scholar and does not indicate the uniqueness of *Black Reconstruction*. Rather, this book is a successful effort to point up positive aspects of the participation of Blacks in the Civil War and Reconstruction. It carries the novel thesis that Radical Reconstruction was overthrown by northern and southern capitalists because of their fear that it represented a nascent form of proletarian rule. Du Bois regards it as the height of folly that southern poor whites did not see in the freedmen fellow members of the proletariat and form a continuing alliance with them against exploiting southern and northern capitalists.

The volume relies heavily on arguments used by the Abolitionists and quotes James Ford Rhodes frequently. Also the author's case appears to be heavily bolstered because he frequently quotes from state histories which generally cast a bad light on Negro participation in government during Reconstruction.[86] Du Bois points out the constructive aspects of Radical Reconstruction, especially of the state constitutional conventions in which freedmen participated, and the work of the Freedmen's Bureau. Also characteristic of the general interpretation of this period by Afro-American historians, there is little but high praise for Thaddeus Stevens and Charles Sumner. Appended to the volume is a list of the main historians of the Reconstruction Period, grouped according to the degree in which Du Bois feels they are favorable or unfavorable to the participation of Blacks in government.[87] At the end of almost every chapter, the author added an eloquent "peroration" which together or singly, reveal his literary genius and poetic nature, although, perhaps such indulgences constitute a violation of the canons of strict objective scholarship.

This volume contains chapters with such titles as "The Black Proletariat of South Carolina," and "The Black Proletariat of Mississippi." In Chapter IV, "The General Strike," it is maintained that though slaves did not stage a general revolt based on violence during the Civil War, they doomed the war effort by refusing to work and absconding the moment northern armies reached their areas.

Black Reconstruction reveals Du Bois "as both the merciless critic and the constructive historian."[88] Rayford W. Logan, in appraising this work, exaggerates the significance of its economic theory. "This fresh interpretation of the economic forces of our era of storm and stress is as significant," he writes, "as was Charles A. Beard's Economic Interpretation of the Constitution of the United States a quarter of a century ago."[89] However, studies of Reconstruction by other historians are far better at casting light on economic aspects of the period. The unique and valuable contribution of Black Reconstruction lies in the great emphasis which it placed on constructive aspects of the period. Again, Logan errs in his agreement with the Marxist theory which one finds in this book. "For the first time," Logan avers, "one clearly understands that America lost during Reconstruction her golden opportunity to found a political and industrial democracy."[90]

As previously stated, from this volume on, Du Bois ties the plight of "exploited" black labor in the United States with that of labor in the colonial world everywhere. He sees American Negro slavery as but one aspect of exploitation by industrialized Europe and America of colored peoples the world over. "It was thus the black worker," he states, "as founding stone of a new economic system in the nineteenth century and for the modern world, who brought the Civil War in America. He was its underlying cause, in spite of every effort to base the strife upon union and national power."[91] He continues:

That dark and vast sea of human labor in China and India, the South Seas and all Africa, in the West Indies and Central America and in the United States —that great majority of mankind, on whose bent and broken backs rest today the founding stones of modern industry—shares a common destiny.

Here is the real modern labor problem. . . . Out of the exploitation of the dark proletariat come the Surplus Value filched from human beasts, which, in cultured lands, the Machine and harnessed Power veil and conceal. The emancipation of man is the emancipation of labor and the emancipation of labor is the freeing of that basic majority of workers who are yellow, brown and black.[92]

Judging from this new position of Du Bois after the Russian Revolution, it seems difficult to believe that in his early years he had sided with the position of Booker T. Washington in the view that his race should compromise with the white South.[93] Henceforth, he was to attack not only the traditional attitude of the United States toward the Black man, but the entire economic orientation of the United States and Western world. In his youth, states this scholar, he saw only the "Negro problem" in the United States. "I did not," he wrote, "face the general plight and conditions of all humankind."[94] After this conversion, he repeatedly stated that "The history of our day . . . may be epitomized in one word—Empire; the domination of white Europe over black Africa and yellow Asia, through political power built on the economic control of labor, income and ideas. The echo of this industrial imperialism in America was the expulsion of black men from American democracy, their subjugation to caste control and wage slavery. This ideology was triumphant in 1910."[95] In his autobiography, as in *Black Reconstruction*, he reiterates his belief that with the end of Reconstruction there was an "expulsion of black men from American democracy."

Reviewers were almost unanimous in their praise of *Black Reconstruction* for giving a needed emphasis to the positive aspects of Reconstruction. They were almost equally unanimous in their denunciation of the bitterness of the author. On this latter point, Avery Craven wrote: "By distorting facts and reviewing abolition propaganda in the name of history he has . . . probably done little toward averting the 'fire and blood' solution of the race question or securing that 'perfect and unlimited equality' with any white man he desires."[96] D. S. Muzzey, with the same general criticisms, praised "the beauty and brilliance of his style," while scoring "his bitterness and lack of judicial balance."[97] Crane Brinton did not feel that the book revealed any hatred on the part of the author, but that Du Bois "shares the desires for justice, for democracy, for free discussion, for gentlemanly competition among individuals, for dispassionate search for scientific truth which was the creed of nineteenth century liberals like Mill."[98] Du Bois will not, he wrote, "if he can help it, repay white scorn with Negro hatred. On the whole, he succeeds. The book is wistful rather than truculent."[99] S. D. Spero, reviewing the book for *The Nation*, stated that "Du Bois's old race consciousness and new Marxism do not allow him to remain content with the demonstration of this major thesis (to show that the Negro 'is an average and ordinary human being'); they lead him to transform the Negro plantation slaves into a revolutionary working class and make the Reconstruction legislatures into dictatorships of the proletariat."[100] A. A. Taylor correctly termed the book "the most comprehensive study of this period by a Negro author."[101]

Black Folk Then and Now

This volume first appeared in 1939,[102] bearing the subtitle "An Essay in the History and Sociology of the Negro Race." Du Bois stated that it was an attempt to do "somewhat more thoroughly, the task which I attempted twenty-three years ago in a little volume . . . called *The Negro*. This book incorporates some of that former essay, but for the most part is an entirely new production."[103]

The author early admitted some basic limitations. "This

is not a work of exact scholarship; far too few studies in history are," he wrote.[104] He continued: "The kernel of this work is, I believe, a body of fairly well-ascertained truth; but there are also areas here of conjecture and even of guesswork which under other circumstances I should have hesitated to publish."[105] He excuses himself for writing the book, despite these limitations, because the race has been so neglected in history, or misinterpreted, and because "millions of black and brown folk today, not to speak of most educated whites, have no conception of any role that black folk have played in history, or any hope in the past for present aspiration."[106]

The larger difficulties of the work Du Bois saw as "the breadth of the field which one mind can scarcely cover; the obstacles to securing data."[107] He also admitted at the outset that his interpretation was probably biased because of his African descent and narrow group culture. "But there is little danger of long misleading here," he charged, "for the champions of white folk are legion. The Negro has long been the clown of history; the football of anthropology; and the slave of industry. I am trying to show here why these attitudes can no longer be maintained."[108] Still, true to his training, Du Bois realized "that the truth of history lies not in the mouths of partisans but rather in the calm science that sits between." "Her cause I seek to serve," he continued, "and wherever I fail, I am at least paying truth the respect of earnest effort."[109]

The author states that he had acquired the urge to write on the past of Blacks after hearing Franz Boaz speak at Atlanta University in 1906 on the richness of the African past. Upon hearing these revealing facts, Du Bois states that he was "too astonished to speak," because "all of this" he "had never heard." It is then that he first began to realize "how the silence and neglect of science can let truth utterly disappear or even be consciously distorted."[110]

In attempting to define "race," he concludes that, "No

scientific definition of race is possible. . . . In this book then we are studying the history of the darker part of the human family, which is separated from the rest of mankind by no absolute physical line and no definite mental characteristics, but which nevertheless forms, as a mass, a series of social groups more or less distinct in history, appearance, and in cultural gift and accomplishment."[111] Throughout the volume the tone is fairly temperate. Chapter Six, on "The Culture of Africa" is not excessively laudatory. "What the facts concerning the culture of Africa begin to tell us," he concludes, "is simply that here we have a normal human stock whose development has been conditioned by certain physical and social factors."[112] Du Bois had already stated that "It is . . . easy to exaggerate the cultural gifts of any particular people," and he steers clear of this pit-fall.[113]

There are not many footnotes in the volume. The author used standard sources, mostly monographs in English, although a few in French and German are cited. Among the standard works are those of Lugard, Frobenius, Chamberlain, and Martineau. Du Bois repeated his oft-stated assertion that "black slavery gave birth" to the industrial revolution.[114] In one place he states that, "England stopped the slave trade in order to defeat Napoleon," yet on the next page he admits that profits from slavery were declining.[115] In another instance, Du Bois states categorically, "There is no doubt that the thirst of the black men for knowledge . . . gave birth to the public school system of the South."[116]

About one-third of the volume deals with the African background. The interpretation given to such topics as the partition of Africa, the slave trade, and the American Civil War is largely that of the economic determinist. Yet, apart from faulty generalization and interpretation in some places, this volume is a mine of facts which are, for this impassioned scholar, very temperately presented. The final chapter is entitled, "Future of World Democracy." Here the author reiterates his faith in socialism as the to-be-desired new economic order, scores again racist explanations for the differences among individuals, disclaims any faith in violent revolution, and pleads for a greater practice of Christian virtues. Thus, it seems that he, in this volume, retreated somewhat from the type of faith in Marxism which he had manifested earlier. "It seems clear today," he wrote, "that the masses of men within and without civilization are depressed, ignorant and poor chiefly because they have never had a chance. . . . For centuries the world has sought to rationalize this condition and pretend that civilized nations and cultured classes are the result of inherent and hereditary gifts rather than climate, geography and happy accident. This explanation . . . is today, because of the decline and fall of [European] hegemony, less widely believed."[117] Mankind, he states, can go on to far greater achievements "if mere political democracy is allowed to widen into industrial democracy and the democracy of culture and art. The possibility of this has long been foreseen and emphasized by the socialists, culminating in the magnificent and apostolic fervor of Karl Marx and the Communists."[118] Although Du Bois here sees the same solution for the world's ills as Marx saw, he advocates not "violence and revolution, which is only the outward distortion of an inner fact, but . . . the ancient cardinal virtues: individual prudence, courage, temperance and justice, and the more modern faith, hope love."[119]

By this time an internationalist outlook on race, together with his Marxist leanings, caused him to write of "the proletariat of the world," which he says, "consists not simply of white European and American workers but overwhelmingly of the darker workers of Asia, Africa, the islands of the sea, and South Central America. These are the ones who are supporting a superstructure of wealth, luxury and extravagance. It is the rise of these people that is the rise of the world. The problem of the twentieth century is the problem of the color line."[120] Nowhere in this volume does he give credit to these exploiters of colored peoples for anything but "wealth, luxury and extravagance."

The book was generally well received by critics. Carter Woodson regretted the omission of certain secondary works, and stated that "the chapters devoted . . . to African kingdoms do not show much relief."[121] Woodson also held that Du Bois omitted the names and exploits of many Africans whom Woodson considered too significant to be overlooked. M. J. Herskovits praised the manner in which Du Bois viewed the race problem as a world problem.[122] Like Woodson, H. J. Seligman criticized the brief allotment of space for the African background. Yet he admitted that "No one can leave [the book] without a deepened sense of the part the Negro peoples have played and must play in world history."[123]

Du Bois later admitted that by the time he wrote *Black Folk Then and Now* his thinking on the race problem had undergone a change. In his autobiography he states that he felt, at first, that a quick revolutionary assault could end the problem. World War I caused him to see, he states, that violence plus the economic bases of race prejudice made "not sudden assault but long siege . . . indicated; careful planning and subtle campaign with the education of growing generations and propaganda."[124] Still, considering the generally restrained and temperate tone of *Black Folk Then and Now*, one might not guess that the wook was written "in tears and blood."[125]

Color and Democracy: Colonies and Peace

In 1945 also appeared his *Color and Democracy: Colonies and Peace.*[126] This volume, like the book *What the Negro Wants,*[127] was designed to help world leaders fashion the new order after World War II. Here the author called for the granting of democracy to all peoples, especially those long subjected to European colonialism. As already seen, Du Bois was convinced that the world could rise above the

wars and depressions which had racked the twentieth century only by allowing the subjected colored masses to escape from their bondage. This, he felt, was the key to future
peace. Such is the thesis of *Color and Democracy*, in which
he "sought to say that insofar as . . . efforts [at peace] leave
practically untouched the present imperial ownership of
disfranchised colonies, and in this and other ways proceed
as if the majority of men can be regarded mainly as sources
of profit for Europe and North America, in just so far we
are planning not for peace but war, not democracy but the
continued oligarchial control of civilization by the white
race."[128]

Topics treated are "Dumbarton Oaks," "The Disfranchised Colonies," "The Unfree People," "Democracy and
Color," "Peace and Colonies," "The Riddle of Russia," and
"Missions and Mandates." Du Bois echoes his oft-stated
position that World War I was caused by colonial rivalry.
Colonies, he states, must be taken from European powers or
there will be "recurring wars of envy and greed because of
the present inequitable distribution of colonial gain among
civilized nations."[129] He also repeats his conviction that the
world's poverty, ignorance and disease are caused by "monopoly." "The possibility of producing wealth in our age,"
he avers, has repeatedly been estimated to be great enough
to furnish all the peoples of the world with the necessities
of life and some of the comforts, but monopoly prevents
this being attained."[130] No where does the author consider
adequately that many of Europe's wars have been expansionist wars—that even in the absence of overseas colonies
European states would probably have been fighting over
one anothers landholdings in continental Europe.[131]

This historian is to be commended for his cosmopolitan
conception of race and for his world humanitarianism. This
high position led Du Bois to an elevated conception of democracy, which he defined as "not simply the self-defense
of the competent; it is the unloosing of the energies and

the capabilities of the depressed."[132] Again, he states his conviction that this is precisely the type of democracy which the Soviet Union is accomplishing.[133]

There is little in *Color and Democracy* which Du Bois had not already repeated many times in other of his writings. The volume ends on a note of optimism. The author felt that the rise of a new liberalism was pointing in the direction which he desired.

The volume was variously received. A reviewer for *Foreign Affairs* stated, "His survey of the whole question of dependent peoples . . . is so brief and episodic that his book constitutes little more than an anti-imperialist—especially an anti-British—tract."[134] Another reviewer called the work "Sound, challenging, thought-provoking."[135] H. A. Overstreet wrote: "This book . . . is a small volume of 143 pages; but it contains enough dynamite to blow up the whole vicious system whereby we have comforted our white souls and lined the pockets of generations of free-booting capitalists. Its chief value lies in what it reveals to us of conditions that hitherto we have merely taken for granted. . . . It is reading that is utterly essential if we want to understand the fullness of the world job that is ahead of us."[136] Amry Vandenbosch called it "a tract for the times, and as such [of] considerable value; but . . . not a scientific analysis of the large and difficult problem with which it deals."[137]

The World and Africa

Also out of his new attitude toward the "race issue," Du Bois wrote and published in 1947 *The World and Africa*.[138] This volume bore the subtitle "An Inquiry into the Part which Africa has played in world History." Like *Color and Democracy*, *The Gift of Black Folk*, and his autobiography, *Dusk of Dawn*, *The World and Africa* played up the theme that European colonialism was the fountain-head of modern industrialism and civilization, with the concomitant chronic warfare and depression. These volumes also sought gen-

erally to reveal what Carter G. Woodson had been attempting to show for almost three decades, that the Afro-American has a rich past and has made contributions to civilization which deserve high praise.

With *The World and Africa*, Du Bois was seeking "to
remind readers of the crisis of civilization, of how critical a
part Africa has played in human history, past and present,
and how impossible it is to forget this and rightly explain
the present plight of mankind."[139] Already he had made
two attempts to write the history of Africa. His first, *The
Negro*, which had appeared in 1915, he now called a "con-
densed and not altogether logical-narrative."[140] He stated
that *Black Folk Then and Now* was an enlargement upon
The Negro, which enlargement he felt was necessary after
World War I because he thought that period represented
the "beginning of . . . a new era."[141] He states that he decided to write *The World and Africa* and reinterpret these
earlier works because the period after World War I actually
was "the end of an age which marked the final catastrophe
of the old era of European world dominance rather than
[being] at the threshold of a change of which he had
dreamed in 1935."[142] He referred to this latest effort as
"not so much a history of the Negroid peoples as a statement
of their integral role in human history from prehistoric to
modern times."[143]

Again, as with *Black Folk Then and Now*, Du Bois admits at the outset the limitations to the task which he was
essaying. "I still labor," he wrote, "under the difficulty
of the persistent lack of interest in Africa so long characteristic of modern history and sociology. The careful detailed researches into the history of Negroid peoples have
only begun, and the need for them is not yet clear to the
thinking world."[144] He continued: "I feel compelled nevertheless to go ahead with my interpretation, even though
that interpretation has here and there but slender historical
proof. I believe that in the main my story is true, despite the

fact that so often between the American Civil War and
World War I the weight of history and science supports
me only in part and in some cases appears violently to con-
tradict me."[145]

On the lack of documentation to support his statements,
he wrote: "I am challenging authority—even Maspero,
Sayce, Reisner, Breasted, and hundreds of other men of highest respectability, who did not attack but studiously ignored
the Negro on the Nile and in the world and talked as though
black folk were non-existent and unimportant."[146] He used
mostly secondary works.[147] Of his research, he stated:

> I have done in this book the sort of thing at which
> every scholar shudders. With meager preparation
> and all too general background of learning, I have
> essayed a task, which, to be adequate and complete,
> should be based upon the research of a lifetime; but
> I am faced with the dilemma, that either I do this
> now or leave it for others. If out of my almost inev-
> itable mistakes and inaccuracies and false conclu-
> sions, I shall have at least clearly stated my main
> issue—that black Africans are men in the same sense
> as white European and yellow Asiatics, and that his-
> tory can easily prove this—then I shall rest satisfied
> even under the stigma of an incomplete and, to
> many, inconclusive work.[148]

Here one finds this author's often-stated positions on the
slave trade, slavery, colonialism, and the two world wars.
True to his moralistic proclivities, after flaying European
exploitation of colonies, Du Bois writes of the "moral plight
of present European culture and what capitalistic invest-
ment and imperialism have done to it." In seeking an explanation for this moral plight, he finds an answer in the
subject matter of his doctoral dissertation. "I believe that
the trade in human beings between Africa and America,"
he wrote, "which flourished between the Renaissance and
American Civil War, is the prime and effective cause of the

contradictions in European civilization and the illogic in modern thought and the collapse of human culture."[149]

In *The World and Africa*, this historian shows the very keen and admirable sympathy and feeling for the underdog and weak which is so characteristic of his life and writings. He depicts a touching scene from the killing of an elephant for the ivory trade and piano keys and billiard balls. "Neither for the keys nor the music," he writes, "was the death of the elephant actually necessary."[150] Topics covered in the volume are: "The Collapse of Europe," "The White Masters of the World," "The Rape of Africa," "The Peopling of Africa," "Egypt," "The Land of the Burnt Faces," "Atlantis," "Central Africa and the March of the Bantu," "Asia in Africa," "The Black Sudan," "Andromeda," and "The Message." The volume is lightly documented.

One reviewer called the book "timely," but criticized it for being "admittedly based on the work of other writers rather than research."[151] Another reviewer, while praising the volume for the attention which it focuses on a neglected field, criticized the "extensive excursions into classical mythology, Biblical literature, and Oriental legend," for being "open to challenge for their validity." This reviewer also criticized some of the sources as being unreliable, and stated that "much of what Du Bois poses here has been substantiated, but its comprehensive treatment is the task of anthropologists and historians of the future."[152] Another reviewer scored the bitterness in the volume. Linton Wells believes that *The World and Africa* "would have been more convincing and would have better served his cause had Dr. Du Bois been less bitter. Imbued with such hate, no one can deal adequately or rationally with his subject," he stated.[153] "Though Dr. Du Bois is a distinguished scholar and his book is based on extensive research," comments another reviewer, "the result is not sober anthropology and history, but poetry and legend. It is full of corroded passion, of anger opening into illumination, of logic dwindling into nostalgia. It moves proudly, like a pageant. This is history as Herodotus understood it. It is also special pleading which will antagonize as much as it convinces."[154]

Other Works

In 1945 appeared the preparatory volume of the *Encyclopedia of the Negro*, which was edited by Du Bois, L. D. Reddick, G. B. Johnson, and Rayford Logan.[155] Carter Woodson, who certainly knew the difficulties of such a task, stated then that the editors should have waited until the entire work was ready for publication before issuing a part of it. He criticized the plan of the work as "inadequate" and expressed doubts that the editors would ever finish such a stupendous task.[156] He was right. This introductory volume had been made possible through a grant from the Phelps-Stokes Fund. Reviewers also criticized the work for "seeming capriciousness in the selection of subjects" and for poor listing of references.[157]

Du Bois made three efforts at writing novels which used the Black theme. In 1911 appeared his *The Quest of the Silver Fleece*,[158] in 1929 *Dark Princess*, a romance,[159] and in 1957, *The Ordeal of Mansart*. What one reviewer said of *Dark Princess* is perhaps characteristic of much of his writing. This work was aptly described as "A piece of symbolic social literature and propaganda, written with fine nervous ardor and scorn for injustice."[160] Two other of his non-historical works were highly similar in content and form. In 1903 he had published his *The Souls of Black Folk: Essays and Sketches*.[161] This book was very widely read, going through sixteen editions by 1928 and it was in its twenty-first edition in 1937. It early revealed, even more clearly than his *Suppression of the African Slave Trade* or *The Philadelphia Negro* had done, the keen sensitivity of Du Bois to the racial discrimination and oppression to which his race was subjected, and the very eloquent form which his protest could take. "Herein lie buried many things," he wrote, "which if read with patience may show the strange meaning of being black here at the dawning of the twentieth century."[162] Some of the essays in this volume had appeared previously in *The Atlantic Monthly, The World's Work, The Dial, The New World* and *Annals*. By 1969 *The Souls of Black Folk* had won a place among the classics of American literature.

In *Darkwater* Du Bois had written that he has been "in the world but not of it." "I have seen the human tragedy," he continued, "from a veiled corner."[163] This work also carried a Credo in which he said, "I believe in God; the Negro race; Service, the Devil, the Prince of Peace; Liberty for all men; the training of children; Patience."[164] Like *The Souls of Black Folk*, this publication is a collection of essays, stories, parables and poetry.

The following criticism of *Darkwater* might also have been made about many of the writings of this scholar, historical or otherwise. "There is a certain weakness in Prof. Du Bois's reasoning," comments this reviewer, "which is that his intense concentration on one subject leads him to turn general universal wrongs into special Negro wrongs. The error runs all through his book and disfigures it."[165] The praise which this reviewer has for the volume might also be given to any of his works. "If we disagree with much in this beautiful book," continues this critic, "it is not possible to withhold the heartiest praise for the power of its statement, the force and passion that inspire it, and the entrancing style in which it is written."[166] In a review of this book, Oswald Garrison Villard called the ability of Du Bois "to suffer and to feel the wrongs of his race as deeply . . . at once his strength, the reason for his leadership, and also his chief weakness," because it carried with it "a note of bitterness, tinctured with hate, and the teaching of violence which often defeats his own purpose." He stated further: "Doubtless, few of us with sympathies so keen, with nerves so rasped, with wounds as raw, would do better. But still, some suppression of the ego, a lesser self-consciousness, and the omission of personal bitterness at all times would carry Mr. Du Bois and his cause much further."[167]

In the *Sturm und Drang* of the first third of the twentieth century many persons lost faith in Classical Liberalism. Total warfare and total depression came to convince many people that the decision of most pressing moment had come to an unequivocal choice between security and liberty. Mussolini, Hitler, Stalin and their supporters typify those who, in the post World War I period, abandoned liberty as an ideal in the interests of supposed security. The United States, faced with similar peril in this period, found a new balance between security and freedom. Du Bois, like some other liberals of his day, came to feel that only in a thorough abandonment of the old ideals and ways lay a permanent solution to the world's ills. True to his economic determinism, he felt too that the capitalistic system, which helped to give rise to Classical Liberalism, must be abandoned.

Du Bois made the jump from being a historian of the Black man, to being a champion of the entire underprivileged population of the earth. He made this jump because he believed that to work further to improve the lot of the black man in American society is only to lop off the branches of a tree which must be killed from its roots. After the 1830's, it was not against racial segregation and discrimination that he directed his blows, but against what he felt produced segregation, discrimination and exploitation—the capitalistic system.[168]

Du Bois reached his zenith as a scholar—in the traditional sense—, at the outset of his career. *The Suppression of the African Slave Trade to the United States*, his sociological study, *The Philadelphia Negro*, and the "Atlanta University Studies," represent his most thorough and objective products. More and more, as he drifted deeper into causes centering around the "race issue," the character of his scholarly productivity changed. Still, perhaps as much because of his "'bad" as well as good qualities as a scholar, he gave a great impetus to interest in the black race and to the scientific study of its history and culture. The body of writings which he contributed to Black studies helped mightily to attract attention to the field of Black history. While he antagonized, he also aroused attention, interest, sympathy and respect—not only for the race, but for Black history. His *Black Reconstruction*, through focusing attention on the neglected aspects of that period, contributed greatly in bringing about a reinterpretation of the period. Because of this, *Black Reconstruction* and his doctoral dissertation must be ranked as outstanding products of American historiography.

CHAPTER II

THE WHY AND WHAT OF AFRO-AMERICAN HISTORIOGRAPHY

[1] Vernon Loggins, *The Negro Author* (New York: Columbia University Press, 1931).

[2] Michael Kraus, *A History of American History* (New York: Farrar and Rinehart, 1937), p. 336.

[3] M. J. Herskovits, "The Present Status and Needs of Afro-American Research," *Journal of Negro History*, XXXVI, April, 1951, pp. 123-147.

[4] Kraus, *op. cit.*, p. 336.

[5] J. H. Franklin, "George Washington Williams, Historian," *Journal of Negro History*, XXXI, January, 1946, p. 61; Vernon Loggins, *The Negro Author*, pp. 278-279; W. J. Simmons, *Men of Mark* (Cleveland, 1887), pp. 549-559.

[6] *History of the Negro Race in America, 1619-1880* (New York: G. P. Putnam's Sons, 1883), pp. v-vi.

[7] *Ibid.*, p. x.

[8] *Ibid.*, pp. 551-2.

[9] *History of Negro Troops in the War of the Rebellion, 1861-1865* (New York: G. P. Putnam's, 1888), p. 32.

[10] *Suppression of the African Slave Trade to the United States of America, 1638-1870* (New York: Longmans, Green, 1896).

[11] H. W. Green, *Negro Holders of the Doctorate* (Boston: Meador Publishing Company, 1946, p. 46.

[12] See sketch of his life in Benjamin Brawley, *Negro Builders and Heroes* (Chapel Hill: University of North Carolina Press, 1937), pp. 186-190; and in Edwin R. Embree, *Thirteen Against the Odds* (New York: Viking Press, 1946).

[13] L. D. Reddick, "A New Interpretation for Negro History." *Journal of Negro History*, XXII, January, 1937, p. 21; and Loggins, *op. cit.*, p. 283.

[14] Du Bois, *Dusk of Dawn* (New York: Harcourt Brace, 1940), p. 58.

[15] In *What the Negro Wants*, edited by Rayford W. Logan (Chapel Hill: University of North Carolina Press, 1944), p. 49.

[16] University of Pennsylvania Press, 1899.

[17] *Ibid.*, p. v.

[18] These facts are taken from Woodson's "Ten Years of Collecting and Publishing the Records of the Negro," *Journal of Negro History*, X, October, 1925, pp. 598-606. Also see C. H. Wesley, "Carter G. Woodson as a Scholar," *loc. cit.*, XXXVI, January, 1951, pp. 12-24; J. G. Van Deusen, in *The Black Man in White America* (Washington, D. C., Associated Publishers, 1944), p. 284 says, "Dr. Woodson has probably done more than any single person to rescue Negro history from oblivion."

[19] Woodson, *loc. cit.*, XI, April, 1926, p. 239.

[20] Woodson, *loc. cit.*, XI, April, 1926, p. 240.

[21] *Ibid.* From Woodson's logic on this point, one is led to wonder whether God is unjust because He made some individuals the inferior of others.

[22] *Ibid.*

[23] Woodson, "Ten Years of Collecting and Publishing the Records of the Negro," *loc. cit.*, p. 600.

[24] Washington, D. C., 1923, p. iii.

[25] Dr. Du Bois describes this change in his outlook in his autobiography, *Dust of Dawn*, pp. 215 ff. 284; See also his "My Evolving Program for Negro Freedom" in *What the Negro Wants*, Rayford Logan, editor. See also Chapter III, this study.

[26] "A New Interpretation for Negro History," *Journal of Negro History*, XXII, January, 1937, p. 20.

[27] Booker T. Washington, *The Story of the Negro: The Rise of the Race from Slavery* (2 vols., New York: Peter Smith, 1940 edition). This statement is from Loggins, *op. cit.*, p. 280.

[28] Washington, *op. cit.*, Preface.

[29] *Ibid.*

[30] "The Reconstruction of History," *Journal of Negro History*, XX, October, 1935, pp. 411-427.

[31] *Journal of Negro History*, XXV, October, 1940, p. 559.

[32] W. E. B. Du Bois, *Black Reconstruction* (New York: Harcourt Brace, 1935), Preface.

[33] J. W. Bell, "The Teaching of Negro History," *Journal of Negro History*, VIII, April, 1923, p. 123.

[34] *Ibid.*, p. 127.

[35] Merl R. Eppse, *An Elementary History of America: including the Contributions of the Negro Race* (Nashville: National Publishing Company, 1943), Preface.

[36] *Ibid.*

[37] Woodson, *loc. cit.*, XI, April, 1926, p. 239.

[38] Vernon Loggins believes that it is a racial trait of the Negro to strive for advancement. "There is something within him," he writes, "undoubtedly a racial inheritance, which stirs him to strive to get on the mountaintop. With our American social organization such as it is, much is denied him. But literature and the related arts are open freely to him. [At least Negro historians have not agreed with this statement.] It is in them that he has his best opportunity to 'rise and shine.'" p. 366 of *The Negro Author*.

[39] Arnold J. Toynbee. *A Study of History*, IV, pp. 289-291.

[40] The phrase is borrowed from Evarts B. Greene, speech before Sixteenth Annual Meeting of the Association for the Study of Negro Life and History, New York, published in *Journal of Negro History*, XVII, January, 1932, p. 9.

[41] See related comments in R. R. Palmer, *History of the Modern World* (New York: Knopf Publishers, 1949, p. 821; Eric Fisher, *Passing of the European Age* (New York: Oxford Press, 1949); Lowell J. Ragatz, *March of Empire* (New York: H. L. Lindquist, 1948), p. 70.

[42] *Loc. cit.*, p. 20.

[43] *Dusk of Dawn*, p. 217.

[44] *Ibid.*, pp. 173-220. It should be noted that, despite this change, Du Bois never gave up entirely the educational aspect of his work.

45 In *What the Negro Wants*, edited by Rayford W. Logan, pp. 56-7.

46 Both studied such topics as the Rural Negro, the Negro Professional Man, the Negro in Business, the College-bred Negro, Negro Crime, the Negro Church, and Negro Artisan.

47 Du Bois, *The Philadelphia Negro*, p. v. See also, *What the Negro Wants*, edited by Rayford W. Logan, pp. 56-7. Since Du Bois had shown in all his earlier writings a keen awareness of economic forces in history, it is highly probable that the manner in which the Bolshevik Revolution affected him was to make him more impatient with gradual progress in race relations. For the rest of his career he was to champion ideas and causes which promised a quick solution to the race problem and other social problems.

48 It is the opinion of the writer that younger students of Negro history are less guilty of a "filio-pietistic" approach than was the case with pioneers in the field.

49 *Loc. cit.*, pp. 21-23.

50 *Op. cit.*, p. 258.

51 *Black Reconstruction*, p. 724.

52 Oswald Garrison Villard, in *The Nation*, Volume 110, May 29, 1920, p. 726.

53 Quoted in *Journal of Negro History*, I. April, 1916, p. 230, in reprint of comment from the *New York Evening Post*.

54 Cf., for example, his reviews in the *Journal of Negro History* of books by: Rayford W. Logan, XXXI, January, 1946, pp. 122-123; Lorenzo J. Greene, XXVIII, No. 4, 1943, pp. 478-479; Merze Tate, XXVIII, April, 1942, pp. 251-253. In a review of Woodson's, *The Rural Negro* (Washington, D. C.: Associated Publishers, 1931), in this same organ, the reviewer comments that, "At times it is an argument against certain forms of peonage, exploitation and other disadvantages which the dominant element of the population has forced upon the less fortunate darker group." (XVI, April, 1931, p. 245).

55 Evarts B. Greene, *loc. cit.*, p. 8. Other outstanding scholars in history indicated the value of Negro history upon the appearance of the *Journal of Negro History* in 1916. At that time A. H. Buffington wrote from Williams College: "The more I think of the matter, the more I do believe there is a place for such a publication. The history of the Negro in Africa, in the West Indies, in Spanish America and in the United States offers a large field in which little appears to have been done." (p. 229). A. C. McLaughlin stated that after a few years it would have "considerable historical value." (p. 228). Charles H. Haskins wrote, "You have struck a good field of work." (p. 228). See also favorable comments by Edward Channing (p. 225), Ferdinand Schevill (p. 227), and Frederick Jackson Turner (p. 228). All of these comments were taken from "How the Public Received the Journal of Negro History," in this organ, 1, April, 1916.

56 On the general development of Negro historiography, see also, John Hope Franklin, "New Perspectives in American Negro history," in *Social Education*, XIV, No. 5, May 1950: Helen Boardman, "The Rise of the Negro Historian," in *The Negro History Bulletin*. April, 1945, pp. 148-154; Carter G. Woodson, "The Negro Historian of our Time," in *Negro History Bulletin*, April, 1945, pp. 155-156. It is interesting that a contemporary Marxist and keen student of Negro history views it as a source of propaganda for a larger purpose. (Cf. Herbert Aptheker, "Negro His-

tory: Arsenal for Liberation," *New Masses*, February 11, 1947, pp 8-9. See also his "Distorting the Negro's History," *New Masses*, September 23, 1941, pp. 21-23; and his, "Negro History—A cause for Optimism," *Opportunity*, XIX, August, 1941, pp. 228-231).

CHAPTER III

THE PHILOSOPHY OF BLACK HISTORY

[1] See Earl E. Thorpe, *Negro Historians in the United States* (Baton Rouge, La.: Fraternal Press, 1958), esp. Chapter I; the 1931 paper, "Perspectives in History" by Professor Evarts B. Greene (*Journal of Negro History*, hereafter referred to as JNH), XXII; L. D. Reddick, "A New Interpretation for Negro History," JNH, XXII, Jan., 1937. Over one-half or ten of the fourteen articles in the Oct., 1940 issue of this journal were devoted to an evaluation of Negro History and what has been termed the Negro History Movement. In this connection, see also, this journal, XX, No. 1, Jan., 1935. It is, perhaps, regrettable that the Presidential Address at each annual meeting of this Association is not published as a permanent record which would reveal shifts and changes in philosophy, as is the case with many historical societies.

[2] Henry Steele Commager, *The American Mind* (New Haven: Yale University Press, 1950), p. 278.

[3] Louis O. Kattsoff, *Elements of Philosophy* (New York: Ronald Press, 1953), p. 66.

[4] George Washington Williams, *History of the Negro Race in America*, 1619-1880 (New York: G. P. Putnam's Sons, 1883), p. x.

[5] JNH, II, p. 443.

[6] Hartford, Connecticut.

[7] JNH, XX, 1937, p. 19.

[8] *Ibid.*

[9] In Hesseltine's "A Quarter-Century of the Association for the Study of Negro Life and History," JNH, XXV, 4, Oct., 1940, p. 442.

[10] John Hope Franklin, "The New Negro History," JNH, XLII, 2, April, 1957, pp. 89-197.

[11] JNH, II, 1926, p. 24.

[12] C. A. Hucker, *Chinese History: A Bibliographic Review* (Washington, D. C.: The American Historical Association, 1958), p. 1.

[13] *Ibid.*

[14] Philip D. Jordan, *The Nature and Practice of State and Local History* (Washington, D. C.: The American Historical Association, 1958), p. 4.

[15] *Ibid.*, oo. 4, 16.

[16] JNH, XIII, p. 12.

[17] *Ibid.*

[18] Charles H. Wesley, "The Reconstruction of History," JNH, XX, 4, Oct., 1935.

[19] Charles G. Sellers, Jr., *Jacksonian Democracy* (Washington, D. C.: American Historical Association, 1958), pp. 3-5.

[20] On the continuing re-appraisal of historical interpretations, see Geoffrey Barraclough, *History in a Changing World* (Norman, Oklahoma: University of Oklahoma Press, 1955).

21 Review by Rayford W. Logan, JNH, XXI, 1, Jan., 1936, p. 62.
22 L. D. Reddick, "A New Interpretation for Negro History," *loc. cit.*
23 *Ibid.*, p. 17.
24 *Ibid.*
25 *Ibid.*, pp. 23-25.
26 Both of whom he refers to, calling Du Bois "brilliant" and Beard "the most eminent of American historians."
27 *Ibid.*, pp. 26-27.
28 *Ibid.*, p. 27.
29 *Ibid.*
30 *Ibid.*, p. 28.
31 At the time Dr. Reddick was teaching at Dillard University in New Orleans, while Dr. Fontaine was employed by Southern University at Baton Rouge.
32 *Journal of Negro History*, XXV, No. 1, Jan., 1940, pp. 6-13.
33 Ralph Bunche, Allison Davis, E. E. Just, and Abram Harris.
34 "Alain Locke sometimes understands."
35 "A much better compiler than interpreter," and "Dr. Johnson seems to be profoundly lacking in a sense of history."
36 *Ibid.*, p. 6.
37 R. R. Palmer, *A History of the Modern World*, 2nd ed. (New York: A. A. Knopf, 1956), pp. 607-612.

CHAPTER IV

THE FATHER OF NEGRO HISTORY

1 Biographical facts are taken from the introduction written by Kelly Miller for Woodson's *The Negro in Our History* (Washington, D. C.: Associated Publishers, 1947, 9th ed.); Charles H. Wesley, "Carter G. Woodson—as a Scholar," *Journal of Negro History*, XXXVI, No. 1, January, 1951, pp. 13ff. For activities of Woodson after 1915, the *Journal of Negro History* is the best source. He founded and edited this work until his death in 1950, and each volume carries information on his activities.
2 Charles H. Wesley, "Carter G. Woodson, as a Scholar," *Journal of Negro History*, XXXVI, January, 1951, p. 17.
3 Kelly Miller, *loc. cit.*, p. xxv.
4 C. G. Woodson, "An Accounting for twenty-five years," *Journal of Negro History*, XXV, No. 4, October, 1940, pp. 422-3.
5 *Ibid.*, p. 422.
6 C. G. Woodson, "Ten Years of Collecting and Publishing the Records of the Negro," *Journal of Negro History*, X, No. 4, October, 1925, p. 600.
7 *Ibid.*, p. 598.
8 *Journal of Negro History*, I, No. 2, April, 1916, pp. 228-229 carries reprints of their comments in letters to the editor.
9 *Ibid.*, p. 229.
10 See Chapter V, for further comments on these persons.
11 Woodson, "Ten Years of Collecting and Publishing the Records of the Negro," *loc. cit.*, p. 600.
12 *Ibid.*, p. 600.

216   *The Central Theme of Black History*

[13] Letter to Woodson, reprinted, *Journal of Negro History*, I, No. 2, April, 1916, p. 227.

[14] Hereafter referred to, at times, in the text as the *Journal*.

[15] Woodson, "Ten Years of Collecting and Publishing the Records of the Negro," *loc. cit.*, pp. 600-601

[16] *Ibid.*, pp. 601-602. In 1920 Edward Channing wrote Woodson: "It would be a great misfortune for the cause of historical truth for you to be obliged to suspend publication." (Letter from Channing to Woodson, March 30, 1920, Harvard University, in Woodson Collection, Library of Congress).

[17] Woodson, "Ten Years of Collecting and Publishing the Records of the Negro," *loc. cit.*, pp. 602-603.

[18] Luther Porter Jackson, "The First Twenty-Five Volumes of the Journal of Negro History Digested," *Journal of Negro History*, XXV, No. 4, October, 1940, p. 433.

[19] *Ibid.*, pp. 433-434.

[20] *Ibid.*, p. 434.

[21] *Ibid.*, pp. 435-436.

[22] Charles H. Wesley, "Carter G. Woodson—as a Scholar," *loc. cit.*, p. 20, quoting letter from Woodson to Wesley of June 19, 1937, Washington, D. C.

[23] Woodson, "Ten Years of Collecting and Publishing the Records of the Negro," *loc. cit.*, p. 598.

[24] *Ibid.*

[25] *Ibid.* Woodson had a voluminous correspondence with persons all over the United States of America and various other countries who became interested in fostering research in Negro history as a result of Woodson's work. Some of these persons founded organizations similar to Woodson's to foster the study of Negro history. Some of these letters gave him little-known facts about the race, while other letters corrected him on errors of fact which appeared in some of his books. (See, for example, letter from D. E. Carney, Freetown, Sierra Leone, West Africa, January 19, 1921; letter from Monroe Work, Tuskegee Institute, July 14, 1920; letter from Bishop B. G. Shaw, Birmingham, Alabama, February 2, 1926; letter from Prof. W. Westergaard, University of California at Los Angeles, October 27, 1925; letter from Prof. A. E. Jenks, University of Minnesota, January 13, 1921; letter from George Washington Cable, Lathen, Mass., Nov. 7, 1916—all in Woodson Collection in Library of Congress).

[26] *Ibid.*, p. 425.

[27] *Ibid.*, p. 426.

[28] *Ibid.*, pp. 426-428. For a full list of the volumes published by the Association to 1940 see this article, pp. 426-427. Woodson asked colored persons from various countries to write articles for the *Journal* on various aspects of their history. (See, for example, letter to Woodson from the Secretary of the National Congress of British West Africa, the Gold Coast, Feb. 7, 1921; and a similar letter from W. Esuman-Givira Seky, Cape Coast, Gold Coast, West Africa, Oct. 14, 1920. These and similar letters are in the Woodson Collection, Library of Congress, Washington, D. C.

[29] C. G. Woodson, "An Accounting for 25 Years," *loc. cit.*, pp. 426-428.

[30] Rayford W. Logan, "An Evaluation of the First Twenty Volumes of the Journal of Negro History," *Journal of Negro History*, XX, No. 4, October, 1935, p. 399.

31 *Ibid.*, p. 400.
32 *Ibid.*, p. 403. Also see L. P. Jackson, "The Work of the Association and the People," *ibid.*, pp. 385-396.
33 *Journal of Negro History*, II, 1917, Foreword.
34 See *The History of the Omega Psi Phi Fraternity*, by Herman Dreer (Published by the Fraternity, Washington, D. C., 1940, 331 pp.).
35 C. G. Woodson, "Accounting for 25 Years," *loc. cit.*, p. 428-420.
36 C. G. Woodson, "Negro History Week," *Journal of Negro History*, II, No. 2, April, 1926, p. 238.
37 C. G. Woodson, "An Accounting for 25 Years," *loc. cit.*, p. 429.
38 *Ibid.*, p. 430.
39 New York and London, G. P. Putnam's Sons, 454 pp. A 2d ed. appeared four years later.
40 *Ibid.*, Preface.
41 *Ibid.*
42 XXI, July, 1915, p. 119.
43 J. F. Gould, *Survey*, XXXV, January 29, 1916, p. 521.
44 Mary C. Terrell, *Journal of Negro History*, I, No. 1, January, 1916, pp. 96-97.
45 Washington, D. C., Associated Publishers.
46 New York, A. Knopf.
47 *The Negro in Our History*, Preface.
48 Alain Locke, in *Journal of Negro History*, XII, No. 1, January, 1927, pp. 99-100.
49 *Ibid.*, pp. 100-101.
50 *The Negro in Our History*, Preface.
51 January 7, 1923, p. 18. This work was also reviewed with comments generally favorable, by *The Springfield Republican*, July 15, 1922, p. 8; *Survey*, XXXXIX, October 15, 1922, p. 119; and, *American Political Science Review*, XVI, November, 1922, p. 727.
52 See p. 360, first edition.
53 Washington, D. C., Association for the Study of Negro Life and History, 221 pp.
54 October 24, 1918, p. 54.
55 *A Century of Negro Migration* was also reviewed by the *Boston Transcript*, Dec. 31, 1918, p. 6; *The Nation*, Jan. 11, 1919; *Review of Reviews*, Dec. 1918, LVIII, p. 661; and, the *Journal of Negro History*, 1918, p. 341. These critics had high praise for Woodson's objectivity and thoroughness of research.
56 Washington, D. C., Associated Publishers, 330 pp. A 2d edition appeared in 1945. See review by F. C. Summer, *Journal of Negro History*, VII, No. 2, April, 1922.
57 *Ibid.*, Preface.
58 *The History of the Negro Church*, Preface. For further comment on this book see section on "Writers of Church History."
59 West Virginia College Institute, 54 pp. This was published as "West Virginia Collegiate Institute Bulletin," Ser. 6, No. 3.
60 See *Journal of Negro History*, VI, No. 1, January, 1921.
61 *Ibid.*, p. 1.
62 Washington, D. C., Associated Publishers.
63 *Ibid.*, Preface.

⁶⁴ XVIII, May 12, 1933, p. 55. This work was also similarly reviewed by Alain Locke for *Survey*, LXIX, October, 1933, p. 363.

⁶⁵ *Mis-Education of the Negro*, p. xi.

⁶⁶ *Ibid.*, p. xii.

⁶⁷ *Ibid.*, p. 1.

⁶⁸ *Ibid.*, pp. 144-145. Italics supplied.

⁶⁹ *Ibid.*, p. 145 ff.

⁷⁰ Washington, D. C., The Association for the Study of Negro Life and History, 78 pp.

⁷¹ Washington, D. C., The Association for the Study of Negro Life and History, 296 pp.

⁷² See the Prefaces of both works.

⁷³ Associated Publishers, Washington, D. C., 711 pp.

⁷⁴ Associated Publishers, Washington, D. C., 672 pp.

⁷⁵ Woodson, *Negro Orators*, Preface.

⁷⁶ *Ibid.*

⁷⁷ October 24, 1926, p. 26.

⁷⁸ CXXIV, December, 1926, p. 427.

⁷⁹ Washington, D. C., Associated Publishers, 362 pp.

⁸⁰ Washington, D. C., Associated Publishers, 369 pp.

⁸¹ See comments by Cyril Clemens, *Commonweal*, XXIV, May 22, 1936, p. 111; *Christian Century*, LILI, June 17, 1936, p. 874; and, *Survey Graphic*, XXV, April, 1936, p. 261.

⁸² Washington, D. C., Associated Publishers, 184 pp.

⁸³ *African Myths*, Preface.

⁸⁴ Washington, D. C., Associated Publishers, 111 pp.

⁸⁵ Washington, D. C., Associated Publishers, 388 pp.

⁸⁶ *Ibid.*, pp. 1 ff.

⁸⁷ Washington, D. C., Associated Publishers, 1930, 265 pp.

⁸⁸ New York *Herald-Tribune Books*, Nov. 23, 1930, p. 14.

⁸⁹ James Browning, *Journal of Negro History*, XVI, No. 2, April, 1931, p. 245.

⁹⁰ This work was also favorably reviewed by the *New York Times*, September 14, 1930, p. 16 and the *Boston Transcript*, August 16, 1930, p. 3.

⁹¹ Washington, D. C., Associated Publishers, 1934.

⁹² *The Negro Professional Man and the Community*, Foreword.

⁹³ May, 1934, XXXXVII, p. 1303.

⁹⁴ March 25, 1934, p. 12.

⁹⁵ Washington, D. C., Association for the Study of Negro Life and History, 1936, 478 pp.

⁹⁶ *The African Background Outlined*, pp. 217-463.

⁹⁷ *Ibid.*, Preface.

⁹⁸ *Ibid.*

⁹⁹ Rayford W. Logan, *Journal of Negro History*, XXI, 1936, p. 323.

¹⁰⁰ *Ibid.*

¹⁰¹ Washington, D. C., Associated Publishers, 1939, 210 pp.

¹⁰² July 22, 1939, p. 3.

¹⁰³ *Ibid.*

¹⁰⁴ *African Heroes and Heroines*, Preface.

¹⁰⁵ *Ibid.*

¹⁰⁶ Washington, D. C., Associated Publishers.

¹⁰⁷ See, for example, his "The Beginnings of the Miscegenation of the

Whites and Blacks," *Journal of Negro History*, III, 1918, pp. 335-353, and the following articles, all in this journal; "Some Attitudes in English Literature," XX, No. 2, April, 1935, pp. 190-243; "The Negro Washer-woman, a Vanishing Figure," XV, No. 3, July, 1930, pp. 269-277; "Notes on the Bakongo," XXX, No. 4, October, 1945, pp. 421-431; "The Relations of Negroes and Indians in Massachusetts," V, January, 1920, pp. 45-57; "The Negroes of Cincinnatti Prior to the Civil War," I, July, 1916, pp. 1-22; and "Some Things Negroes Need to do," in *Southern Workman*, LI, January, 1922, p. 33. Woodson also wrote, "The Negro in Education," for the *Encyclopedia Americana*, XX, pp. 52-53, and biographical sketches of Richard Allen, Richard Henry Boyd, Morris Brown, Williams Wells, Brown and Blanche K. Bruce for *The Dictionary of American Biography* (See volumes I, p. 204; II, p. 528; III, pp. 145, 161, and 180 respectively).

108 Charles H. Wesley, "Carter G. Woodson—as a Scholar," *loc. cit.*, pp. 14-17.

109 C. G. Woodson, "Negro History Week," *Journal of Negro History*, XI, No. 2, April, 1926, p. 239.

110 *Ibid.*, pp. 239-240.

111 *Ibid.*, p. 239.

112 C. G. Woodson, "The Celebration of Negro History Week," *Journal of Negro History*, XII, No. 2, April, 1927, p. 103.

113 *Negro Makers of History* (Washington, D. C.: Associated Publishers, 1928). Preface.

114 *Journal of Negro History*, X, No. 4, October, 1925, p. 600.

115 See review of *The Negro in Our History*, in *New York Tribune*, January 7, 1923, p. 18.

116 Kelly Miller, *loc. cit.*, p. xxvi.

117 Charles H. Wesley, "Carter G. Woodson—As a Scholar," *loc cit.*, p. 21.

118 Melville J. Herskovits, "The Present Status and Needs of Afro-American Research," *Journal of Negro History*, XXXVI, No. 2, April, 1951, pp. 123-124.

119 John G. Van Deusen, *The Black Man in White America* (Washington, D. C., Associated Publishers, 1944), p. 284. The May, 1950 issue of the *Negro History Bulletin* was devoted exclusively to Woodson. The eight brief articles in this issue were written by persons who knew Woodson intimately.

CHAPTER V

MEDIA AND AFRO-AMERICAN HISTORY TO 1930

1 In this essay, unless otherwise indicated, the page references are to Marshall McLuhan, *Understanding Media*, Signet book, New York: New American Library, 1964. The page referred to often only suggests the idea being presented in this essay, hence no claim is made that Mr. McLuhan would concur with these extensions of his study of "the extensions of man."

2 *Ibid.*, p. 40.

3 *Ibid.*, p. 86.

4 *Ibid.,* p. 30.
5 *Ibid.,* p. 32.
6 *Ibid.,* p. 34.
7 *Ibid.,* p. 25.
8 *Ibid.,* p. 234.
9 *Ibid.,* pp. 56-67.
10 *Ibid.,* p. 144.
11 *Ibid.,* p. 251.
12 *Ibid.,* pp. 210-11.
13 *Ibid.,* p. 213.
14 *Ibid.,* p. 207.
15 *Ibid.,* p. 208
16 *Ibid.,* p. 215.
17 Marshall McLuhan and Quentin Fiore, *War and Peace in the Global Village,* paperback ed., p. 173.
18 *Ibid.*
19 *Understanding Media,* p. 220.
20 *Ibid.,* p. 40.
21 *Ibid.,* p. 208.
22 *Ibid.,* p. 40.
23 *Ibid.,* p. 36.
24 *Ibid.,* p. 144.
25 *Ibid.,* p. 297.
26 *Ibid.,* p. 298.
27 *Ibid.,* p. 204.
28 *Ibid.,* p. 162.
29 *War and Peace in the Global Village,* p. 58.
30 *Ibid.,* pp. 112-13.
31 *Understanding Media,* p. 223.
32 *Ibid.,* p. 262.
33 *Ibid.,* pp. 73-74.
34 *Ibid.,* p. 171.
35 *Ibid.,* p. 177.
36 *Ibid.,* p. 120.
37 Cf. Ch. 14.
38 *Ibid.,* p. 27.
39 *War and Peace in the Global Village,* p. 81.
40 *Understanding Media,* p. 206.
41 *Ibid.,* p. 250.
42 *Ibid.,* p. 173.
43 *War and Peace in the Global Village,* pp. 160-64.
44 *Understanding Media,* p. 197.
45 *Ibid.,* p. 199.
46 *War and Peace in the Global Village,* p. 16.
47 *Understanding Media,* p. 54.
48 *Ibid.,* p. 264.
49 *Ibid.,* p. 262.
50 *Ibid.,* p. 133.
51 *War and Peace in the Global Village,* p. 132.
52 *Understanding Media,* p. 270.
53 *Ibid.,* pp. 36ff.

54 *War and Peace in the Global Village*, p. 79.
55 *Understanding Media*, p. 241.
56 *Ibid.*, p. 244.
57 *Ibid.*, pp. 244-45.
58 *Ibid.*, p. 229.
59 *Ibid.*, p. 267.
60 *Ibid.*, p. 58.
61 *Ibid.*, p. 63.
62 *Ibid.*, p. 161.
63 *Ibid.*, p. 239.
64 *Ibid.*, p. 285.
65 *Ibid.*, p. 206.
66 Edited by R. Crossman.
67 *War and Peace in the Global Village*, p. 9.
68 *Ibid.*, p. 11.
69 *Ibid.*, p. 7.
70 *Ibid.*, p. 133.

CHAPTER VI

BLACK AND WHITE TRIBALISM

1 *Understanding Media*, p. 274.
2 *Ibid.*, p. 290.
3 *Ibid.*, p. 20.
4 *Ibid.*
5 *War and Peace in the Global Village*, p. 93.
6 *Ibid.*, pp. 66-67.
7 *Ibid.*, p. 128.
8 *Ibid.*, p. 71.
9 *Understanding Media*, p. 48.
10 *War and Peace in the Global Village*, p. 82.
11 *Ibid.*, pp. 58-59.
12 *Ibid.*, p. 64.
13 *Understanding Media*, p. 275.
14 *Ibid.*, p. 239.
15 *Ibid.*, p. 205.
16 *Ibid.*, p. 56.
17 *Ibid.*, p. 297.
18 *War and Peace in the Global Village*, p. 123.
19 *Ibid.*, p. 129.
20 *Ibid.*, p. 97.
21 *Ibid.*
22 *Ibid.*, p. 10.
23 *Identity: Youth and Crisis*, paperback ed., p. 315.
24 *Ibid.*, pp. 315-16.

222   *The Central Theme of Black History*

CHAPTER VII

THE NEGRO AND THE CENTRAL THEME OF SOUTHERN HISTORY

[1] C. Vann Woodward, *The Burden of Southern History* (Baton Rouge: 1960), p. 8. See also James C. Bonner, *Plantation and Farm: The Agricultural South*, in A. Link and R. W. Patrick, eds., *Writing Southern History* (Baton Rouge: 1965), pp. 149ff.

[2] Louis D. Rubin, Jr., and J. J. Kilpatrick, eds. (Chicago: 1957).

[3] C. Vann Woodward, *op. cit.*, p. 8.

[4] See F. E. Vandiver, ed., *The Idea of the South: Pursuit of a Central Theme* (Chicago: 1964).

[5] David Potter, *Yale Review*, LI (Autumn, 1961).

[6] Carl Bridenbaugh, *Myths and Realities: Societies of the Colonial South* (Baton Rouge: 1952). One evidence of the absence of a unique mind of the South during much of the colonial period is the relative absence of a sectional emphasis in the histories produced by Southerners on the Age of the American Revolution (See C. G. Sellers, Jr., *The American Revolution: Southern Founders of a National Tradition*, in Link and Patrick, eds., *op. cit.*, pp. 59ff.

[7] A. Nevins, *Ordeal of the Union*, II (New York: 1947), pp. 540ff.

[8] Merrill Jensen, *The New Nation: A History of the United States During the Confederation, 1781-1789* (New York: 1950), pp. 74ff.

[9] John R. Alden, *The South in the Revolution, 1763-1789* (Baton Rouge: 1957). Also *The First South* (Baton Rouge: 1961).

[10] L. D. Rubin, Jr., J. J. Kilpatrick, eds., *op. cit.* (Chicago: 1957), p. 37.

[11] See William B. Hesseltine and D. L. Smiley, *The South in American History*, 2nd ed. (New Jersey: 1960).

[12] Jesse T. Carpenter, *The South as a Conscious Minority, 1789-1861* (New York: 1930).

[13] F. B. Simkins, *A History of the South* (New York, 1953).

[14] R. S. Cotterill, *The Old South: The Geographic, Social, Political and Cultural Expansion, Institutions, and Nationalism of the Antebellum South* (Glendale, California: 1936).

[15] William B. Hesseltine, *A History of the South* (New York: 1936).

[16] U. B. Phillips, "The Central Theme of Southern History," *American Historical Review*, XXXIV (1928), pp. 30-43; E. M. Coulter, eds., *The Course of the South to Secession* (New York: 1939).

[17] New York: A. Knopf, 1941. See also James C. Bonner, *Plantation and Farm: The Agricultural South, loc. cit.*, pp. 160-164; P. A. Waring and C. S. Golden, *Soil and Steel* (New York: 1947); W. D. Wyman and Avery Craven, "The Turner Thesis and the South," *Journal of Southern History*, V (August, 1939), pp. 291-314; and Henry C. Allen, *Bush and Backwoods* (East Lansing, 1959), which compares the Australian and United States frontiers.

[18] New York: 1930.

[19] David Potter, "The Enigma of the South," *loc. cit.*, p. 148.

[20] In his *90° in the Shade* (Chapel Hill), p. 15.

[21] *Ibid.*, p. 8.

[22] Cf. his, "The Enigma of the South," *loc cit.*, 1961.

[23] See his essay in L. D. Rubin, Jr. and J. J. Kilpatrick, eds., *op. cit.*

[24] *Journal of Southern History*, XXI (November, 1955), pp. 447-455.

[25] *Ibid.*, p. 451.

[26] James McBride Dabbs, "The Land," in L. D. Rubin, Jr. and J. J. Kilpatrick, eds., *op. cit.*, p. 75.

[27] Cf. A. W. Griswold, *Farming and Democracy* (New York: 1948), pp. 35-36.

[28] *Ibid.*, pp. 86-87.

[29] *Ibid.*, pp. 179-181.

[30] "The Enigma of the South," *loc. cit.*, p. 148.

[31] *Ibid.*

[32] *Ibid.*, pp. 148-149.

[33] *Ibid.*, p. 146.

[34] *Ibid.*, p. 149.

[35] *Ibid.*

[36] *Ibid.*, pp. 150-51.

[37] James McBride Dabbs, "The Land," in L. D. Rubin, Jr., and J. J. Kilpatrick, eds., *op. cit.*, 77.

[38] *Ibid.*, pp. 77-78.

[39] From his, "Tolerating the South's Past," in G. B. Tindall, ed., *The Pursuit of Southern History* (Baton Rouge: 1964), p. 316.

[40] See C. W. Ramsdell, "The Changing Interpretations of the Civil War," *Journal of Southern History*, III (February, 1937).

[41] See his *America's Shame and Redemption* (Marquette, Michigan: 1965), pp. 36-37, 142.

[42] "The Enigma of the South," *loc. cit.*, p. 147.

[43] *Ibid.*

[44] Cf. his "Mythology: A new Frontier in Southern History," in F. E. Vandiver, ed., *op. cit.*, p. 15. "The Central Theme Revisited" is in the volume, *The Southerner as American*, ed. by C. G. Sellers (Chapel Hill: 1960).

[45] *The Burden of Southern History*, p. 11.

[46] *Ibid.* See also D. Potter, *loc. cit.*, p. 150.

[47] In his *The Burden of Southern History*, p. 11.

[48] New York: 1932.

[49] Cambridge, Massachusetts.

[50] Chapel Hill: 1955.

[51] Baton Rouge: 1952.

[52] See his "A Comparative Analysis of Economic Development in the American West and South," *Journal of Economic History*, XVI (Dec., 1956), pp. 558-574.

[53] See his "Americans Below the Potomac," in C. G. Sellers, ed., *op. cit.*, p. 33.

[54] *Ibid.*

[55] Volume I, New York: 1930.

[56] Frank Vandiver, "The Southerner as Extremist," in book which he edited entitled, *The Idea of the South*, p. 44.

[57] See their *Southern Regions of the U. S.* (1936), and comment on this work in David Potter, "The Enigma of the South," *loc. cit.*

[58] David Potter, "The Enigma of the South," *loc. cit.*, p. 145.

CHAPTER VIII

THE WHITE TEACHER OF BLACK HISTORY

1 Harlan pamphlet, p. 2.
2 *Ibid.*, p. 2.
3 *Ibid.*, pp. 21-22.
4 *Ibid.*, p. 22.
5 *Ibid.*, p. 22.
6 *Ibid.*

CHAPTER IX

W. E. B. DU BOIS

1 E. R. Embree, *Thirteen Against the Odds* (New York: Viking Press, 1946), p. 153.
2 W. E. B. Du Bois, *Dusk of Dawn*, pp. 11-13.
3 *Ibid.*, p. 14. Biographical facts on his life are also taken from *Who's Who in Colored America*, 1931-3, p. 717; *Who's Who in America*, 1934-5, XVIII, p. 753, and B. G. Brawley, *The Negro in Literature and Art*, pp. 50-55.
4 Du Bois, *Dusk of Dawn*, p. 14.
5 *Ibid.*, p. 34. See also Earl E. Thorpe, "Frederick Douglass, Booker Washington, and W. E. B. Du Bois," *Negro History Bulletin*, January, 1957.
6 *Dusk of Dawn*, pp. 139-140.
7 *Ibid.*, p. 32.
8 Du Bois, *Dusk of Dawn*, pp. 37-39.
9 *Ibid.*, p. 36.
10 *Ibid.*, p. 42.
11 *Ibid.*, pp. 42-43.
12 *Ibid.*, pp. 42-46.
13 *Ibid.*, p. 47.
14 *Ibid.*, p. 50.
15 *Ibid.*, p. 51.
16 *Ibid.*, p. 28. See also Earl E. Thorpe, "The Booker Washington—W. E. B. Du Bois Controversy," *Quarterly Review of Higher Education Among Negroes*, October, 1955.
17 *Ibid.*, p. 28.
18 *Dusk of Dawn*, pp. 95-96. See also, Mary W. Ovington, *Portraits in Color* (New York: Viking Press, 1927), p. 85.
19 *Ibid.* Du Bois gives a comprehensive account of his differences with Washington in his *Souls of Black Folk* (Chicago: A. C. McClurg and Co., 1904). 264 pp.
20 *Dusk of Dawn*, p. 26.
21 *Ibid.*, p. 296.
22 *Dusk of Dawn*, p. 215.
23 *Ibid.*
24 *Ibid.*, pp. 286-287. See also the excellent study by D. W. Wynn entitled, *The NAACP Versus Negro Revolutionary Protest* (New York: Exposition Press, 1955. Esp. Ch. III.
25 *Dusk of Dawn*, p. 304.
26 *Ibid.*, p. 314.

27 *Ibid.*
28 *Black Reconstruction* (New York: Harcourt Brace, 1935).
29 *Dusk of Dawn,* pp. 320-321.
30 See pp. 126-132, this study.
31 See pp. 132-135, this study.
32 *Dusk of Dawn,* 172.
33 Mary W. Ovington, *op. cit.,* p. 78.
34 *Ibid.,* p. 86.
35 *Ibid.,* p. 91.
36 *The Suppression of the African Slave Trade to the U.S.A., 1638-1870*
(New York: Longmans, Green and Co.), 335 pp.
37 Loggins, *The Negro Author,* p. 281.
38 *Ibid.*
39 Loggins, *op. cit.,* p. 282.
40 Unnamed reviewer, *The Nation,* LXIII, Dec. 31, 1896, pp. 498-500.
41 *Suppression of the African Slave Trade,* p. v.
42 *Suppression of the African Slave Trade,* p. v.
43 *Ibid.,* p. 1.
44 One of the few examples where one might expect to find documentation, and does not, is the statement on page 15 that "As a whole, it may be said that whatever opposition to the slave-trade there was in the planting colonies was based principally on the political fear of insurrection."
45 *Ibid.,* p. 39.
46 *Ibid.,* p. 151.
47 *Ibid.,* p. 197.
48 *Suppression of the African Slave Trade,* pp. 197-199.
49 *Ibid.,* p. 197.
50 *Ibid.* p. 198.
51 *Suppression of the African Slave Trade,* p. 198.
52 *Ibid.*
53 Ginn and Co., Boston, for the University of Pennsylvania Press. 520 pp. This volume was published as No. 13 in the University of Pennsylvania Series in Political Economy and Public Law.
54 *Ibid.,* Preface.
55 *The Philadelphia Negro,* Introduction, by S. M. Lindsy.
56 *Ibid.,* p. 352.   .
57 *Ibid.,* p. 385.
58 Benjamin Brawley, *Negro Builders and Heroes* (Chapel Hill: Universty of North Carolina Press, 1937), p. 190.
59 G. W. Jacobs and Co., Philadelphia, 222 pp.
60 *Ibid.,* pp. 81-82.
61 *Ibid.,* pp. 82-83.
62 *Ibid.*
63 *Ibid.,* p. 85.
64 *Ibid.,* p. 90.
65 The two chapters in the volume by Du Bois are entitled "The Economic Revolution in the South," pp. 77-122, and "Religion in the South," pp. 123-192.
66 *John Brown* (Philadelphia: G. W. Jacobs and Co.).
67 *Ibid.,* p. 2.
68 *Ibid.,* p. 8.
69 *Ibid.,* p. 338.

[70] *Ibid.*, p. 395.
[71] Cf. *His Color and Democracy*, p. 382.
[72] New York: Holt and Co., 1915, 326 pp.
[73] *Ibid.*, Preface.
[74] Boston: The Stratford Co., 349 pp.
[75] *Ibid.*, Foreword.
[76] *Ibid.*
[77] *The Gift of Black Folk*, Foreword.
[78] See for example, review by Walter White, in New York *Tribune*, September 21, 1924, p. 12.
[79] Harcourt Brace, New York, 746 pp.
[80] Du Bois, *Dusk of Dawn*, p. 318.
[81] Du Bose, *Dusk of Dawn*, p. 319.
[82] *Ibid.*, p. 41.
[83] *Ibid.*
[84] *Black Reconstruction*, p. 724.
[85] *Ibid.*, Preface.
[86] In addition to Dunning's *Reconstruction, Political and Economic*, he used the following state histories: Simkins and Woody, *South Carolina During Reconstruction*; Garner, *Reconstruction in Mississippi*; Fleming, *Civil War and Reconstruction in Alabama*; Ramsdell, *Reconstruction in Texas*; Coulter, *The Civil War and Reconstruction in Kentucky*.
[87] *Black Reconstruction*, pp. 731-736.
[88] Review by Rayford W. Logan, *Journal of Negro History*, XXI, NO. I, January, 1936, p. 61.
[89] *Ibid.*, p. 62.
[90] *Ibid.*
[91] *Black Reconstruction*, p. 15.
[92] *Ibid.*, pp. 15-16.
[93] *Dusk of Dawn*, p. 55.
[94] *Dusk of Dawn*, p. 26.
[95] *Ibid.*, p. 96.
[96] *American Journal of Sociology*, XXXXI, January, 1936, p. 535.
[97] New York *Herald-Tribune Books*, June 23, 1935, p. 1.
[98] *Christian Science Monitor*, August 7, 1935, p. 12.
[99] *Ibid.*
[100] 141: 108, July 24, 1935. For other reviews see: Lewis Gannett, in the New York *Herald-Tribune*, June 13, 1935, p. 17; John Chamberlain, in *Current History*, XIV, August, 1935, p. 42, and, Charles S. Johnson, in *Survey Graphic*, XXXXVIII, January, 1936, p. 25.
[101] In his "Historians of the Reconstruction," *Journal of Negro History*, XXIII, No. 1, January, 1938, p. 32.
[102] New York: Harcourt Brace.
[103] *Ibid.*, Preface.
[104] *Ibid.*, vii.
[105] *Ibid.*
[106] *Ibid.*, vii-viii.
[107] *Black Folk Then and Now*, p. vii.
[108] *Ibid.*, p. ix.
[109] *Ibid.*
[110] *Ibid.* p. vii.
[111] *Black Folk Then and Now*, p. 1.

112 *Ibid.*, pp. 92-93.
113 *Ibid.*, p. 92.
114 *Ibid.*, p. 128-129.
115 *Ibid.*, pp. 177-178.
116 *Ibid.*, p. 210.
117 *Black Folk Then and Now*, p. 382.
118 *Ibid.*
119 *Ibid.*
120 *Ibid.*
121 In *Journal of Negro History*, XXIV, No. 4, October, 1939, p. 461.
122 In *New Republic*, LV, August 16, 1939, p. 100.
123 In *Saturday Review of Literature*, XX, July 29, 1939, p. 18. Other reviews, mostly favorable, are: C. G. Stillman in New York *Herald-Tribune Books*, June 25, 1939, p. 12; W. S. Meacham in *New York Times*, July 2, 1939, p. 3.
124 *Dusk of Dawn*, pp. 5-6.
125 *Ibid.*, p. viii.
126 Harcourt, Brace and Co., New York.
127 Rayford W. Logan, editor.
128 *Color and Democracy*, Preface.
129 *Ibid.*, p. 57.
130 *Color and Democracy*, pp. 74-75.
131 See, for example, the statements by Dr. Walter Dorn on the expansionist tendencies of the European states system in his *Competition for Empire*, 1740-1763 (New York. Harper and Bros., 1940), 426. pp.
132 *Color and Democracy*, p. 116.
133 *Ibid.*
134 *October*, 1949, XXIV, p. 159.
135 D. R. Homer, in *Library Journal*, LXX, May 15, 1955, p. 486.
136 In *Saturday Review of Literature*, XXVIII, June 23, 1945, p. 17.
137 In *Annals of the American Academy of Political and Social Science*, 242: 174 November, 1945. See also reviews by Alain Locke, in *Survey Graphic*, XXXIV, October, 1945, p. 415; Carter G. Woodson, *Journal of Negro History*, XXX, No. 2, July, 1945.
138 New York, Viking Press, 1947, 276 pp.
139 *The World and Africa*, p. vii.
140 *Ibid.*
141 *The World and Africa*, p. vii.
142 *Ibid.*
143 *Ibid.*, p. viii.
144 *Ibid.*
145 *The World and Africa*, p. viii.
146 *Ibid.*
147 Works which he used most include Robert Briffault's *The Decline and Fall of the British Empire*; George Padmore's *How Britain Rules Africa*; Eric Williams's *Capitalism and Slavery*; his own *Suppression of the African Slave Trade*; Rayford Logan's *The United States and Haiti*; Chapman Cohen's *Christianity, Slavery and Labor*; E. D. Moore's *Ivory: The Scourge of Africa*.
148 *The World and Africa*, pp. xi-xii.
149 *The World and Africa*, p. 43.
150 *The World and Africa*, p. 75.

151 In *Booklist*. XXXXIII. February 15, 1947, p. 182.
152 Review by W. M. Brewer, *Journal of Negro History*, 1948.
153 *Saturday Review of Literature*, XXX, March 29, 1947, p. 10.
154 Robert Peel, in *Christian Science Monitor*, February 10, 1947, p. 14.
155 New York, H. W. Wilson and Co., 207 pp.
156 In *Journal of Negro History*, XXX. No. 3, July, 1945, pp. 341-342.
157 See above review by Woodson, and *Subscription Books Bulletin*, XVI, July, 1945, p. 38.
158 A. C. McClurg and Co., Chicago, 434 pp.
159 Harcourt, Brace, New York.
160 In *The World Tomorrow*, XI, November, 1928, p. 473.
161 A. C. McClurg and Co., Chicago, 264 pp.
162 *Ibid.*, Foreword, 21st ed., 1937.
163 *Ibid.*, p. vii.
164 *Ibid.*, pp. 3-4.
165 In New York *Times*, August 8, 1920, p. 19.
166 *Ibid.*
167 *Ibid.*
168 On the loss of the old ideals which succeeded World War I, see R. R. Palmer, *op. cit.*, chapter on "The Decline of Classical Liberalism," or Crane Brinton, *op. cit.*, pp. 447-526. For other works by W. E. Du Bois, see the work which he edited entitled *From Servitude to Service* (Boston: American Unitarian Association, 1905), 232 pp.; his "The Enforcement of the Slave-trade Laws," *Annual Report of the American Historical Association* (Washington, D. C.: 1892), pp. 163-174; his *In Battle for Peace: the Story of My 83rd Birthday* (New York: Masses and Mainstream, 1952), 192 pp.

INDEX

A

A Century of Negro Migration, 62
A Story of Liberia, 99
A Study of History, 46
Abolitionism, 87
Abolitionists, 165, 184, 194
Accra, 182
Adam, 104
Adams, Samuel, 154
Africa, 39, 44, 45, 46, 156, 157, 176, 185, 195, 196, 199, 200, 201, 205
Africa, history of, 4, 71, 141; medieval kingdoms, 8, 13
Africans, 131
African, 51, 55, 70, 71, 131, 149; culture, 79; tribalism, 80, 81
African Heroes and Heroines, 71, 95
African Myths, Together with Proverbs, 68, 95
Afro-American (Baltimore), 160
Age of the Frontier, 170
Age of the Global Village, 106, 170
Age of Print, 76
Agrarianism, 85
Agrarians, Southern, 136, 138
Agrarianism, 136, 139
Alabama, 58
Alabama State College, 58
Alden, John R., 135
Aldrin, Edwin, 123
Altizer, Thomas J., 46, 47, 103, 170
Ambler, Charles W., 50, 59
American Academy of Political and Social Science, 188
American Colonization Society, 116
American Crisis Biographies, 190
American Historical Association, 39, 192
American Historical Review, 51, 56

American Way, 136, 139
American Negro Academy, 91
American Revolution, 135
Amos and Andy, 94
Amsterdam News, 91
America, 37, 39, 41, 43, 45
Anderson, Eddie "Rochester," 94
Anger, of W. E. B. Du Bois, 206
Anglo-Saxon-Protestant, 129
Anti-slavery Convention, New England, 7
Anthropology, 198, 206
Appeal to the Slaves, 7
Appomattox, 146
Aptheker, Herbert, 59
Arabic, 56
Aristocracy, plantation, 138
Armstrong High School, 51
Armstrong, Louis, 78
Armstrong, Neil, 123
Arrogance, 128; of power, 128
Art, 83
Asia, 49, 176, 196, 200
Asians, 131
Asiatics, 205
Asiento, 186
Assassins, 11
Association for the Study of Negro Life and History, 4, 10, 12, 20, 23, 28, 34, 35, 37, 40, 42, 43, 50, 53, 57, 58, 182
Associated Publishers, 10, 53, 54
Atlanta, 58, 90, 188
Atlanta University, 97, 150, 181, 198
Atlanta University Studies, 28, 189, 209
Atlanta University System, 181
Atomic bombs, 122
Attucks, Crispus, 110
Automobile, 93

K

Kansas City, 188
Karenga, Ron, 44
Keil, Charles, 172
Keller, Helen, 57
Kentucky, 6, 49
Kerner Commission, 170
Kierkegaard, Soren, 103
King, Martin Luther, Jr., 9, 16, 44, 78, 99, 101, 111, 113, 161
Knights of Columbus, 192
Korean War, 110
Ku Klux Klan, 111, 132, 143, 155, 167

L

Laissez-faire, 41
Latin America, 56; and slavery, 79-80, 191
Lawson, James, 162
Legend, 206
Legree, Simon, 155
Lewis, Robert Benjamin, 10, 33, 39
Liberal democracy, 140
Liberals, White, 130, 168
Liberalism, 168; attacked, 41-44
Library of Congress, 50, 193
Life Against Death, 46, 169
Lincoln, Abraham, 13, 39, 87
Lindsey, Arnett, 59, 68
Literacy, impact of, 83-84, 88, 97, 98
Literalism, 80, 103
Literature, field of, 13
Locke, Alain, 25, 42, 97, 110, 162
Locomotives, 88
Logan, Rayford W., 40, 52, 56, 59, 87, 154, 166, 195
Loggins, Vernon, characterizes Negro History, 14, 18, 31, 184
Louisiana, 13
Los Angeles, 59
L'Ouverture, Toussaint, 13, 185
Love, 123, 144, 200
Love's Body, 46, 126
Low, Augustus, 59
Lugard, Frederick, 199
Luther, Martin, 80, 154
Lynchings, 90, 99, 135, 180

M

Magic, 81, 85, 105
Malcolm X, 9, 44, 46, 47, 78, 97, 103, 104, 106, 107, 111, 161, 169
Mandates, 202
Manhood, 3-17, 148
Marcuse, Herbert, 103
Martineau, Harriet, 199
Marx, Karl, 46, 127, 170, 180, 200
Marxism, 40, 42, 130, 139, 162, 179, 181, 190, 193, 195, 197, 200
Masochism, White, 168, 169, 170, 171
Mays, Benjamin, 81
McCarthyism, 132
McKay, Claude, 90, 100
McKissick, Floyd, 44
McLaughlin, A. C., 51
McLuhan, Marshall, 46, 47, 76-86, 88, 89, 91-94, 96, 98-108, 113, 169
Mechanical Age, 102
Media, and Afro-American history to 1930, 76-100
Medicine, 13
Meier, August, 152
Medievalism, 139
Mehlinger, Louis R., 58, 59
Memorial, Laura Spelman Rockefeller, 52, 66
Michigan, 58
Middle Atlantic Colonies, 157
Militancy, of Latin American slaves, 79-80; 92
Miller, Kelly, 50
Mills, C. Wright, 127
Mirrors, 91-92
Mis-Education of the Negro, 15, 63, 64, 65
Missouri Compromise, 111, 135
Money, 86, 170
Monistic theories, 142
Monopoly, 202
Moon, men land on, 123
Moorland Collection, 150
Morals, 120
Morison, Samuel E., 147
Morse, Samuel, 86
Movies, 92
Muhammed, Elijah, 9, 44, 97, 104, 105, 106, 161